C o n t e n t s

The Object Database Handbook: How to Select, Implement, and Use Object-Oriented Databases

Douglas K. Barry

WILEY COMPUTER PUBLISHING

JOHN WILEY & SONS, INC.

New York • Chichester • Brisbane • Toronto • Singapore

Publisher: Katherine Schowalter

Editor: Robert Elliott

Managing Editor: Robert S. Aronds

Text Design & Composition: Pronto Design & Production Inc.

Designations used by companies to distinguish their products are often claimed as trademarks. In all instances where John Wiley & Sons, Inc. is aware of a claim, the product names appear in initial capital or all capital letters. Readers, however, should contact the appropriate companies for more complete information regarding trademarks and registration.

This text is printed on acid-free paper.

This publication is designed to provide accurate and authoritative information in regard to the subject matter covered. It is sold with the understanding that the publisher is not engaged in rendering legal, accounting, or other professional service. If legal advice or other expert assistance is required, the services of a competent professional person should be sought.

Library of Congress Cataloging-in-Publication Data:

Barry, Douglas K.
  The object database handbook: how to select, implement, and use
  object-oriented databases / Douglas K. Barry.
          p. cm.
  Includes index.
  ISBN 0-471-14718-4 (pbk: alk. paper)
  1. Object-oriented databases.   I. Title.
QA76.9.D3B3685   1996   96-10800
005.75—dc20   CIP

Printed in the United States of America
10 9 8 7 6 5 4 3 2 1

P r e f a c e

It is no longer true that Object Database Management Systems (ODBMSs) are coming—they have, in fact, arrived. This became evident recently at the Real-Ware Awards ceremony at DB/Expo 1995, a large database show in San Francisco. This was the third time this event had been held. Among others, there is one category that is intended to feature successful deployment of object technology. Each award in this category jointly honors a product vendor and a company that has successfully deployed an application with object technology. In prior years, no award entries had even been received from the ODBMS vendors. Instead, most entries involved some type of graphical user interface using relational database management systems. In 1995, the entries from all three finalists in this category included ODBMS companies. All of the applications had been deployed near the beginning of 1995, each one involving over a gigabyte of data and hundreds of users. This is strong evidence that the technology has arrived. It also provides evidence for my observation that 1995 was the year when we started to see many significant applications using ODBMSs.

A look at Database Management System (DBMS) history over the last forty years illustrates that ODBMSs are merely the latest form of DBMS in our evolution to an information society. If you look at Figure P.1, you will note that a new form of DBMS has appeared every decade, each time meeting new data needs in society. Perhaps a new kind of DBMS will arise in the latter part of this decade that will make it possible to automate yet another kind of data. The illustration also shows another phenomenon: The DBMSs and file systems that were invented in the past still are very much in use today. The advent of ODBMSs does not mean they will replace existing DBMS installations; that was not the case when Relational DBMSs came on the scene. And there are still many installations of Hierarchical and Network DBMSs in the world today.

The question still comes up, though, about whether ODBMSs are real. This may be a common reaction to a new DBMS technology, because the same question was asked of relational DBMSs in the early 1980s. The answer to that question seems obvious now, and ODBMSs are now on the cusp of being accepted as real—as can be seen from implementations such as those that were submitted at DB/Expo.

This book is written for those people who want to use an ODBMS and be successful in doing so. It is oriented to the practical concepts and ideas that make a project workable. A hands-on approach is woven into the book based on my own experiences and those of my clients. In addition, I have drawn on interviews that I have had for my columns in *Object Magazine*; in

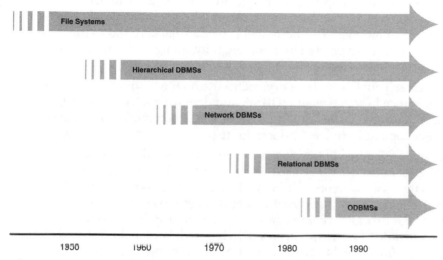

Figure P.1 *Evolution of DBMS technology.*

these interviews, I have talked to those who have pioneered applications using this technology. Practical lessons learned from those pioneers are included in the book as well.

This book is a practical guide to selection and deployment of ODBMSs. Along the way, I am drawing on concepts from many sub-fields of computer science such as object technology, DBMSs, team development, analysis and design methodologies, software management, and software testing. Because each of these sub-fields is extensive, this book does not go into any one of them in great depth. There are many other fine books on these subjects. The focus of this book is to introduce just enough of these concepts to show how they interplay in the selection and deployment of ODBMSs. For those interested in studying some of the other books in more depth, a listing is provided in the Appendix.

In particular, the book is intended for four distinct groups of people. The first group is those with an object programming background who want to store data in a DBMS. This book will provide them with the basics of DBMS properties that allow the data to be safely shared among multiple, concurrent users.

The second group is made up of people with a DBMS background who are looking for different ways to store data. They might be looking for better performance or better modeling capabilities. This book will provide them with examples that compare the object and relational models—and the aspects of relational models that might indicate they should be considering an object model and storing data in an ODBMS.

A third sct includes people who manage projects and are wondering if the technology is real. If it is, they want to know the advantages and disadvantages of the technology. This book will provide a background to the technology and where it can be used most successfully, along with a model of how to best ensure such success.

Finally, those people who have decided to use a DBMS for objects and need some guidance in selecting an ODBMS and deploying a successful application will find the book helpful. It provides a selection model that addresses the larger context including business strategies and selection team needs.

The book is organized in three parts to allow those with varying levels of expertise to access what they need directly. Part I, "Laying the Foundation," presents the basic concepts of using ODBMSs, with a focus on providing simple-to-understand explanations of concepts. These basic concepts are covered in a way that provides a commonality of reference for the rest of the book. This is a high-level view with details deferred until later in the book when specific features/functionality are discussed. Several sample cases are developed and used throughout the book to allow readers to see the basic concepts as well as more advanced concepts later in this book using familiar diagrams.

Part II, "Selecting and Deploying," focuses on selecting and deploying ODBMSs. A model for successful implementation is presented and developed in detail. Of particular interest to many will be Chapter 8, which provides an overview of feature interaction focusing on the features of locking granularity and the location of method and query execution in a client/server environment. This is a topic of interest to nearly all developers and provides a detailed hands-on view of the importance of feature interaction. Chapter 10 concentrates on how to rework an existing relational data model into an object model and walks the reader through the steps required to do this. This can be used by readers in several ways. First, it provides a mapping between an object schema and a relational schema for those readers more accustomed to relational schema. Second, it provides steps needed for those readers who want to keep existing data in a relational DBMS, while mapping the data into an object structure that can be used either by an ODBMS that supports a gateways to relational DBMSs or directly by an object programming language. Third, it provides a mapping technique for converting data from a relational DBMS to an ODBMS.

Part III, "Detailed Selection Checklists," is made up of detailed checklists aggregated into 13 categories. These checklists will help readers to understand the possible features available to them in ODBMS products and will prompt a fresh examination of their application needs. These checklists, the most extensive listing of ODBMS features available, go far beyond any of the marketing and sales literature you might receive from the vendors. They cover the details that will likely spell the difference between success and failure when you deploy your application.

Terminology can be confusing to readers and can make the text difficult to read. As a remedy, I will use the term DBMS in this book for any type of database management system. Relational DBMSs will be identified as RDBMSs. The term ODBMSs refers to products that work with objects: Object-Relational Mapping, Object Manager DBMSs, Object DBMSs, and Object-Relational DBMSs (these are defined in Chapter 4). I will spell out Object-Relational Mapping, Object Manager DBMSs, Object DBMSs and Object-Relational DBMSs in referring to specific types of products. Although this varies from the "official" definition of an ODBMS put out by the Object Database Management Group (ODMG), I believe this will make the reader's task an easier one. In addition, I sometimes use the term *application* in the singular. This has no special meaning. All of the material in this book applies to the common situation of selecting an ODBMS for use by multiple applications. Finally, a glossary is provided as a reference for terminology used in this book.

Acknowledgments

There are, of course, many people to whom I owe a debt of gratitude for their help and inspiration both in my work in ODBMSs and in the development of this book. The following people deserve a special acknowledgment.

My wife, Rosie, who has contributed to this book in more ways than anyone could ever know.

My daughter, Katie, who was remarkably patient with her grouchy old dad as he worked through some of the details in this book.

The ODBMS vendors without whom this book would not be possible.

My clients whose struggles with the technology formed the basis of much of what is written here.

Janet Gardner and Joshua Duhl for their excellent comments and suggestions as technical reviewers. Both have been in the ODBMS industry as long as I have and I value their technical expertise.

Marie Lenzi who gave me the wonderful opportunity to practice writing about the ODBMS industry when she asked that I be the Database columnist for Object Magazine.

My cohorts—both vendors and users—in the Object Database Management Group for working so hard to bring standardization to the ODBMS industry.

Won Kim and the many members of his research team at the Micro-

*electronics and Computer Technology Corporation (MCC) for intro-
ducing me to ODBMS technology back in 1987.*

Jim Ruble who has encouraged me to do what is right over the years.

*Bruce Holmberg who introduced me to Framastats back in high
school—although he never explained their actual operation at the
time, they have taken a form of their own in this book. Bruce still
needs explain to me what exactly is a left-handed Framastat.*

About the Author

Doug Barry is an independent consultant, speaker, and author specializing in ODBMS technology. In his current practice, he works with a broad array of clients who are applying this new technology to their products. His area of particular specialty is the selection of an ODBMS that makes successful product development and deployment possible. Through his work as Executive Director of the ODMG, an industry standards group, Mr. Barry has been involved with efforts to create ODBMS standards and promote those standards in the industry.

Mr. Barry has worked with DBMS technology for over 20 years and has been working with ODBMSs since 1987, when he was the Control Data Corporation database liaison to MCC during the development of the ORION ODBMS project. He maintained that connection to MCC when he co-founded Itasca Systems, where he guided the technical development of ORION into the commercial product ITASCA.

Upon leaving ITASCA Systems in 1992, Mr. Barry founded Barry & Associates. To simplify the ODBMS selection process and focus it on product features, he compiled and published *The DBMS Needs Assessment for Objects*, a data book on ODBMS features, which he now updates and publishes on an annual basis. In addition, he speaks widely on this topic. Mr. Barry provides an informed, unbiased source of information about ODBMSs and the companies that develop them.

Laying the Foundation

Part 1 is intended to provide information on the basics you need to understand before you can implement object database technology. In Chapter 1, the basic concepts of using an ODBMS are overviewed for those readers new to the topic. Chapter 2 focuses on complex data. The need for excellent performance on complex data is at the heart of object database technology, so a clear understanding of it is essential. Then for those who understand the relational model, Chapter 3 compares the relational model to the object model. In Chapter 4, the spectrum of object products is categorized by product architecture to make it easier for you to begin to evaluate the best fit between your application needs and the products available. Finally, Chapter 5 presents information about the standards that can be helpful in understanding the direction in which the industry is moving.

This part of the book is designed to provide a basic understanding needed in order to use the more technical material presented in Parts II and III. If you, like me, jump into new things without reading the directions, you might be tempted to skip ahead. That may be okay if you have a thorough grounding in the object concepts. If not, this section will give you the foundation you need. With this foundation, the material in Part II, Selecting and Deploying, will be more meaningful. It also provides the depth of understanding required to make use of Part III, Detailed Selection Checklists.

1

Basic Concepts for Using Object Databases

My first encounter with object technology took place in 1987. At that time, ODBMSs were merely prototypes or pioneer products. If you are just getting started in object technology, I can understand what you are going through. In 1987, object concepts seemed completely contrary to my Relational DBMS (RDBMS) training. Frankly, as I worked with the concepts, I mainly got a headache trying to put what seemed to be round pegs into square holes.

At that time, I was responsible for finding ways to apply this new ODBMS technology at the company for which I worked. A colleague from the company's Computer Aided Design (CAD) group approached me with a challenge. It seemed the CAD group had a benchmark that they used to compare DBMS products—it was a door hinge with the pin missing. In other words, it was half of a hinge, and it had 18 objects in it. The CAD group's benchmark was to create hundreds of half door hinges. My colleague wanted to know what impact an ODBMS might have on the benchmark. Because of the headaches I gave myself thinking about object technology, I was dubious that there could be any benefit that wouldn't be achieved by just using an RDBMS.

So I put a research ODBMS prototype, a pioneering ODBMS product, and an RDBMS product through their paces on the same computer system. As I looked at the outcome, I realized that I had better get over my object technology headaches. On the early ODBMS product and prototype, the hinge benchmark ran between 7 and 100 times faster than it ran on the RDBMS. And not only did it run faster, it required much less code.

This little vignette illustrates not only my original insight into object technology, but also a recognition of my blind spot. As a relational person, I had little appreciation for the performance on complex data that an ODBMS could achieve. The training that had made me pretty good at Relational DBMS work gave me a blind spot about what other aspects of computer technology could do. And I know others have blind spots as well. I can see them when I work with clients. Programmers don't really understand DBMSs. Relational DBMS people don't understand object technology. RDBMS people don't appreciate how object programming languages are integrated into many ODBMSs. In implementing an application using ODBMSs, be aware of your blind spot as you go forward. When you ignore the blind spot as you roar down the freeway, you may be on a collision course before you know it. The same is true in the implementation of object technology. Check your blind spot by getting the facts before you find yourself on a collision course that will jeopardize your company's large investment or your career.

This chapter is intended to help you begin to identify the blind spot before it becomes a problem for you. It focuses on the basic concepts of the object model, DBMSs, and the integration of object programming languages with DBMSs. Information about the notation that will be used throughout this book is woven into these basic concepts.

Key points to be covered in this chapter include:

- The basic object concepts.

- A brief overview of relational concepts and terminology.

- The theory behind what DBMSs provide. These are called the ACID properties—atomicity, consistency, isolation, and durability.

- A discussion of the various ways object programming languages can be integrated with DBMSs.

Object Model Concepts

Just as a blueprint creates a symbolic representation of a building, we create many different types of symbols to represent items that are too complex to say in a few words. An object model, the core of object technology, is a set of concepts that defines how complex entities and processes in the real world can be modeled into an object schema, or data definition. Examples of things that might be represented in an object schema are a bill of materials, a manu- facturing process, a telecommunications network, or the relationship of vari- ous financial instruments in banking, investment, or insurance industries.

For those of you familiar with the relational model, as you look at the exam- ples you may note that an object schema may represent more complex data than a relational schema. This ability to portray greater complexity makes it possible to create a model of complex data, which is one of the great strengths of object technology.

Three concepts—data abstraction, encapsulation, and inheritance—are critical to understanding object models. These basic concepts are shown in Figure 1.1.

Data Abstraction

In illustrating a real-world situation, a large amount of information must be distilled down to its essentials. This process is data abstraction—making an abstract model of a tangible reality to meet needs of a set of applications. In an object schema, the abstract data model is usually implemented as a graph. Figure 1.2 and Figure 1.3 illustrate two very different examples of data

Data Abstraction

Encapsulation

Inheritance

**Object concepts for
all object technology**

Figure 1.1 *Basic object model concepts.*

abstraction. In the first example, a family tree illustrates how a complex set of people and relationships can be reduced to a simple drawing. The second illustration portrays a business example of a simple parts explosion, which again takes a set of interrelationships and reduces them to a drawing.

Object Instances

In abstracting a real-world item or process into an object schema, many entities are created. Each single entity is called an object instance. In Figure 1.4, you see the circles representing real-world entities of a person named Doug and a part called a Fram Mount. In this book, circles will be used to illustrate single entities or object instances.

Object Identification (OID)

In object models, every object instance has a unique, unchanging identity called an object identification, or OID for short. OIDs are used to reference object instances.

There are several important characteristics of OIDs. First, OIDs are generated by the object system. Users or programs have no control over identifica-

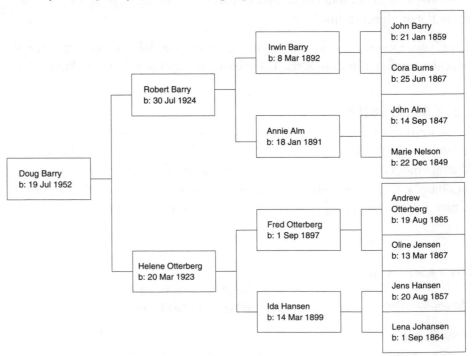

Figure 1.2 *A family tree as a data abstraction.*

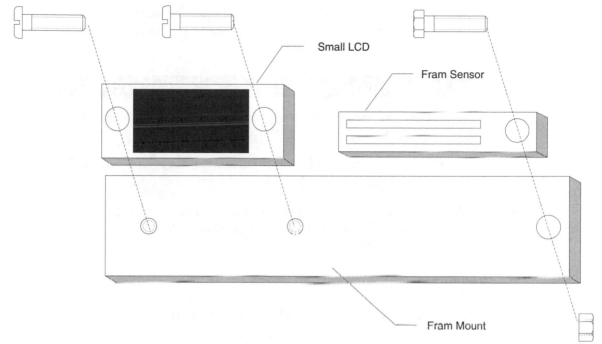

Figure 1.3 *Parts explosion abstraction of a Framastat.*

tion or the form of the OID. Second, OIDs are independent of the data contained in the object. The internal data values are not used to generate identification, so there is nothing in the data itself that is reflected in the OID.

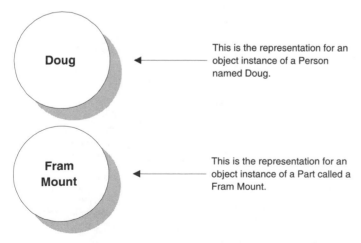

Figure 1.4 *Instance object notation.*

Finally, the OID lasts the lifetime of the object. The identification of the object never changes even when the data contents may change.

Characteristics of OIDs

- OIDs are independent of the data contained in the object. The internal data values are not used to generate identification.

- OIDs are generated by the object system. Users or programs have no control over identification.

- OIDs last the lifetime of the object. Identification of the object never changes even when the data contents may change.

References using OIDs are represented as arrows in this notation. This is illustrated in Figure 1.5. As we get deeper into the aspects of storing objects, you will see why the use of OIDs is one of the reasons many of the ODBMS products are noted for high performance.

Relationships

An ODBMS differs from an RDBMS in that an ODBMS directly supports relationships. As is the case in real life, most object instances are "related" to one

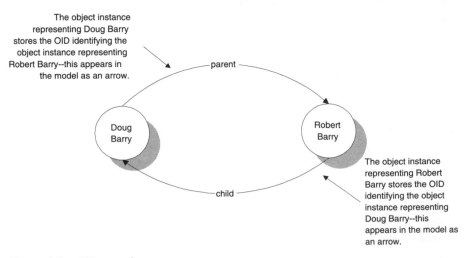

Figure 1.5 *OIDs as references.*

another in some way. People in a family aren't just isolated people; they are parents and children, sisters and brothers, cousins and in-laws. Parts in a parts explosion aren't just isolated items; they are pieces that fit together in some way. These relationships are illustrated in an object schema diagram by arrows.

A new graph of the family tree first shown in Figure 1.2 is illustrated using object notation in Figure 1.6. Relationships are represented by the arrows. The arrows in this case go in either direction because in one direction it's a child relationship and in the other direction it's a parent relationship. This is a way to simplify the appearance of the model by collapsing the two arrows shown in Figure 1.5. The OIDs mentioned earlier are used for representing these relationships. There is an OID for each object instance. Different object instances refer to each other by using the OIDs. So, in Figure 1.6, Robert Barry has a single OID that identifies that object instance. Irwin Barry and Doug Barry refer to Robert Barry using that OID.

When real life is abstracted and represented in an object schema, the OIDs are critical for keeping track of who's who and what's what. In some cases, there may appear to be other options for identification. In the genealogy example, Social Security Numbers (SSNs) might be used to keep track of the object instances. Take a look at Figure 1.2, however, and identify the draw-back to that approach. The people to the far right did not have SSNs because this form of identification was not in place until the 1930s. Their only identi-fication is positional—it is determined by those to whom they are related. Object systems deal directly with identification by using OIDs, which are generated automatically from the object system and can be used for refer-ences in situations such as that shown in Figure 1.6.

Classes

Object instances can be grouped together into a class, which is a grouping of objects that have similarity. The class defines the structure and the data items for each of the objects. A class, when it is part of a larger object schema, is sometimes referred to as a class object because it serves as an instance of a class. If this is confusing to you, it is not critical to this discussion to get into the more sophisticated aspects of the object model at this time. Look at some of the texts on object models if you want to study the object model further. To simplify our discussion here, the term *class* will be used and we won't worry about classes as instances of something else.

In our genealogy example, the class is Person. In Figure 1.6, many different people, each an object instance, are represented. The class, Person, defines a basic structure or characteristic of all of the object instances. Each class also has attributes, which are its characteristics, such as name or the person's date

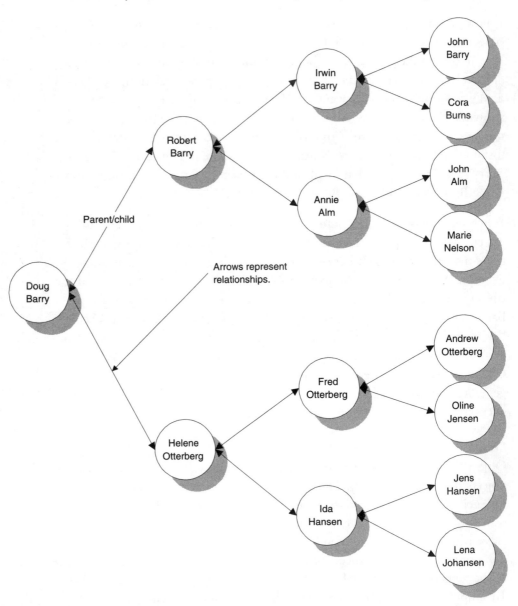

Figure 1.6 *Graph structure for genealogy example.*

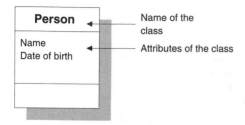

Figure 1.7 *Class notation.*

of birth. In Figure 1.6, other possible class names might be Human Being, People, or Family Members. Other attributes in Figure 1.6 might be place of birth, date of marriage, and date of death. Figure 1.7 provides a view of notation for classes used in this book. It is based on the Object Modeling Technique (OMT) notation (*Object-oriented Modeling and Design*, James Rumbaugh et al., Prentice-Hall, 1991).

The notation for a class includes the name of the class at the top with its attributes or characteristics of note shown below the name. Attributes can also contain a reference to object instances of the same class or object instances of other classes. As shown in Figure 1.5, this is where the OIDs that refer to other objects are kept. Similarly, every Person object instance in Figure 1.6 refers to two parents. (As an adoptive parent, I know this is an oversimplification of the real world where we have birth parents, adoptive parents, stepparents, foster parents, and so on. For the examples in this book, I will use two parents.) The Parents attribute is where those references are stored. In Figure 1.8, the Parents attribute is a reference back to the Person class showing that a Person has two parents.

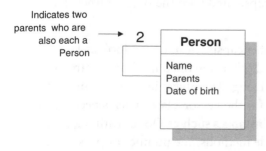

Figure 1.8 *Class notation with Parents references.*

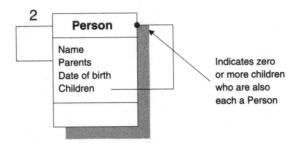

Figure 1.9 *Class notation with Parents and Children references.*

To complete the class, the Children attribute is added in Figure 1.9 to show zero or more children. This is where the OIDs that refer to the Children of a Person are kept. The genealogy chart in Figure 1.6 is based on the notation in Figure 1.9.

Encapsulation

The second important concept for the object model is encapsulation. Encapsulation refers to the concept of including processing or behavior with the object instances defined by the class. Encapsulation allows code and data to be packaged together.

The definition of methods for the class is an integral part of encapsulation. A method is programming code that performs behavior an object instance can exhibit. In the genealogy example, the object instances could have behavior such as marrying and dying. Calculating the age of a person would be another example of such behavior. Figure 1.10 shows a way of looking at encapsulating the Age method with a Doug instance object. The code for the age method is "attached" to or encapsulated with the object rather than part of the application.

To better understand the concept of encapsulation, take a look at Figure 1.10. Note that the Age method and other unnamed methods wrap around or encapsulate the object instance, Doug. The object instance is shown here even though the method is defined for the Person class. This is because the Age method acts on Person object instances such as Doug. Although the figure illustrates space for four possible methods, the number of possible methods is arbitrary, based on the needs of the class. It is not uncommon,

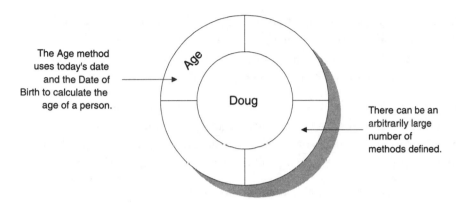

The Age method uses today's date and the Date of Birth to calculate the age of a person.

There can be an arbitrarily large number of methods defined.

Figure 1.10 *Encapsulation notation.*

however, to find more than 50 methods defined for a given class. For that reason, although we have shown the wrapping for illustrative purposes, you do not usually see methods shown in object instance drawings such as the genealogy example because it clutters the drawing.

The notation for encapsulation builds on the notation that we saw earlier in the chapter. Appropriate methods, which are limited to Age in the genealogy example, are shown at the bottom of the class notation, as illustrated in Figure 1.11.

Code and data were not always packaged together. At one time, for example, it was necessary to define an age calculation in each application or have a library that contained the age calculation routine. Having an age calculation, or any routine, replicated in many applications may make it difficult to ensure that a change in the routine was made everywhere that it is used.

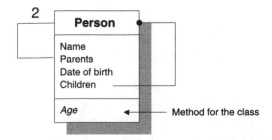

Method for the class

Figure 1.11 *Notation for methods associated with a class.*

Using a library improves this situation if use of the library is enforced. Nevertheless, with a library, you can never be sure which routine is supposed to be used with which data. It is entirely possible to execute the right code on the wrong data or the wrong code on the right data.

Object systems recognize which methods belong to which data. You cannot execute the right method on the wrong data as you could with library systems. The correct execution of methods is called *dispatching*, and it is handled by the object system. Dispatching will be explained further in Chapter 3.

Encapsulation makes it possible to maintain routines, such as the calculation of age, conceptually as part of the data. There are several ways to store methods depending on where the methods execute in the system. This might be a critical factor for you in choosing an ODBMS. We will look at it in more detail in Chapter 8 as well as Checklist 3, "Procedures and Programming," in Part III.

Associating code and data together is especially helpful in large systems with lots of code and data; this is sometimes termed *programming in the large*. By modeling your system with the processing (methods) directly associated with the appropriate data (classes), it is easier to manage the development and maintenance of the system. In short, it is not necessary to manage a set of routines separately from the management of the data.

Inheritance

The third concept is inheritance. Inheritance is a concept we use all the time. We say a robin is a type of bird. Of course, we all know what a robin is. But if I said a fwizzle is a type of bird, what would you know about a fwizzle? Actually, you know quite a bit about it. It can probably fly, it probably builds nests, it probably sings, and so on. These are concepts a fwizzle inherits from the basic characteristics of birds.

In short, inheritance is a means of defining one class in terms of another. In the example above, we made some assumptions about a fwizzle based on what we know about the class, Bird.

The University example in Figure 1.12 further illustrates this concept. A Student is a type of Person. Likewise, a Professor is a type of Person. Both Student and Professor inherit all the attributes and methods of Person. They each also have attributes defined that are unique to each of them. A Student "takes" courses and a Professor "teaches" courses. Because Student and Professor inherit the attributes and methods of Person, you can obtain the Name of a Student as well as determine the age of a Student using the Age method.

Reuse

There is one additional note related to the concepts of object technology. In this University example, we *reused* the Person class from the Genealogy example. This is actually one of the biggest design challenges of object technology—to be effective in designing class definitions for reuse and then to be effective at reusing the definitions. Some practical considerations for reusability will be discussed in Chapter 9.

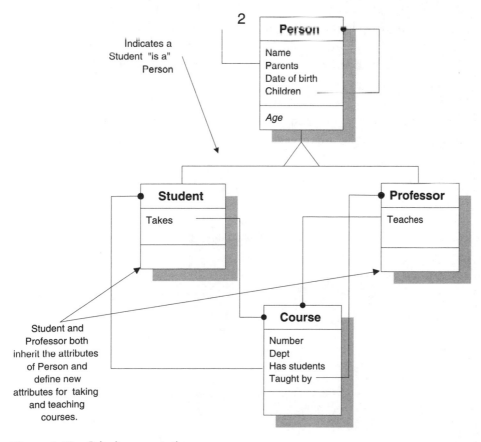

Figure 1.12   *Inheritance notation.*

Relational Model Terminology

Some discussion of basic terminology in the relational model is necessary because the terms are used throughout this book. This will cover only the terminology and is not meant to be a comprehensive discussion of the relational model. A more detailed comparison of the object and relational models can be found in Chapter 3.

The basic concept in the relational model is the *relation* or table, which contains the definition of the data. The *columns* or fields in the table identify attributes such as name, age, and so on. A *tuple* or row contains all the data of a single instance of the table such as a person named Doug.

In the relational model, every tuple must have a unique identification or *key* based on the data. In Figure 1.13, an SSN is the key that uniquely identifies each tuple in the relation. Often, keys are used to join data from two or more relations together based on matching identification. The relational model also includes concepts such as *foreign keys*, which are primary keys in one relation that are kept in another relation to allow for the joining of data. An example of foreign keys is storing your mother's and father's SSNs in the tuple that represents you. Your parents' SSNs are keys for the tuples that represent them and there are foreign keys in the tuple that represent you.

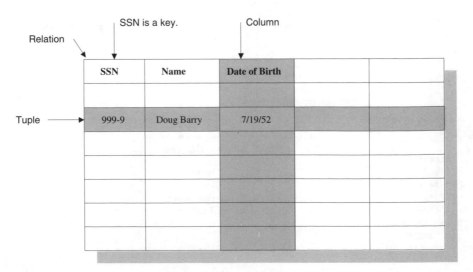

Figure 1.13 *Basic relational components.*

DBMS Concepts

With the basic concepts of the object and relational models in place, we can build on this understanding by taking a look at basic DBMS concepts. These concepts apply to both RDBMSs and ODBMSs. One of the most critical benefits of DBMSs is that they allow the safe sharing of data by more than one user. If you and I both wanted to check the Age of Doug at the same time that would be an example of sharing data. When we are doing this, it would be important that neither of us change Doug's date of birth because that would affect what the other person is doing. DBMSs manage this sharing behavior.

The properties of a DBMS that allow this sharing of data to be safe are known as the ACID properties—atomicity, consistency, isolation, and durability. Without these ACID properties, everyday occurrences such as the transfer of funds between bank accounts would be difficult and the potential for inaccuracy would be huge. Imagine more than one person transferring funds out of a single account—a regular occurrence. The ACID properties make it possible for the bank to keep these multiple bank transfers from overlapping each other—potentially causing erroneous bank balances. These ACID properties are the focus of this section.

Atomicity

The first of the ACID properties to consider is atomicity, which refers to the "all or nothing" flavor of an entire sequence of operations as it is applied to the database. Simply put, as the user performs updates to the database, either all or none of the updates are visible to the outside world. This is called a *transaction*. A transaction either commits or aborts. In this way you get the whole change or no change, and not just a part of the change should something go wrong in either the software or the hardware of your computer system.

Consistency

Consistency refers to the preservation of the integrity of the information in the database despite the actions of multiple users working at the same time. A simple example is to consider multiple designers working on different aspects of a new Framastat. As each person updates drawings, this can impact all others. The DBMS gives each designer a consistent view of the

Framastat for the duration of their transaction. You would not want the Framastat you are working on to be changed by someone else while a transaction is in process.

Isolation

As shared objects are accessed by multiple users, the DBMS must manage possible conflicts between *concurrent transactions*. Concurrent transactions are those that occur at the same time, illustrated as activities occurring over time at the top of Figure 1.14. The series of safeguards that a DBMS uses to prevent conflicts between concurrent transactions is referred to as *isolation*.

If two people are updating the same Fram Mount object, it's not acceptable for one person's changes to be written over when the second person saves a different set of changes. Both users should be able to behave as though each user is the only user and his or her changes are isolated from those of the other users.

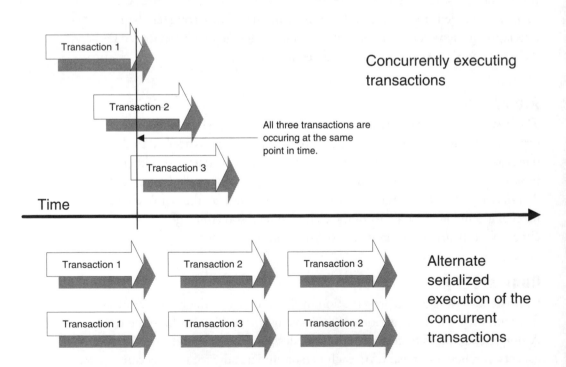

Figure 1.14 *Serializing transactions.*

Serializability is a concept basic to understanding isolation through transactions. Transactions are serializable if the interleaved execution of their operations produces the same effects on the database as their execution in some serial order. This is illustrated in Figure 1.14. At the top of Figure 1.14, you can see Transaction 1 through Transaction 3 executing concurrently over time. What happens in the DBMS is that the transactions may execute in serial order based on consistency and isolation requirements. Possible ways in which these transactions may execute are shown at the bottom of Figure 1.14. Serialized execution does not imply the transactions that start first are necessarily the ones guaranteed to terminate before other transactions in the serial order.

It is possible to relax this serializability in some cases—but it can result in unexpected behavior. Even the terms for that behavior sound unpleasant—*lost updates* and *dirty reads*—yet they are sometimes needed. They are described in detail in Checklist 7, "Transactions," in Part III.

There is an inverse relationship between the level of isolation and the throughput of concurrent transactions. More specifically, the more transactions are isolated from one another, the higher the likelihood of conflicts and hence, transaction aborts.

Different DBMS products provide different levels of isolation between concurrently executing transactions. Some products also allow the choice of different levels of isolation. Checklist 7, "Transactions," in Part III illustrates this.

Durability

Once a transaction is committed, the updates of that transaction must never be lost. Durability refers to the ability of the system to recover committed transaction updates if either the system or the storage media fails. Checklist 1, "General Architecture," and Checklist 7, "Transactions," in Part III identify key characteristics to be considered.

DBMSs and Objects

The ACID properties allow a DBMS to provide safe, secure, multi-user access to shared data. The ACID properties make the objects *persistent*. An object is persistent when it can be manipulated in a programming language and saved in

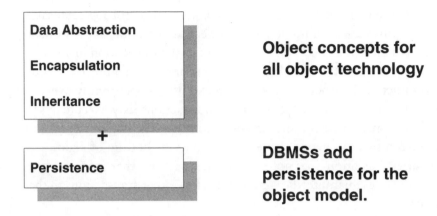

Figure 1.15 *ODBMSs retain the object model concepts while adding persistence.*

the database before exiting the program; when you return at a later time that object is available to you. That object is persistent. A way to make persistence more tangible is to imagine the impact a power outage can have. Because of the persistence provided by the ACID properties, work that has been saved prior to the power outage will remain stable despite the problem.

Taking the object model and applying DBMS concepts to it gives you the capability of making the objects persistent, as illustrated in Figure 1.15. A DBMS that allows the storing of objects will retain all the capabilities of the object model and will add the ability to make the objects persistent. This section will cover some basic architectural components for using objects with DBMSs.

Client/Server Architecture

This section provides a high-level set of concepts for client applications, as well as a view of how objects are stored on the disk. A later section in this book will put these components together to show the different that approaches vendors have taken in developing ODBMSs.

A client/server environment is created when you combine an application running on a client with a DBMS on a server. In this environment, the programming language is used in the client and the DBMS is the server managing the data stored on the disk. Some of the DBMS software is also on the client, which will be covered at a later point.

Basic notation used in this book to indicate a multi-user, client/server DBMS architecture is shown in Figure 1.16. The clients, usually some type of application, are shown at the left. This may be either an interactive application or

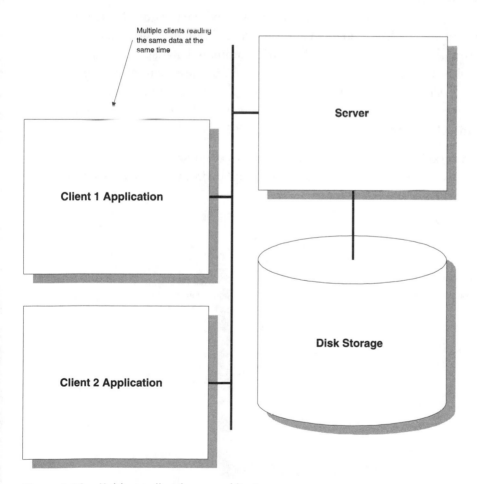

Figure 1.16 *Multi-user client/server architecture.*

a program running by itself. Either type of application will be seen as a user of the DBMS. The clients and server are shown as if they are on separate machines connected via a network. They could be on the same machine. Various types of clients will be described in the next section.

As indicated in the discussion of the ACID properties, DBMSs allow multiple users to read/write data at the same time with safety. Figure 1.16 illustrates this capability.

Client Applications

Clients can be programmed in three ways—with embedded Structured Query Language (SQL), through an application program interface (API), or transparently integrated with an object programming language. Examples of each will be highlighted over the next few pages. In these examples, assume that the desired type of programming language is an object programming language. This means that the application will see the data as objects—not in any other form.

The graph shown in Figure 1.17 illustrates the notation that will be used for the examples. The objects get into the application workspace in a variety of ways. Each will be described.

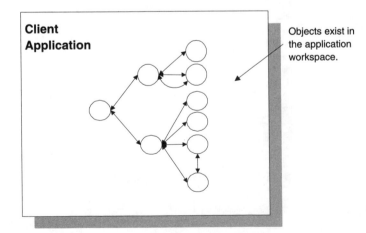

Figure 1.17 *Objects in the client application.*

```
host language statement
host language statement

    embedded SQL statement

host language statement

    embedded SQL statement

host language statement
```

Figure 1.18   *Embedded SQL in host programming language.*

Embedded SQL

The approach used by RDBMSs with programming languages is embedded SQL, a database sublanguage. This technique is also used by some ODBMSs. Embedded SQL requires interleaving the host programming language with SQL statements as shown in Figure 1.18. The host programming language could be C, C++, Smalltalk, COBOL, FORTRAN, Ada, or other languages.

The embedded SQL does all the database manipulation. The host programming language does all the application work. As a result, the application program using embedded SQL must contain the necessary code to convert the relational data in the form of tuples to the host programming language data structures. The notation for this is shown in Figure 1.19.

Application Program Interface (API)

A second approach is to provide some type of call-level or application program interface (API) that does not require the use of embedded SQL and looks more like the host programming language (see Figure 1.20). This is done with special function or procedure calls in the host programming language. The most well-known form of such an API is ODBC (see Chapter 5), but there can be many other, often proprietary, APIs.

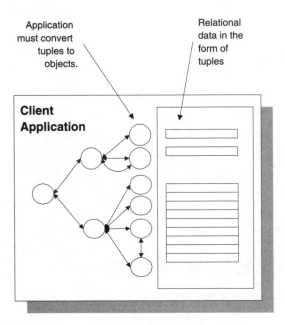

Figure 1.19 *Embedded SQL in client application.*

With an API, the client application still may need to convert the results to objects for use in an object programming language. The notation for this is shown in Figure 1.21.

```
host language statement
host language statement

database call in host language statement

host language statement

database call in host language statement

host language statement
```

Figure 1.20 *Database API calls for a host programming language.*

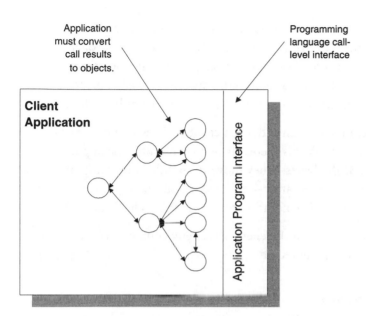

Figure 1.21 *Application Program Interface notation in client application.*

Transparent Program Integration

The third approach is to transparently integrate the object programming language with the DBMS interaction. When this is done, the object manipula-

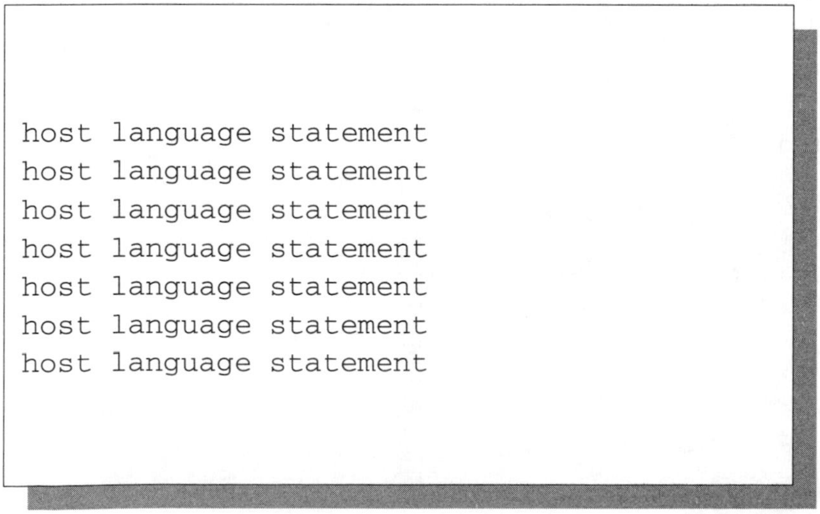

```
host language statement
host language statement
host language statement
host language statement
host language statement
host language statement
host language statement
```

Figure 1.22 *Transparent integration of DBMS in host programming language.*

tion (updating, deleting, traversing objects, etc.) is done the same way for all objects whether or not they are stored in the DBMS. In this approach, only a few additional commands for DBMS functions, such as starting transactions or committing transactions, are added to the programming language to achieve the DBMS interaction. Figure 1.22 shows an example of the code.

When this transparent integration is done, a client cache is set up as part of the application work space. With this cache, there is no need for the application to explicitly translate DBMS objects—they move from disk storage automatically into program memory representation—either as a result of a query or from traversing the graph structure. The notation for this is shown in Figure 1.23.

The clients are only one part of the client/server environment. Next we will look at what occurs on the server side.

Server Disk Storage

Objects can be stored using DBMSs in two ways, as relational tuples or directly as objects on disk. The notations for each type of storage will be shown in this section.

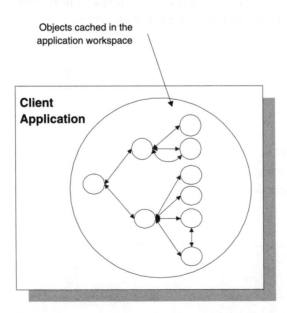

Figure 1.23 *Transparent program integration in client application.*

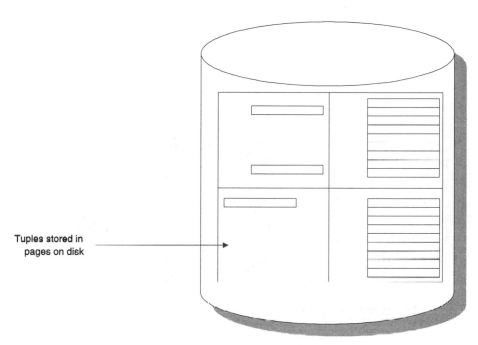

Tuples stored in
pages on disk

Figure 1.24 *Tuple disk storage.*

Tuple Disk Storage

When objects are stored as tuples, the OID references between objects must
be converted to some other type of data so that the OID references can be
stored on disk since RDBMSs have no concept of OIDs. The tuples are then
stored in tables that are in pages on the disk. These pages may be managed
by the file system or they might bypass the file systems and be stored directly
on the disk using what is called a *raw partition*. The notation for this type of
storage is shown in Figure 1.24.

Object Disk Storage

The second way objects may be stored on the disk is direct storage, which
maintains the OID references between objects (see Figure 1.25). The objects
are stored on pages much like the tuples are. These pages may be managed
by the file system or they may be raw partitions.

The impact of the different storage formats on the servers with the different
types of clients will be covered in Chapter 4.

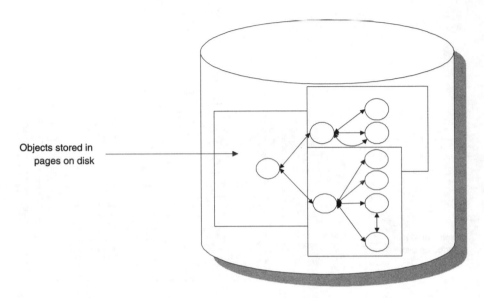

Figure 1.25 *Object disk storage.*

Summary

Basic concepts about object technology, relational terminology, database theory, and the ways object programming languages can be integrated with DBMSs were introduced in this chapter. They provide a basic understanding that will be useful in the next chapter on complex data.

Complex Data

When I look back about ten years, I clearly remember a project where I was involved in the development of a corporate personnel system designed to use an RDBMS. By the time we finished modeling the data, the relational schema covered all the walls of a large conference room. Now, if you've never worked on a personnel system, it may seem like a simple project and you might think the data would be very simple. The conference room walls should provide a hint of the level of complexity for you. They certainly did for me.

As an individual employee, it can appear that everyone has the same employee status as you do. But, as it turns out, there are many. Employee status is based on logical things such as different kinds of jobs with different pay systems—such as salespeople with commissions or managers with bonuses based on performance. There may be different benefits systems as well, and, of course, some people work part-time. Then as a reflection of contemporary business, there are also the parts of the company that have been acquired over time. These parts probably have employees with one of several possible editions of grandfathered status sets. And on it goes.

That personnel system seemed simple to me at the beginning, but as I got more involved, the complexity of the data began to dawn on me. You may also have had an experience of something that looks to be simple turning out to be complex. Complex data is everywhere; sometimes we only recognize it too late, unfortunately.

An RDBMS can be successful with complex data to a point, but somewhere along the line the data becomes too complex. In those cases, as well as others, an ODBMS can be a project saver. An ODBMS often can excel in situations where large amounts of complex data must be stored and retrieved. Representing complex data in a relational schema, which is the alternative, can be difficult to do efficiently. Complex data and how it is handled in RDBMSs and ODBMSs are the focus of this chapter.

The key points in this chapter include:

- Complex data often lacks unique, natural identification.

- Complex data can often be identified in a relational schema by a large number of many-to-many relationships (this was one reason why the personnel model mentioned above was so large).

- Complex data often requires traversing a graph structure.

- Complex data often requires the use of type codes in the relational schema.

Complex Data Is Everywhere

Once you know how to look for complex data, you will notice it everywhere. For an example of how seemingly simple data becomes complex, let's go back to the family tree example described earlier and shown again in Figure 2.1.

The family tree in Figure 2.1 shows only part of the data about a family. The same family is shown in Figure 2.2, but now from another point of view, that of the descendants of John Barry and Cora Burns. Although both figures illustrate members of the same family, only some of them appear in both figures—John, Irwin, Robert, and Doug Barry, as well as Cora Burns. Neither figure shows all the marriages, the descendants, the ancestors of those who married into this family, and many other family situations that may be too complex to mention here. So, Figure 2.2 still does not show all the data, but it does indicate how complex it can become. In your mind, try to imagine Figure 2.1 and Figure 2.2 together. If you can do that, now imagine a graph of the combined figures, this time with all the descendants of the people in Figure 2.1. It can get pretty complex.

Other examples of complex data include data models for multimedia, banking, insurance, investment trading, telecommunications, and manufacturing. Some of the ways to recognize complex data will be shown along with examples. You can recognize complex data by looking for a lack of unique identi-

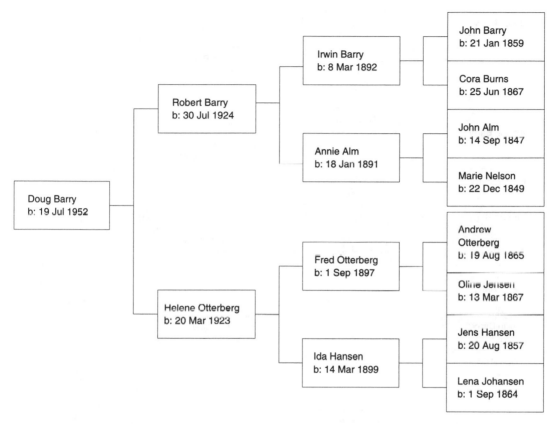

Figure 2.1   *A family tree as a data abstraction.*

fication in your data, many-to-many relationships in your data, data access using traversals, or frequent use of type codes in your data.

Lack of Unique Identification

Many things come into the world without unique identification built into them. Without their license plates or serial numbers, vehicles cannot be described individually. Color, make, model, and age can go a long way to describe a vehicle, but the license plate and the vehicle identification stamped on the car itself are the only unique identifiers for a vehicle.

A person is another example of something that comes into the world without a unique identifier (other than DNA). In the United States, Social Security Num-

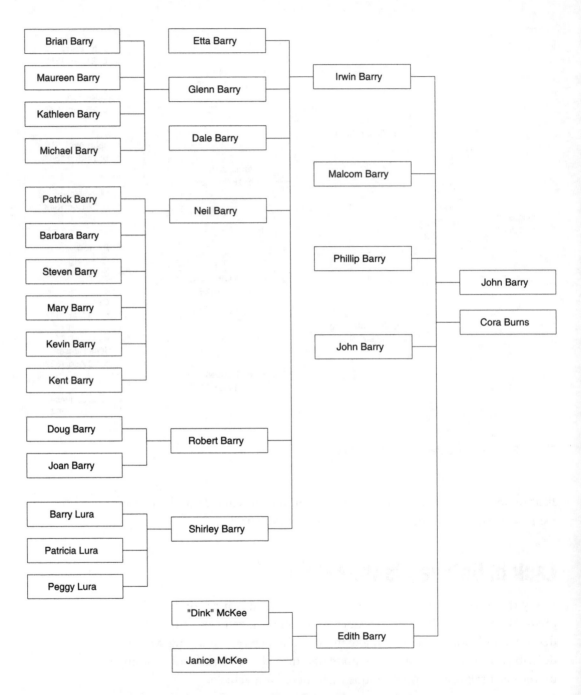

Figure 2.2 *Some of the descendants of John Barry and Cora Burns.*

bers (SSNs) were created in the 1930s to overcome this problem. As explained in Chapter 1, a group of people called a family can be depicted in a graph. In Figure 2.1, you will see some people in that family who never had an SSN because they died before receiving one, and whose only identification is, therefore, positional—to whom are they related. This is common with complex data.

A street address is still another example of a tangible thing that lacks unique identification since there is no natural unique identification for this other than the entire address itself.

Some less tangible things that lack unique identification would be things such as a feeling, a sound, or a movement. The data compiled as part of brain research would very likely include feelings and movement or even sound. These less tangible things do exist in the real world and you may want to reference such things as part of a data definition.

Object systems generate OIDs to provide system-level identification for things that have meaning based on only who or what is related to it or uses it. The OIDs allow easy representation of data that lacks unique identification as well as data that has unique identification. Chapter 1 illustrated how OIDs are used for references. For data without inherent unique identification, the OID provides a unique, unchanging way to reference that data. For data with an inherent unique identification, the OID provides an alternate unchanging way of referencing that data even if the unique identification changes. An example of where you may want to retain references even if the unique identification changes may be in the case where, for whatever reason, your company decides to change the structure of Part ID numbers. By using references based on OIDs, you can change the Part ID structure without affecting anything that references those parts.

A common characteristic of complex data is that it is represented by a graph in the object schema. OIDs provide the way of referencing data in such a graph structure.

Many-to-Many Relationships

Many-to-many relationships provide another sign of complex data. If you say x relates to many y and y relates to many x, you have a many-to-many relationship. For example, a Student can take many courses and a Course can be taken by many students. This is a many-to-many relationship—each instance in the relationship, Student and Course, has many options, as shown in Figure 2.3. The notation for a many-to-many relationship is shown in Figure 2.4.

A Word About Notation

The notation used in this and other sections of this book are a variant of the OMT notation. This is a conscious decision that will make the material easier to understand for readers new to object technology. It is nonstandard to use separate lines for each relationship, but using the standard notation—a single line with filled-in circles at each end—would make it impossible to illustrate the points that must be covered simply.

DBMSs that use the object model have no problem storing these many-to-many relationships. They are stored much like you see them in Figure 2.3.

These many-to-many relationships can create a problem, however, in an RDBMS because the relational model does not allow for repeating groups. A

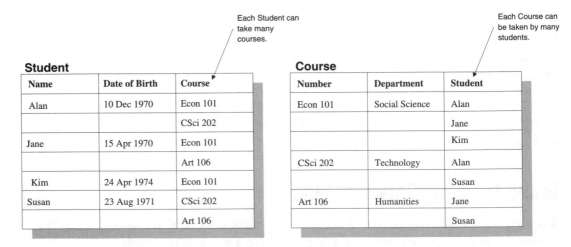

Figure 2.3 *Data having many-to-many relationships.*

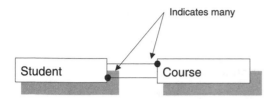

Figure 2.4 *Many-to-many relationship notation.*

repeating group in Figure 2.3 is the multiple courses a Student can take or the multiple students a Course can have. So, the data that is repeating must be removed as shown in Figure 2.5. Now, however, you have a lot of repeated data, which makes for all sorts of update problems if you want to change the data. For example, simply changing Alan's date of birth requires updating two records in the same Student table. Removing Alan from Econ 101 involves updating two records in two different tables, Student and Course. Storing data redundantly is dangerous because it can result in *update anomalies*—inconsistencies that occur when something that exists in two places is changed in one place but not in another. An example of an update anomaly would be removing Alan from Econ 101 in only the Student table. This is shown in Figure 2.6. If you then look at Student, Alan is not taking Econ 101, but if you look at Course, it appears that Alan is still taking Econ 101.

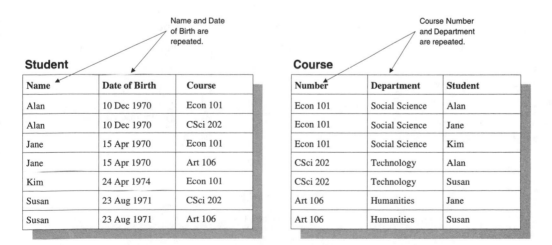

Figure 2.5 *Removal of repeating groups for the relational schema.*

Alan is removed from Econ 101 in this table.

An update anomaly occurred because Alan was not removed from Econ 101 in this table.

Student

Name	Date of Birth	Course
~~Alan~~	~~10 Dec 1970~~	~~Econ 101~~
Alan	10 Dec 1970	CSci 202
Jane	15 Apr 1970	Econ 101
Jane	15 Apr 1970	Art 106
Kim	24 Apr 1974	Econ 101
Susan	23 Aug 1971	CSci 202
Susan	23 Aug 1971	Art 106

Course

Number	Department	Student
Econ 101	Social Science	Alan
Econ 101	Social Science	Jane
Econ 101	Social Science	Kim
CSci 202	Technology	Alan
CSci 202	Technology	Susan
Art 106	Humanities	Jane
Art 106	Humanities	Susan

Figure 2.6 *Update anomaly when data stored redundantly.*

To fix this problem, the people designing a relational schema *normalize* or simplify the data as shown in Figure 2.7. This introduces an intersection entity of Student/Course. Note that now there is no data stored redundantly other than data used to reference an entry in another table such as a student's name or a course number. The notation for an intersection entity is shown in Figure 2.8.

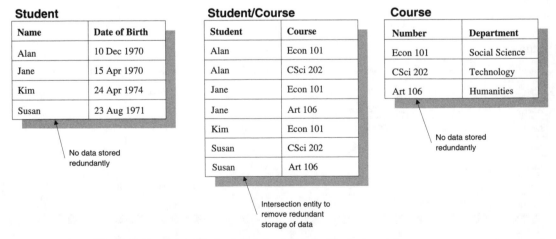

Student

Name	Date of Birth
Alan	10 Dec 1970
Jane	15 Apr 1970
Kim	24 Apr 1974
Susan	23 Aug 1971

No data stored redundantly

Student/Course

Student	Course
Alan	Econ 101
Alan	CSci 202
Jane	Econ 101
Jane	Art 106
Kim	Econ 101
Susan	CSci 202
Susan	Art 106

Intersection entity to remove redundant storage of data

Course

Number	Department
Econ 101	Social Science
CSci 202	Technology
Art 106	Humanities

No data stored redundantly

Figure 2.7 *Normalized relational schema for Student and Course.*

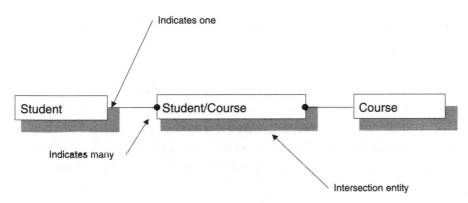

Figure 2.8 *Intersection entity for normalized relational schema.*

This solves the data modeling problem and allows many-to-many relationships to be normalized with the resulting intersection entity in a relational schema. But another problem can occur at this point. To put this data together, an RDBMS must *join*, or combine the data-based identifiers such as Student Name (or more likely a Student ID Number) and Course Number.

Name	Date of Birth	Course	Department
Alan	10 Dec 1970	Econ 101	Social Science
		CSci 202	Technology
Jane	15 Apr 1970	Econ 101	Social Science
		Art 106	Humanities
Kim	24 Apr 1974	Econ 101	Social Science
Susan	23 Aug 1971	CSci 202	Technology
		Art 106	Humanities

Figure 2.9 *Report generated by joining Student, Student/Course, and Course.*

An example of a join would be to take all entries in the Student table, Student/Course table and the Course table to produce a report that looks like Figure 2.9.

So far so good! Joins can be a performance issue for RDBMSs, however, and many joins can kill performance. This performance problem occurs because multiple tables with some matching key information, such as SSNs, are being accessed to combine data from all the tables by matching that key information. The more tables needed, the more joins are needed, and the slower the process becomes.

Let's expand this example to see how performance can be affected by adding departments and teachers to create the classic university example. Here are some of the significant relationships illustrated in the university course schedule: A Course can have more than one Teacher, a Student can take more than one Course, a Course has many Students, a Department lists many Courses, and the same Course can be listed by more than one Department. The illustration for this example is shown in Figure 2.10.

In this model there are three intersection entities: Teacher to Course, Student to Course, and Department to Course. The entire relational schema illus-

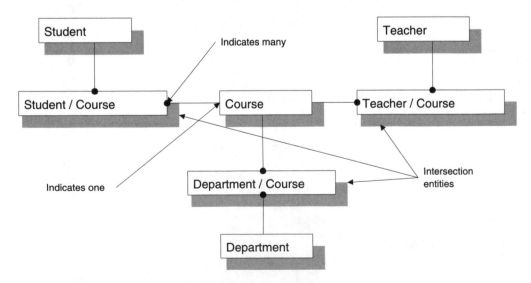

Figure 2.10 *Relational schema for university example.*

Name	Date of Birth	Course	Department	Teacher
Alan	10 Dec 1970	Econ 101	Social Science	Don
		CSci 202	Technology	Don
				Donna
Jane	15 Apr 1970	Econ 101	Social Science	Don
		Art 106	Humanities	Pat
Kim	24 Apr 1974	Econ 101	Social Science	Don
Susan	23 Aug 1971	CSci 202	Technology	Don
				Donna
		Art 106	Humanities	Pat

Figure 2.11 *Expanded report for the university example.*

trated in Figure 2.10 has seven entities: the three intersection entities plus one each for Teacher, Student, Course, and Department. To get the expanded report shown in Figure 2.11 requires joining all seven entities. In real life, because of the joining that must take place, this could be significantly slow in some RDBMS products if this database has any size at all.

Using intersection entities to resolve many-to-many relationships in a relational schema indicates complex data. Having many intersection entities makes a database a likely candidate for an ODBMS because these intersection entities can result in either high performance or high maintenance costs when using an RDBMS. The performance cost results from the slowness of using relational joins to combine data when there are many intersection entities. One solution in an RDBMS is to move away from intersection entities where possible (the term for this is *de-normalizing*). This may lead, however, to improper data modeling. Increased maintenance costs can occur when the data is no longer modeled properly.

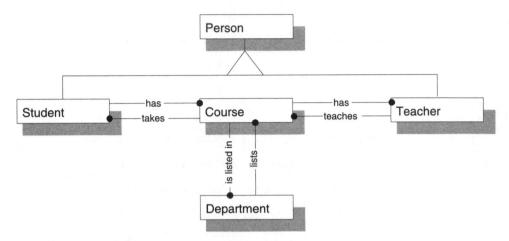

Figure 2.12 *Object schema for university example.*

The object model handles many-to-many relationships easily, which is illustrated in Figure 2.12 and Figure 2.13, using the university example. There would be only the four entities—Teacher, Student, Course, and Department. There would be no joins—only *traversals* of the relationships. A traversal follows the link or pointer using OIDs to other objects, which are shown in Figure 2.13 as arrows. There would be no need to de-normalize to obtain performance, so there are no lurking maintenance issues resulting from de-normalization.

As we have seen from this example, many-to-many relationships are an indication of complex data. To use many-to-many relationships in an RDBMS requires joining of the data; this can be a performance problem if there are many joins. In contrast, many-to-many relationships can be expressed directly in an ODBMS. Instead of joining data, the data can be traversed as graph structure. In the next section, we will see that traversals themselves are another indicator of complex data.

Access Using Traversals

Another indicator of complex data is access using traversals. As we saw in Figure 2.13, traversal access occurs when there is movement from one object instance to the object instances that are connected to it. A parts explosion from a bill-of-materials is one example of using connections of instances, as illustrated in Figure 2.14. A parts explosion is often represented in object

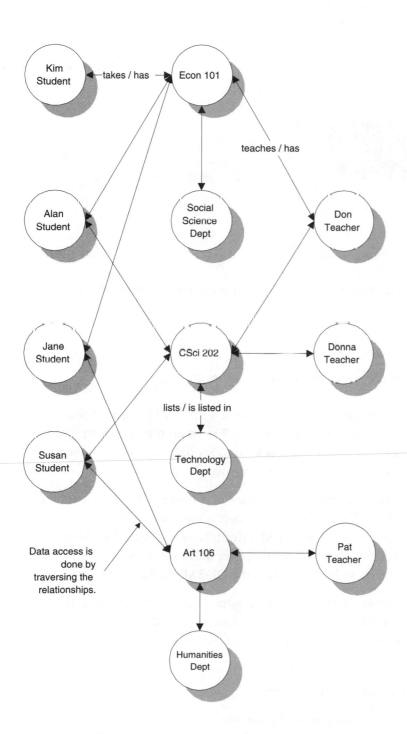

Figure 2.13 *Graph structure for instances in the university example.*

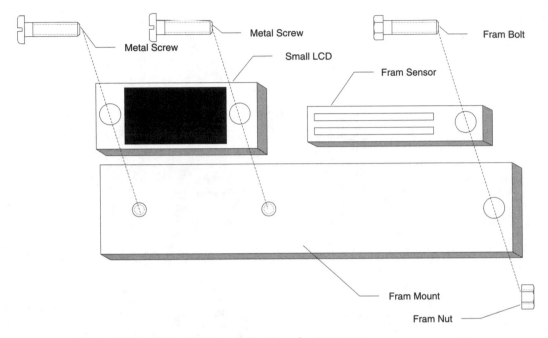

Figure 2.14   *Parts explosion abstraction of a Framastat.*

programming languages as a graph structure. The parts explosion illustrated
in Figure 2.14 is now shown in Figure 2.15 as an abstract graph structure.
Object programming languages access complex data by traversing the relationships represented in Figure 2.15 as arrows.

Graph structures in general are indications of complex data. Your first hint
that you have a graph structure often occurs when you traverse a relationship
between data instances. In an RDBMS, this traversal is often done by successive index searches or joins. These successive index searches generally mean
the RDBMS is likely to be slower than the ODBMS in this type of application.

As we saw in the Framastat example, if your data is naturally represented in
a graph structure that is traversed when accessing the data, you likely have
complex data. Other forms of graph structures include:

- Communications networks

- Real ways organizations work

- Work-flow processes such as manufacturing

- Portfolios of financial instruments such as stocks and bonds

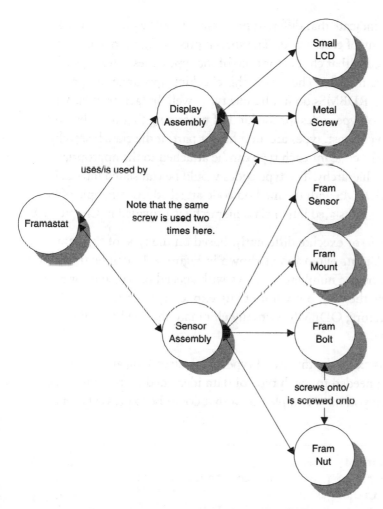

Figure 2.15 *Graph structure for the parts explosion example.*

Frequent Use of Type Codes

A final sign of complex data is the frequent use of type codes, which require different processing in the DBMS. Type codes are a common way of classifying data in a relational schema. For example, you could assign type codes to the types of birds, types of employees, types of students, types of parts, and so on. They are often numbers or alphanumeric codes—but in the examples here, the types will be spelled out instead of using type codes. For this example, we have one set of type codes for the types of parts in a Framastat.

Type codes often indicate that different processing must be done for each type and that a hierarchy of types exists. The special processing needs for each type require program code that checks for each of the type codes. This type checking is shown in Figure 2.16. The reason this checking appears in program code is that commercial RDBMSs do not handle types well. In fact, they have no "understanding" of type codes for the kind of processing that must be done in program code. In contrast, types are an inherent part of the class hierarchy in an ODBMS and the code for each type can be attached to the appropriate classes in the class hierarchy. The type codes would be translated into a class hierarchy in an ODBMS with the method code attached. An example of how type codes may be translated into a class hierarchy is provided in Chapter 10.

ODBMSs *dispatch*, or execute differently, based on the type of the data in a class hierarchy. A parts explosion as shown in Figure 2.17 can be traversed in the order shown on the numbered arrows with special processing for each type of part along the way, but without any explicit type checking in the program code. Therefore, ODBMSs virtually eliminate the need for "if then else if" program code.

As we saw in this example, the use of type codes often indicates there is different processing needed for each type of data identified by the type code. This is a sign that you have complex data that could be expressed as a class

```
if type is Assembly then
      ... specific processing for Assembly ...
else if type is LCD then
      ... specific processing for LCD ...
else if type is Screw then
      ... specific processing for Screw ...
else if type is Sensor then
      ... specific processing for Sensor ....
else if type is Mount then
      ... specific processing for Mount ...

... and so on ...
```

Figure 2.16 *Type checking in application code.*

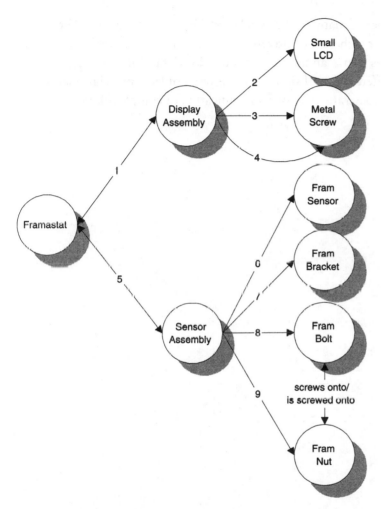

Figure 2.17 *Object schema traversal without type checking in the application.*

hierarchy with specialized methods attached to the classes. Examples in Chapters 3 and 9 show specifically how type codes can be replaced by a class hierarchy and methods can replace the "if then else if" program code.

Summary

Complex data is generally best handled by an ODBMS. This chapter focused on ways to identify complex data. One indicator is data that lacks unique, natural identification. A second way to identify complex data is recognition of a large number of many-to-many relationships within the data. Yet another indicator is the use of traversals to access the data. Finally, frequent use of type codes also is an indicator of complex data. The next chapter will highlight the differences and similarities between object and relational models that will demonstrate most of these indicators of complex data.

Comparing the Object and Relational Models

System developers often ask me whether an RDBMS or an ODBMS is better. The answer, of course, is that there is no one right answer to this question. I believe the correct answer depends on an array of factors. RDBMSs might be better in one situation while ODBMSs might be better in another.

Relational technology has been around for well over a decade and it is familiar to many, but where did object technology come from? Since we are comparing models in this chapter, it is worthwhile to briefly discuss the roots of object technology. Some people will tell you object technology can be traced back to simulation programming work in the late 1960s. Others believe that it developed when engineering and CAD departments found that they needed greater performance than they could achieve with RDBMSs. The performance they needed simply wasn't available. Integrating object technology with DBMSs was seen as a way to meet this performance demand on the complex data found in Engineering and CAD applications. Interestingly enough, that same demand for performance is now being raised in industries such as telecommunications and others as far removed from engineering and CAD settings as the insurance business or securities trading. All these businesses have complex data.

This chapter will use tangible examples to explain the object and relational models in terms that will be helpful in making a specific choice for a specific situation. The differences between object and relational models will be examined by showing how a complex data model would be implemented in each system. I chose a model that should be familiar to many of you. It is called a parts explosion by some and a bill-of-materials by others.

The key points in this chapter include:

- The similarities and differences in RDBMS and ODBMS concepts will provide the start of a translation guide for those of you with a RDBMS background.

- How useful data abstraction and inheritance are for complex data.

- How helpful encapsulation is for developing large, complex systems.

Similarities and Differences in Terms

Figure 3.1 presents some of the basic terms used in relational and object technology. It often happens that a new industry creates new terms along with new technology. Concepts are similar to, yet different from, their predecessor concepts. An example is the term *relation*; although it is similar to the predecessor concept of a record, it was different enough to require a new term when it was introduced. Object technology also introduces a whole set of new terms. For example, a relation is similar to a class. Yet, a relation and a class are not really the same thing. Thus, the new term was born.

Figure 3.1 compares terminology in relational and object models. The term *relation* from the relational model is similar to a *class*, which was defined in Chapter 1. Both relations and classes define the structure from a similar group of instances. *Tuple* from the relational model is similar to the term *object instance* defined in Chapter 1; both contain instance data. The term

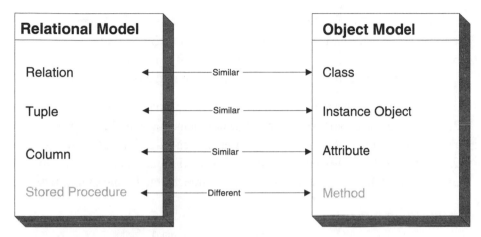

Figure 3.1 *Comparison of relational and object terminology.*

column from the relational model is similar to the term *attribute*, defined in Chapter 1; both contain a single data item, such as a person's date of birth.

A significant difference between relational and object terminology exists because of the way executable code is associated with data. The relational model uses stored procedures and the object model uses methods. The stored procedures of the relational model are not similar to methods of the object model. Methods are computationally complete because they are written in full object programming languages such as C++ or Smalltalk, while stored procedures from the relational model are usually extensions of SQL and are not complete programming languages.

Similarities and Differences in Concepts

Three concepts basic to the object model—data abstraction, inheritance, and encapsulation—were defined in Chapter 1. These three concepts make it possible to model complex data. In this chapter, these three concepts will be used to compare and contrast the object and relational models, using a simplified example of complex data.

Data Abstraction

Data abstraction is the simplification of data. When dealing with complex data, the data is often simplified to a graph. In this section, an abstract data structure will be illustrated in both an object and a relational schema to show the differences between the two models. You will see that the object schema is simpler than the relational schema. This simplicity should provide a higher level of performance for applications using the object schema.

An example of data abstraction from an object perspective is illustrated in Figure 3.2, using the parts explosion example that originally appeared in Chapter 1. This illustrates a bill-of-materials for a simple part called a Framastat. In this figure, the relationships between the components of a Framastat are shown using arrows. In an ODBMS, these relationships are implemented using Object IDs or

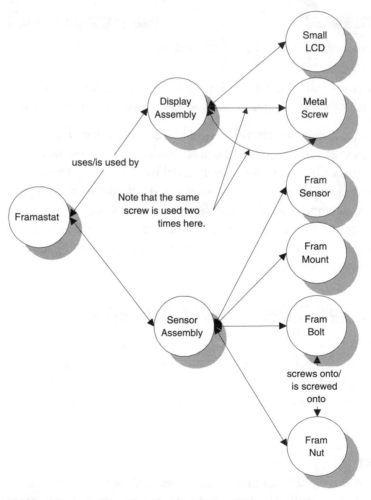

Figure 3.2 *Graph structure for the parts explosion example.*

OIDs. OIDs allow the direct expression of the relationships shown as arrows in Figure 3.2. This direct representation means that the graph structure will be stored as a graph structure in most ODBMSs—not requiring the translations of data in one format in storage to another format in the application program.

A relational approach to the parts explosion is shown in Figure 3.3. Although this is grossly simplified, Figure 3.3 illustrates several important concepts. First, each instance in the relational schema must have an identifier that is provided by the data itself. In this specific relational example, that identifier is Part ID. Second, the references between parts require Part IDs, which are implemented with the Uses relation. For example, in Figure 3.3 a Sensor Assembly (Part ID of P8) uses a Fram Mount (Part ID of P4)—both are foreign keys as described in Chapter 1. This is the relational implementation of the arrows shown in Figure 3.2 of the parts explosion.

A more realistic model that shows the differences in the data is illustrated in Figure 3.4. The simplistic rendering in Figure 3.3 does not reflect that different parts and assemblies might have the need for varied data storage despite their shared columns and attributes.

Part

Part ID	Part Name	Weight
P1	Small LCD	0.5
P2	Metal Screw	2
P3	Fram Sensor	1.2
P4	Fram Mount	0.9
P5	Fram Bolt	14
P6	Fram Nut	6
P7	Display Assembly	
P8	Sensor Assembly	
P9	Framastat	

Uses

Part ID	Uses Part
P7	P1
P7	P2
P7	P2
P8	P3
P8	P4
P8	P5
P8	P6
P9	P7
P9	P8

Calculated

Figure 3.3 *Overly simple set of relations for the parts explosion example.*

LCD

Part ID	Part Name	Weight	Volts
P1	Small LCD	0.5	0.1
...more			

Part

Part ID	Part Type
P1	LCD
P2	Screw
P3	Sensor
P4	Mount
P5	Bolt
P6	Nut
P7	Assembly
P8	Assembly
P9	Assembly

Screw

Part ID	Part Name	Weight	Head
P2	Metal Screw	2	Phillips
...more			

Sensor

Part ID	Part Name	Weight	Threshold
P3	Fram Sensor	1.2	95
...more			

Bracket

Part ID	Part Name	Weight	Height
P4	Fram Mount	0.9	30
...more			

Uses

Part ID	Uses Part
P7	P1
P7	P2
P7	P2
P8	P3
P8	P4
P8	P5
P8	P6
P9	P7
P9	P8

Bolt

Part ID	Part Name	Weight	Diameter	Screws Onto
P5	Fram Bolt	14	7	P6
...more				

Nut

Part ID	Part Name	Weight	Diameter	Screws Onto
P6	Fram Nut	6	7	P5
...more				

Assembly

Part ID	Part Name
P7	Display Assembly
P8	Fram Assembly
P9	Framastat

Note that different data is stored for different Parts

Figure 3.4 *A more realistic set of relations for the parts explosion example.*

In Figure 3.4, a Part Type column was added to the Part relation so that the type of the part can be determined. A type of part indicates whether it is an LCD, Screw, and so on. In the relational schema, there is a separate relation for each Part Type since different data is stored for each type. This is needed in order to understand what relation is needed for which type. The use of Part Type will be covered in greater depth in the encapsulation discussion later in this chapter.

Inheritance

The second object concept that we will cover is *inheritance*. Inheritance is a means of defining one class in terms of another. In this section, we will see how inheritance in the object model takes the place of type codes in the relational model.

In the university example in Chapter 2, we saw that both a Student and a Professor inherit the attributes and methods of the class Person. Another aspect of inheritance is that it eliminates the need for many type codes. For example, a Student is a *type* of Person as is a Professor a *type* of Person, yet no type codes are used in the class hierarchy. In the preceding section, a type column was added to the relational schema. These type codes are not necessary in the Framastat object model because types are part of the inheritance hierarchy. An inheritance hierarchy for the data model underlying the Framastat parts explosion is portrayed in Figure 3.5. Inheritance, in this example, allows defining parts in terms of other parts. For example, in Figure 3.5, a Basic Part is a type of Part, an Assembly is a type of Part, and, further down in the hierarchy, an LCD is a type of Basic Part. More generally, an LCD is a Part also. Each of these rectangles shown in Figure 3.5 represents a *class*.

Since a Basic Part is a type of Part, it inherits Part ID, Part Name, and Used By from Part. If you would look at an instance of LCD class in Figure 3.5, it would look exactly like the instance of an LCD as shown in Figure 3.4 with the addition of a Used By attribute. The Used By attribute in the Part class replaces the Uses relation in Figure 3.4. This attribute has a set of object IDs or OIDs for the parts that use it. Since Used By is an attribute of Part, the OIDs are stored in instances of Part as well as any instances that are subtypes of Parts. All the attributes (columns in relational terms) are inherited except for Volts, which is unique to LCDs in this model.

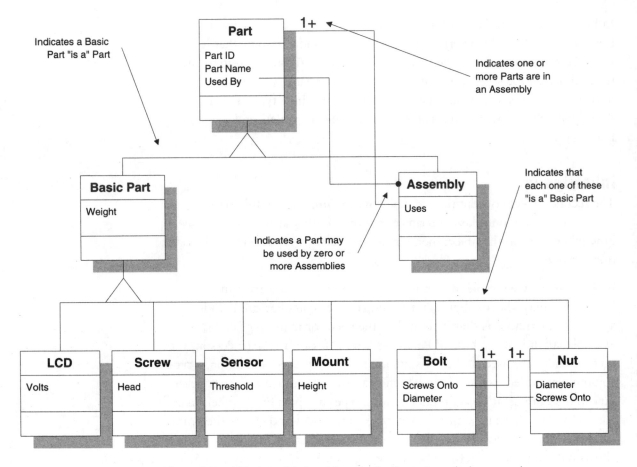

Figure 3.5 *Object model class hierarchy for the parts explosion example.*

Using Data Abstraction and Inheritance

Let's use the two concepts of data abstraction and inheritance and produce a report in order to see what impact they might have on such a task. A Framastat parts explosion report is shown in Figure 3.6. Examining what goes into producing such a report illustrates how the object and relational schemas are used differently.

To create this report using the object model, traversing the data structure is a simple matter. Follow the numbers on the relationship lines in Figure 3.7. These numbers show the order in which the traversals take place. These tra-

Framastat P9, Weight: 98.3 grams
        Display Assembly P7, Weight: 18.3 grams
                Small LCD, P1, Weight 14.3 grams, Volts: 0.1
                Metal Screw, P2, Weight: 2 grams, Head: Phillips
                Metal Screw, P2, Weight: 2 grams, Head: Phillips
        Sensor Assembly P8, Weight: 80 grams
                Fram Sensor, P3, Weight: 34.3 grams, Threshold: 95
                Fram Mount, P4, Weight: 25.7 grams, Height 30 mm
                Fram Bolt, P5, Weight: 14 grams, Diameter: 7 mm
                Fram Nut, P6, Weight: 6 grams, Diameter: 7 mm

Figure 3.6   *Report for the parts explosion example.*

versals use the OIDs, but from the perspective of the program, traversals are done in the standard way for the object programming language, and the translation from OIDs to the programming language is done by most ODBMSs. See Chapter 1 for more information on how this translation is transparent with object programming languages.

The same traversal in the relational schema is illustrated in Figure 3.8. Again the numbers on the arrow lines show the order in which the traversals take place. Note how the Uses and Part relations must be checked repeatedly. The Uses relation is used to determine the relationships that are directly described in the object diagram. The Part relation is checked to determine the type of the part that is needed because different code must be executed for different types of parts. Understanding the types of the instances is something that must be done in the application. A fragment of the code in the application that takes types into consideration is shown in Figure 3.9. All this extra work to assemble data stored in relations into an object structure and back is

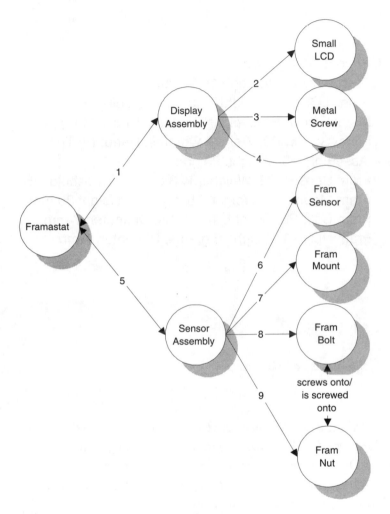

Figure 3.7 *Object model traversal to create report.*

sometimes described as *impedance mismatch*. Because the structures do not match in form, a translation process is required.

A DBMS that uses an object model does not need the Uses relation since traversal is handled by the relationship represented by the OID, nor does a DBMS that uses an object model need to check the type of the Part in determining the right code to execute to display information on a particular type

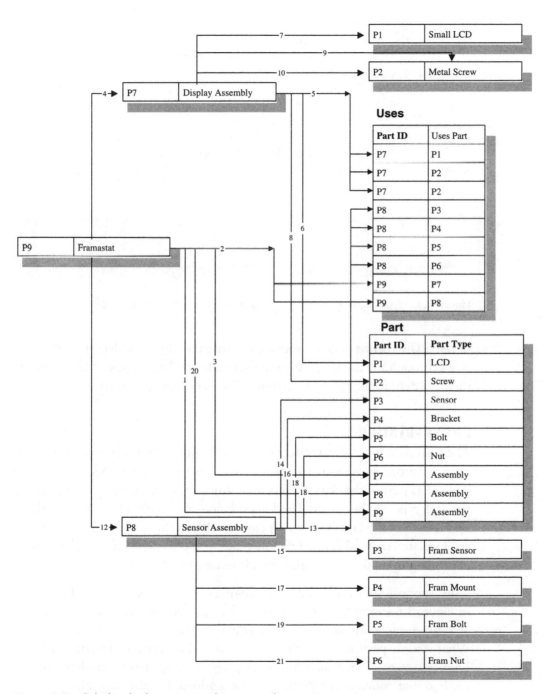

Figure 3.8   *Relational schema traversal to create the report.*

```
if type is Assembly then
      ... specific processing for Assembly ...
else if type is LCD then
      ... specific processing for LCD ...
else if type is Screw then
      ... specific processing for Screw ...
else if type is Sensor then
      ... specific processing for Sensor ....
else if type is Mount then
      ... specific processing for Mount ...

... and so on ...
```

Figure 3.9 *Type checking in application code for the relational schema traversal.*

of part. The correct code is executed because the object model understands types through the use of classes and that code can be *encapsulated* as part of the class definition. The next section will describe the use of encapsulation.

Encapsulation

The final concept to differentiate between the object and relational models is encapsulation. As noted in Chapter 1, encapsulation allows code to be defined as part of the class definition. In this example, the specific processing for each type can be encapsulated in each class definition rather than in the application code. This is shown in Figure 3.10. In this section, we will see the encapsulated method defined that has the same name but different behavior, depending upon the class with which it is associated.

Now, suppose something really challenging exists in this example. The report in Figure 3.6 shows "weight" in the data displayed on each part. "Weight" is an ambiguous term since it could be either an English or a Metric number. What if some parts have weight stored in the Metric system and others in the English system? That makes for messy programming. To encapsulate this, a method that converts Weight into grams is added. For the parts already storing Metric weight, this is a simple method that just passes the data through.

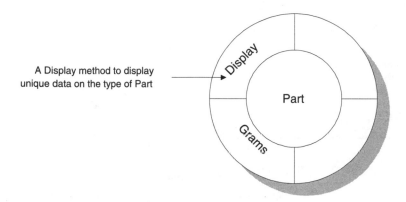

A Display method to display unique data on the type of Part

Figure 3.10 *Object model encapsulation of methods for the parts explosion example.*

For parts that store in the English system, the conversion to the Metric system takes place. A Display method then could also use the Grams method in addition to displaying the attributes of a given class. Both methods are illustrated in Figure 3.10.

Figure 3.11 shows the encapsulated Display and Grams methods in the object model class hierarchy. Note that the Screw, Bolt, and Nut classes do not have a Grams method. They use the inherited Grams method defined in the Basic Part class. That method assumes Weight is already stored in the Metric system. The other parts must convert from the English system using the Grams method. Also, note that Assembly also has a Grams method. This method adds the grams in all the parts used by the Assembly. This is similar to the fields shown to be calculated in Figure 3.3.

The same method is used in more than one class. There is a Display method for the LCD class, the Sensor class, and so on. The object model allows this multiple use of the same method, which is called *overloading*. The overloaded definition of Display in the LCD class *overrides* the definition of Display in the Basic Part class because it is lower in the class hierarchy. Overloading of method definitions allows for specialized processing based on the type of the object.

Another capability of the object model mentioned in Chapter 1 is dispatching, which is executing the correct code based on type of a class. In this example, the object system *dispatches* or executes the correct code based on the type of part. Remember that "if then else if, . . . else if" code in Figure 3.9? The rea-

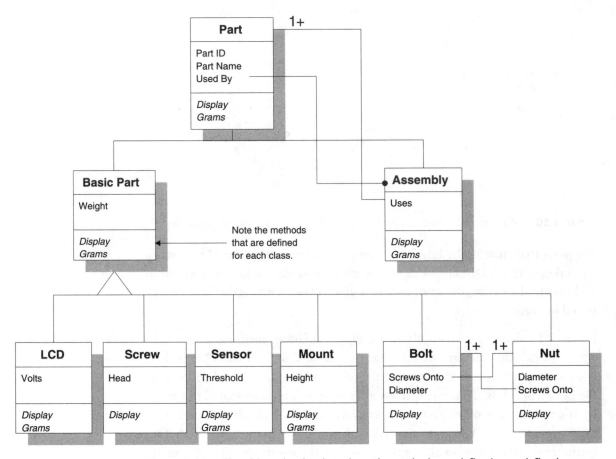

Figure 3.11 *Class hierarchy showing where the methods are defined or re-defined.*

son you do not find this kind of code in an object system is that it has *dispatching* on the type. So if the object system is working on an object instance of the LCD class, it uses the Display method for the LCD class. If it is working on an object instance of the Sensor class, it uses that Display method.

Using Encapsulation

Now let's see what impact encapsulation has on tasks such as the production of a report, building on the example used earlier. If the Display method displays any parts that are used by the object, the entire application to produce the report shown in Figure 3.6 is illustrated in Figure 3.12 with the weight shown in grams. The object application does not need information about

Application Code Fragment using the Relational Model

```
if type is Assembly then
      ... specific processing for Assembly ...
else if type is LCD then
      ... specific processing for LCD ...
else if type is Screw then
      ... specific processing for Screw ...
else if type is Sensor then
      ... specific processing for Sensor ....
else if type is Mount then
      ... specific processing for Mount ...

... and so on ...
```

Application Code using the Object Model

```
Display <Framastat Object ID>
```

Figure 3.12   *Comparison of application code to create the report using relational and object models.*

how a particular object must be displayed or how the weight is calculated. The application code is much shorter than that shown in the relational schema in Figure 3.9, which is repeated for comparison in Figure 3.12.

Although this is a simple example, it represents a very real benefit of encapsulation—the reduction of application code.

Of course, there is more code encapsulated in each of the classes for Display and Grams. Nevertheless, the application program does not contain that knowledge. It simply displays the object. In object model terms, the message Display is sent to the Framastat object in the bottom example in Figure 3.12.

Programming in the Large

Encapsulation makes *programming in the large* more possible. This term refers to large software systems. These systems have lots of data entities and lots of code. After a while, managing what code works with what data can create problems that result in duplication or incorrect execution of code. Encapsulation ensures the correct code is executed on the correct data through dispatching. Even reusing the name of a method in different classes does not cause a problem.

Object model concepts	Relational model technique	Object model technique	Object model benefits
Data abstraction	Intersection entities and indexing to represent references between tuples	OIDs to directly represent references between objects	Simpler schema to represent complex data
Inheritance	Type codes	Class hierarchy	Direct representation of the relationship between type and subtypes as well as support for specialized processing for each type
Encapsulation	"If then else if" code based on type codes	Built-in dispatching to ensure the correct code executes on the correct data	Reduced application code and reduced chance of error where the wrong code executes on the right data

Figure 3.13 *Comparison of relational and object models for data abstraction, inheritance, and encapsulation.*

Summary

This chapter used the parts explosion or bill-of-materials for a mythical Framastat part to compare the object and relational models. It is easier to represent complex data using the object model. The differences in the models were shown using data abstraction, inheritance, and encapsulation; they are summarized in Figure 3.13

The next chapter will provide information on the types of products available, using the approach of architecture to illustrate the variety of products available, and the importance of the differences between object and relational models when it comes to complex data.

4

Types of Products that Handle Objects

I have heard a story many times about one large corporation or another that completed an in-depth comparison of the ODBMS products on the market. Asked what their choice was, the answer came back that they decided against all of them "because of SQL."

There are several important points to be made about that story. First of all, there is a common misconception floating around that if you want to use SQL, you'd better stick with an RDBMS. Nothing could be further from the truth. SQL is a query language that can be used with most ODBMS products on the market. In fact, SQL is the basis of the Object Query Language (OQL) that was adopted by the ODBMS vendors and other parties in the Object Database Management Group (ODMG). More information about the ODMG is in Chapter 5.

Even more important is the point that the company in the story was led astray by a misleading "SQL" label. If they had really dug into ODBMS technology and the various products available, they would have understood the technology. They also would have understood how misleading the marketing labels that are placed on products can be.

A quick look at an industry magazine such as *Object Magazine* illustrates the number of ODBMS products that are available. Each product, naturally, has marketing people identifying key factors about their products. The products, therefore, get labeled by their developers and by their competition. To really understand the types of products, it's important to get beyond the simple, and oftentimes misleading, labels and look at the architecture of the products.

This chapter provides a high-level view of the various architectural approaches taken by vendors, as well as a brief overview of the impact that architecture has on development and performance costs. This provides a look at the similarities, as well as the differences, between the products.

There are several categories of products that allow storing of objects in DBMSs. First, persistent languages are covered. Then the DBMS products that store objects are discussed, categorized as follows: RDBMSs, products that use Object-Relational Mapping, Object Manager DBMSs, Object DBMSs, and finally Object-Relational DBMSs. This categorization allows a view of products based on architectural distinctions. These architectural distinctions can be detected in the way data is stored and in the way the application programming language is integrated on the client side with the storage mechanism. These are key performance and development concerns. Interestingly, architectural distinctions do not include whether a product supports such things as SQL or ODBC.

The information in this chapter was written with the assumption that an object programming language will be used in your application. As mentioned in Chapter 2, the complex data used with object programming languages often ends up being a graph. For this reason, graph structures in this chapter are shown in each of the client applications as a representation of the complex data structures that object programming languages handle. Other notation used in this section is explained in Chapter 1.

Important specifics to consider when selecting DBMS products, such as what is the locking granularity, where methods execute, and where queries execute, will be covered in Chapter 8.

The key points in this chapter include:

- Persistent languages do not provide sufficient capabilities for a multi-user database.

- The server side of many of these products is very similar in operation even though it may store objects, relational tables, or both.

- The client side is where most of the architectural distinctions can be found even though nearly all work with object programming languages.

Product Classification Overview

Figure 4.1 provides an overview of the various types of products that will be covered in this chapter. They are classified by whether the products have an object programming language binding and a database engine as well as by the format of data storage in the database. A checkmark in a category indicates that the products in this category universally have that capability. If there is no checkmark, a comment on how common the capability happens to be among products in the industry is provided. Each of the product categories is one of your options for storing objects.

Persistent Languages

Some non-DBMS products such as persistent languages provide solutions in some cases where storage of objects, but not a DBMS, is needed. Smalltalk is

Product Categories	Object Programming Language Bindings	Database Engine	Database Storage Format
Persistent Languages	✔	None	Same format as the language
RDBMSs	None	✔	Tuples
Object-Relational Mapping	✔	Not in product, but provided by some other underlying RDBMS	Tuples
Object Manager DBMSs	None	✔	Objects
Object DBMSs	✔	✔	Objects
Object-Relational DBMSs	Most Products	✔	Tuples and Objects

Figure 4.1 *Overview of product classifications.*

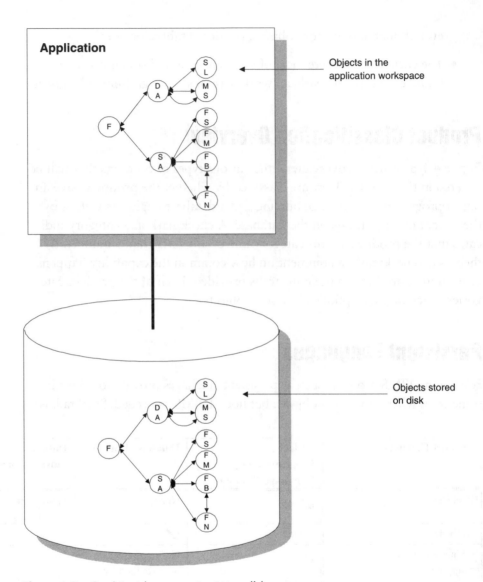

Figure 4.2 *Persistent language storage on disk.*

an example of a persistent language because it allows saving both the data and the application code on disk as part of the standard Smalltalk environment.

The development cost and performance costs of using a persistent language are minimal since the persistence capability is part of the language. Persistent languages are, however, a viable alternative only if the application is a single-user situation. Any situation with more than one user where objects will be shared is extremely risky because the persistent languages do not provide the ACID properties, those properties that make it possible for a DBMS to provide safe, shared access to data in a multi-user environment. See Chapter 1 for an overview of the ACID properties.

The objects in the application workspace and on the disk are identical when using a persistent language, as illustrated in Figure 4.2. These same objects are stored directly on disk in the same format as used by the application.

DBMS Products

Moving beyond persistent languages, DBMS products that also store objects provide a safer environment because of their ACID properties. Although the products may provide the ACID properties in a variety of ways, the data is safe. All the DBMS products provide the DBMS characteristics that allow for the safe sharing of data among multiple users. A basic discussion of the ACID properties can be found in Chapter 1. Details on the variety of ways the ACID properties can be provided are in Checklist 7, "Transactions," in Part III.

In this section, the variants on the client/server architecture that ODBMS products provide will be reviewed. The capability of each type of product will be discussed. Finally, a summary comparing each type of product on complex data is provided. All the examples here show a client/server architecture. The discussion of the client/server concepts and the notation used are in Chapter 1.

Relational DBMSs

Using an RDBMS with objects can have both high development and performance costs. It is possible, nevertheless, to store most object schemas in an RDBMS. RDBMSs, however, are not designed to work transparently with object programming languages. Thus, it is necessary to convert from tuples to objects in the client application. This is the impedance mismatch described in Chapter 3. Applications using object programming languages use objects in the application workspace, and they must access data in the RDBMS, which is stored in tuples. These tuples must be converted to objects upon retrieval from the database and then back to tuples upon storage. This must

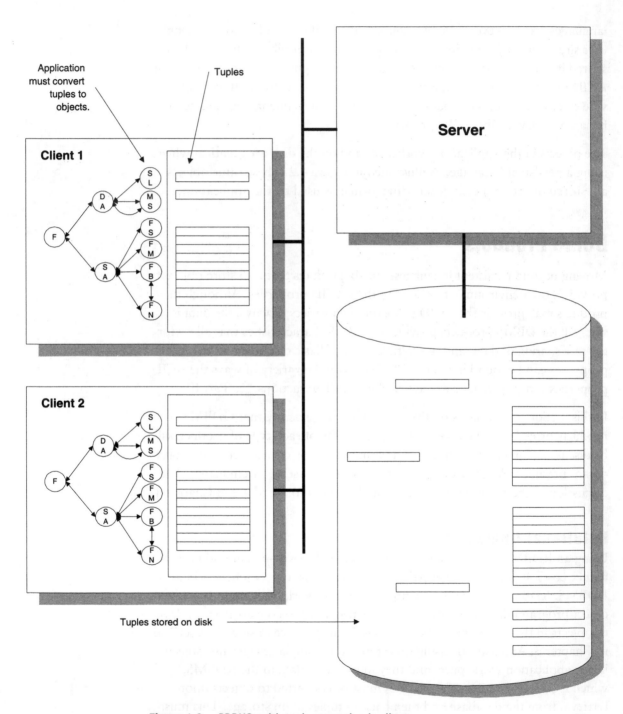

Figure 4.3 *RDBMSs with tuple conversion in clients.*

either be programmed in each client application or in a set of interface routines, which entails a development cost and therefore increased development risk. It could also result in a significant performance cost if a great deal of data is used off the disk. On the other hand, if that data is read once, converted to objects, and then manipulated in the application for a significant period of time before converting any updates to tuples and storing them—the performance cost of the impedance mismatch may be minimal.

An illustration of how RDBMSs store tuples on the disk and present tuples to the application is shown in Figure 4.3.

Object-Relational Mapping

Object-Relational Mapping reduces the development cost of using RDBMS with objects, and can in some cases reduce the performance cost. In Object-Relational Mapping, the RDBMS is used for storing data in a similar manner to that described in the previous section.

The development cost of using RDBMSs with objects is reduced because the Object-Relational Mapping software takes care of the object-to-tuple and tuple-to-object conversion needed when using RDBMSs with objects. It is not necessary, therefore, to program that conversion in each client application as described in the previous section on RDBMSs.

The performance cost of using RDBMSs with objects can be reduced because most Object-Relational Mapping products provide a transparent program integration with object programming languages and the caching that goes with this integration. Transparent program integration and the related caching are explained in Chapter 1. There is no need to program this caching in each application since it is part of the product. Caching can help improve performance if the client applications read the same data multiple times in a single transaction. Caching can, in some cases, reduce the effect of the impedance mismatch problem. It does not, however, eliminate the underlying impedance mismatch problem between objects in your application and tuples on the disk. Using an Object-Relational Mapping product could result in a significant performance problem if you are using a great deal of data off the disk that needs to be converted to objects and you only use that data a few times in your application. On the other hand, if the data is read once, converted to objects, and then manipulated in the application for a significant

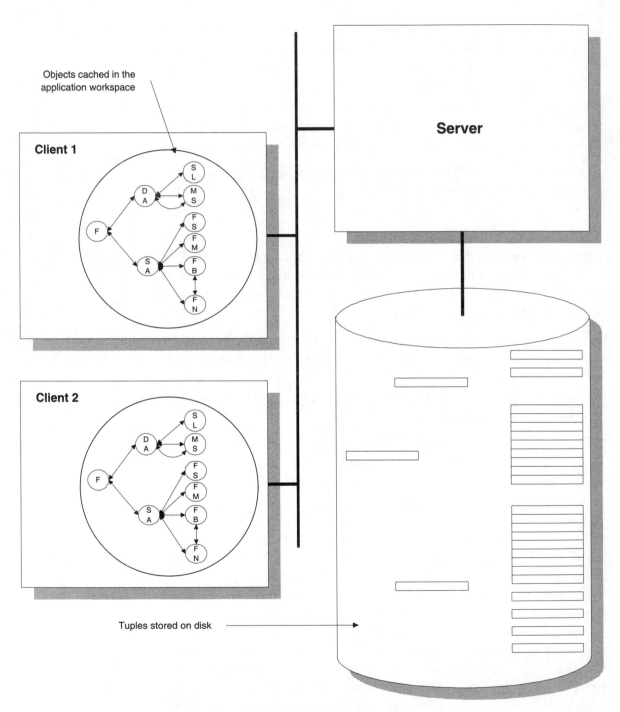

Figure 4.4 *Object-Relational Mapping with caching in clients.*

period of time (effectively using the cache) before converting any updates to tuples and storing it—the cost of the impedance mismatch may be minimal.

The Object-Relational Mapping products basically hide the "tuple-to-object-and-back-to-tuple" mapping needed with RDBMSs, as is illustrated by a comparison of Figure 4.4 and Figure 4.3. The two figures are similar except that Figure 4.4 illustrates the caching that occurs in the client using an Object-Relational Mapping product.

Object Manager DBMSs

Object Manager DBMSs provide fast access to objects on the server disk because they store objects without conversions; performance cost is minimal in accessing objects on the disk. Object manager DBMSs may, however, have a development cost because they do not provide the transparent program integration of the objects on disk to an object programming language. Transparent program integration of object programming languages is described in Chapter 1. As a result, the application still must be written in a manner that allows the application objects to be mapped to server objects as appropriate. This Application Program Interface is also described in Chapter 1. The interface provided by Object Manager DBMS is often a C interface. It usually does not provide the automatic, integrated caching mechanism that Object DBMSs and some Object-Relational DBMSs have.

Figure 4.5 shows the Application Program Interface for Object Manager DBMSs. The client application must convert the data from the DBMS to the objects in the application program workspace.

Object DBMSs

Object DBMSs provide the lowest cost for development and best performance combination when using objects because they store objects on disk and have the transparent program integration with object programming languages as described in Chapter 1. Storing objects directly on disk eliminates the impedance mismatch described in Chapter 3 since tuples are not used. As part of this transparent program integration with object programming languages, Object DBMSs provide caching for the client application. There is no need to program the caching for the application programs because it is part of the product. The result of caching is usually high-performance object manipula-

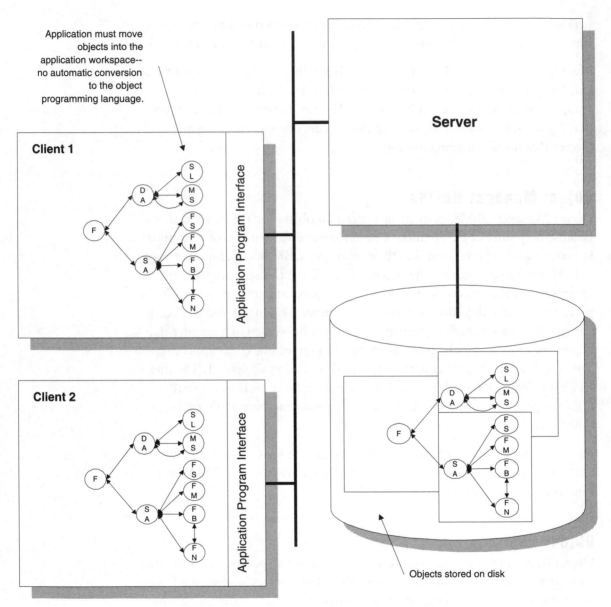

Application must move objects into the application workspace-- no automatic conversion to the object programming language.

Figure 4.5 *Object Manager DBMSs with object conversion using an API.*

tion on the client side when the data is read once and then manipulated many times in your client application. So the architecture of Object DBMSs is geared for fast access of objects from server disk storage and transparent access of objects on the client side using an object programming language.

Figure 4.6 shows the objects stored on server disk as well as the objects cached in each of the client application workspaces in the same form as they were in on disk.

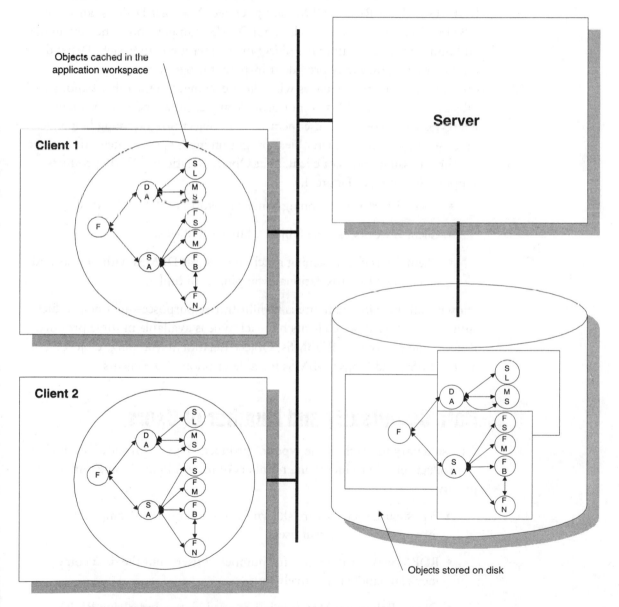

Figure 4.6 *Object DBMSs with object storage on disk and client caching.*

Object-Relational DBMSs

Object-Relational DBMSs have characteristics of both an RDBMS and an Object DBMS in that Object-Relational DBMSs store both objects and tuples in the DBMS. Object-Relational DBMSs can have clients that are similar to RDBMSs, Object-Relational Mapping, Object Manager DBMSs, and Object DBMSs. As a result, Object-Relational DBMSs can have both the advantages and disadvantages of either the object or the relational approach. Depending on the product, they may provide transparent program integration with object programming languages with client caching. On the other hand, some Object-Relational DBMSs do not provide any caching and look more like RDBMSs when you try to use them with an object programming language. Because of the differences in object programming language integration, there are three possible forms of clients that Object-Relational DBMS products support, as shown in Figure 4.7.

- Client 1 performs mapping similar to working with RDBMSs.

- Client 2 works like the Object Manager DBMSs.

- Client 3 has client caching much like Object DBMSs with objects and much like Object-Relational Mapping with tuples.

Showing all three in one figure is for illustrative purposes—no one product supports all three type of clients but each type is available in some product. Refer to the sections on RDBMSs, Object-Relational Mapping, Object Manager DBMSs, and Object DBMSs for a description of the clients.

Data Complexity and Number of Users

As a summary for each of the types of products, Figure 4.8 shows each type of product relative to increasing numbers of users and increasing data complexity.

- Persistent Languages are shown for the full range of complexity, but for very few concurrent users.

- RDBMSs cover the range for number of users, but the data complexity they can handle is relatively low.

- Object-Relational Mapping is restricted by the underlying RDBMSs.

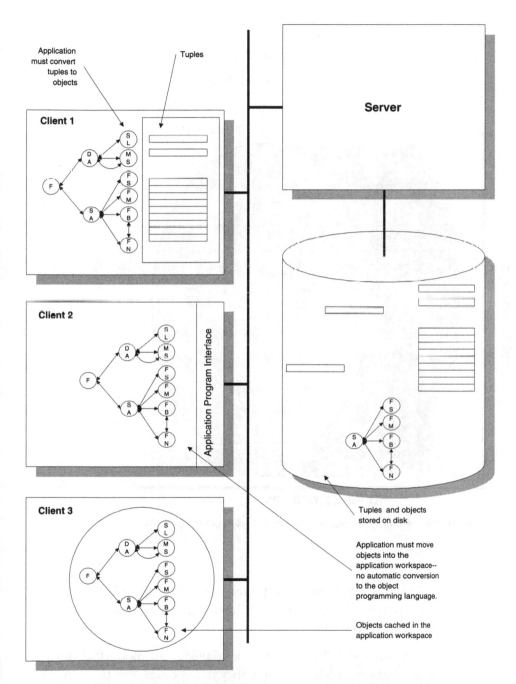

Figure 4.7 *Object-Relational DBMSs showing three approaches for clients used by various products.*

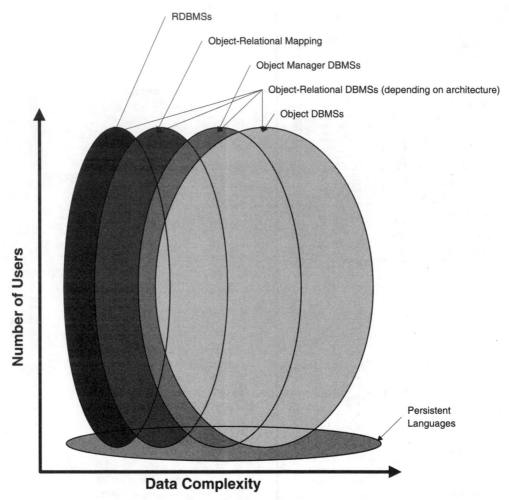

Figure 4.8 *Areas where each of the product types generally apply.*

The caching capability of the products and the integration with object programming allow, however, the handling of data with greater complexity than RDBMSs.

- Object Manager DBMSs can handle complex data more efficiently than Object-Relational Mapping since they store objects directly. They do not, however, have transparent program integration with object programming languages, which may limit their use for very complex data.

- Object DBMSs cover the range for number of users; these products also handle the most complex data because of both the transparent program integration with object programming languages and the ability to store objects directly.

- Object-Relational DBMSs cover a much larger spectrum, mainly because the category has three different types of client architectures, depending on the product. Those products that have transparent program integration with an object programming language can handle data as complex as is handled by Object DBMSs. On the other hand, the other possible clients for Object-Relational DBMSs are much like either RDBMSs, Object-Relational Mapping, or Object Data Managers.

Of course, any generalization such as Figure 4.8 needs to be qualified. This chart does not take into account the product features that will be important to product selection for your application. Chapter 7 covers the selection process and Part III provides detail on the possible features these products have. Nevertheless, based on their respective architectures, Figure 4.8 reasonably represents how each of these products stacks up in terms of handling complex data.

At the beginning of this chapter, I stated that there is no one correct answer to the question of whether an RDBMS or an ODBMS is better. It depends upon many factors, but key to the answer is what needs you are trying to meet with a DBMS. Imagine for a moment that you are choosing a vehicle to meet a particular need. A pick-up truck, an all-purpose vehicle, and a luxury car will all get you there. If you are trying to move a refrigerator, though, a pick-up truck will probably best suit your needs. If you are heading into the woods, an all-purpose vehicle would probably work best. And if you are trying to impress someone in a social setting, the luxury car would probably fit the bill. The same situation exists with DBMSs—all the products store data, but given your particular application, some would make a better choice.

Summary

ODBMS products can be categorized in many different ways. Looking at the architectural differences between products will help to determine which product will provide a satisfactory outcome with minimal development and performance problems. This chapter illustrated the differences between various architectural approaches. Actually, making a selection requires much greater study into the detail of product features and how they fit with your application needs, which will be presented in Part III. Clearly understanding those details may well alter your view of what might be best for your application. The next chapter focuses on standards for using DBMSs with objects.

5

DBMS Standards for Objects

When you travel to another country or part of the world, you sometimes find that the electrical system in place locally can make it difficult to use the electrical appliances, such as a shaver and blow dryer, that you have brought along for use during your travels. Each local area or government has the right to set the standards for the electrical system. It would, however, be more helpful to electrical users if there was a single electrical standard. This is a practical example of the difference that standards can make.

Standards make it easier for everyone to make choices and use the technology. Many of you can remember back some years when you had to choose between BetaMax and VHS formats at the time you purchased a VCR. The two formats were incompatible. Do you still have any old BetaMax cassettes? Now it is easy to choose; VHS won the contest and is the standard. In this case, competition between two formats resulted in one format emerging as a winner.

It works better for everyone when agreement is reached on standards first, rather than having products fight for dominance as the market creates the standard. This kind of agreement was reached in the stereo component industry, so your stereo components all work together even though they are from different manufacturers. In the software industry, there are several groups working on standards that affect the ODBMSs—the Object Database Management Group (general Object DBMS standards), Object Management Group (Common Object Request Broker Architecture [CORBA] standard for object request brokers and other general object standards), ANSI X3H2 (SQL standard), ANSI X3J16 (C++ standard), and ANSI X3J20 (Smalltalk standard). These standards are all aimed at portability of code in one way or another.

The chapter focuses on standards set by several groups and what you need to know about these standards. It will cover the standards specifications that should be considered when choosing an ODBMS—ODMG-93, SQL3, and the CORBA standard for object request brokers. Some information on object programming standards is also provided.

Key points covered in this chapter include:

- Background on the ANSI X3H2's SQL3 specification and the Object Database Management Group's ODMG-93 specification.

- Standards you need to be concerned about when considering ODBMSs.

- How the Object Request Broker standard works with ODBMSs.

DBMS Standards

There are three DBMS standards—SQL-92, ODMG-93, and SQL3—that will be important to you in your selection and deployment of an ODBMS. The following section compares these standards so that you can make an informed decision about what is relevant to your specific application. It is important to understand the background and heritage of the standards. The two groups responsible for the standards are ANSI X3H2 (SQL-92 and SQL3 standards) and the Object Database Management Group (ODMG-93 standard).

Background on ANSI X3H2 and the ODMG

The two main groups working on DBMS standards are the ODMG and ANSI X3H2. Although these two groups have very different heritages, they are trying to find as much common ground as possible for the use of objects with DBMSs. ANSI X3H2 focuses on the SQL standard and is currently working on the next revision, SQL3, which adds objects to the existing relational SQL-92 standard. ODMG works on Object DBMS standards and has published ODMG-93, which uses X3H2's SQL-92 specification as a starting point for queries, but also builds on other standards related to object technology such as the Object Management Group's (OMG) Object Model and Interface Definition Language along with object programming languages such as C++ and Smalltalk.

ANSI X3H2

Formed in 1978, ANSI X3H2 is a technical committee of American National Standards Institute (ANSI) Standard Planning and Requirements Committee (SPARC). X3 affairs are managed by the Computer and Business Machine Manufacturer's Association (CBEMA). In turn, ANSI is the USA representative to International Organization for Standardization (ISO), which has a technical committee, JTC1, that handles SQL standards.

The X3H2 committee was originally assigned to the development of a data definition language for CODASYL or network databases. As part of the work, the committee developed a data sublanguage for network databases, called Database Language NDL. During development of NDL, it became apparent that the relational model was increasingly important and in 1982 the development of the relational standard was assigned to X3H2. This became the well-known SQL standard. The current version of SQL is SQL-92. ANSI X3H2 has recognized the importance of adding objects to their specification and has been working on SQL3, which extends SQL-92 with a form of object capability. Contact information on X3H2 is in the Appendix.

Object Database Management Group

ODMG is a consortium of ODBMS vendors and interested parties working on standards to allow portability of customer software across ODBMS products. It was conceived in the summer of 1991, and its first meeting occurred in the fall of 1991. Version 1.0 of the ODMG-93 specification was published in August 1993. The ODMG has established liaison relationships with the following ANSI committees: X3H2 (SQL), X3H7 (Object Models), X3J16 (C++), and X3J20 (Smalltalk). The ODMG is also affiliated with the OMG. Contact information on the ODMG is in the Appendix.

SQL-92

SQL-92 is the standard for RDBMSs. SQL-92 does not address objects in any way. The specification is mentioned here because it is a portion of the basis of the two database specifications for storing objects: SQL3 and ODMG-93.

SQL-92 is the culmination of work on several earlier standards versions. It is based on SQL-89, which in turn was based on SQL-86. SQL-92 was developed by the ANSI X3H2 committee, which originally began work on an SQL standard in 1982. Although SQL-86 can be best characterized as a minimal standard, SQL-89 added a number of features such as default values, check constraints, and simple referential constraints. SQL-92, which is significantly larger than SQL-89, added varying length character strings, bit string, multiple character sets, datetime and interval, outer joins, domain assertions, temporary relations, referential actions, schema manipulation language, dynamic SQL, scrolled cursors, connections, and information schema relations. These various sets of additions culminated in SQL-92.

No RDBMS product is fully compliant with all of SQL-92, although most are compliant at the SQL-89 level through backwards compatibility. Some are compliant at higher levels and greater compliance can be expected in the future. The SQL-92 Compliance checklists in Part III highlight each product's level of compliance to SQL-92. The term *backwards compatibility* here refers

```
host language statement
host language statement

    embedded SQL statement

host language statement

    embedded SQL statement

host language statement
```

Figure 5.1 *Embedded SQL in host programming language.*

to each successive version of SQL supporting all of the previous versions. This is the philosophy of the X3H2 committee. So, anything compliant with SQL-86 should work in SQL-89. Likewise, anything compliant with SQL-89 should work in SQL-92.

SQL-92 uses a database sublanguage that results in a programming style illustrated in Figure 5.1. Some issues with embedded SQL were described in Chapter 1. Note the style shown in Figure 5.1. It requires the mixing of host programming language statements and embedded SQL statements. This will be contrasted with what is being done with object programming languages in ODMG-93 later in this chapter.

ODMG-93

The work of the ODMG is to create standards for ODBMSs. The initial standard, ODMG-93, is a portability specification that will allow much of the code written for one ODBMS product to run on other ODBMS products. This is seen as something that is good for the ODBMS industry in general.

The first ODMG specification was released in 1993 by a consortium of ODBMS vendors and other interested parties. The ODMG standard, in contrast to SQL3, builds on other object standards in the industry, as illustrated by Figure 5.2. ODMG-93 is a strict superset of OMG's Common Object Model and their Interface Definition Language (IDL). Extensions beyond the OMG standard have been added for database-related features like transactions, keys, extents, and various attribute specifications. In addition, the Object Query Language (OQL) in ODMG-93 is closely based on the query portion of SQL-92. There are some areas where OQL deviates from the query portion of SQL-92 because SQL-92 assumes a relational model and OQL assumes an object model. This set of model differences also creates problems for SQL3 as we will see later in this chapter.

ODMG-93 uses the C++ and Smalltalk language standards as much as possible, which allows the transparent integration of object programming languages described in Chapter 1, as illustrated in Figure 5.3. This is significantly different from the embedded SQL as shown earlier in Figure 5.1. Here only the programming language appears in an application program using the ODMG-93 specification. ODMG-93 integration with other object programming languages in addition to C++ and Smalltalk can be expected in the future.

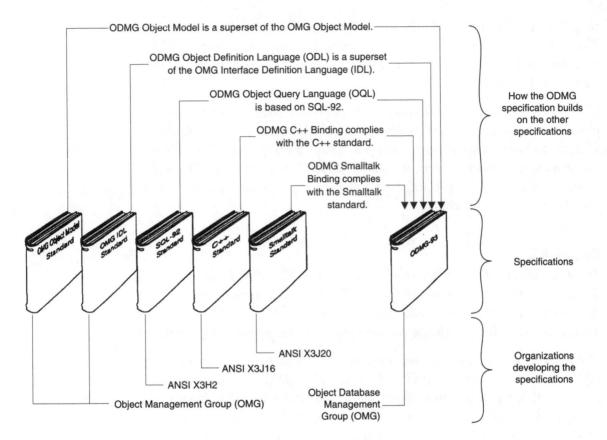

ODMG Object Model is a superset of the OMG Object Model.

ODMG Object Definition Language (ODL) is a superset of the OMG Interface Definition Language (IDL).

ODMG Object Query Language (OQL) is based on SQL-92.

ODMG C++ Binding complies with the C++ standard.

ODMG Smalltalk Binding complies with the Smalltalk standard.

How the ODMG specification builds on the other specifications

Specifications

Organizations developing the specifications

ANSI X3J20

ANSI X3J16

ANSI X3H2

Object Management Group (OMG)

Object Database Management Group (OMG)

Figure 5.2   *ODMG-93 heritage.*

Figure 5.2 also shows that the OMG Common Object Model is used as the basis for the ODMG object model. The Common Object Model was designed to be a common denominator for object request brokers, object database management systems, object programming languages, and other applications. In keeping with the OMG architecture, the ODMG has designed an ODBMS profile for the model, adding components (e.g., relationships) to the OMG Common Object Model to support ODBMS needs. This definition is illustrated in Figure 5.4. It shows the instance is a first-class object not contained in any other structures. It means the instance can be queried and manipulated directly. Later in this chapter, this figure will be used to contrast the ODMG object model with that of SQL3 model.

```
host language statement
host language statement
host language statement
host language statement
host language statement
host language statement
host language statement
```

Figure 5.3 *Transparent integration of DBMS in host programming language.*

Issues of backwards compatibility often come up in the software business. Because work began on the ODMG standard in 1991, the ODMG decided to build on events in the industry since the development of SQL and procedural programming languages. It relied on the concepts of object technology that have come from the OMG and from object programming languages. The issue of backwards SQL-92 compatibility is not a problem for the ODMG since the only point of desired compatibility in ODMG-93 is on queries and not the rest of the SQL-92 standard. Issues of backwards compatibility will also be discussed for SQL3.

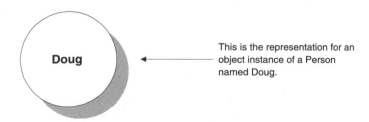

Figure 5.4 *ODMG instance object definition.*

Another difference between SQL3 and the ODMG-93 is in the nature of the object model. In ODMG-93, a classical object model is used to dispatch on the first argument that is the type of the object to which the message is being sent. (Dispatching is discussed in Chapter 3.) This is what the OMG specifies and is also found in object programming languages such as C++ and Smalltalk. We will see later that SQL3 uses a different model.

SQL3

The work of ANSI X3H2 has been to focus on DBMS standards. It is best known for the SQL standard. The current version of that standard is SQL-92. ANSI X3H2 is working to add objects to its standard while at the same time maintaining backwards compatibility with SQL-92.

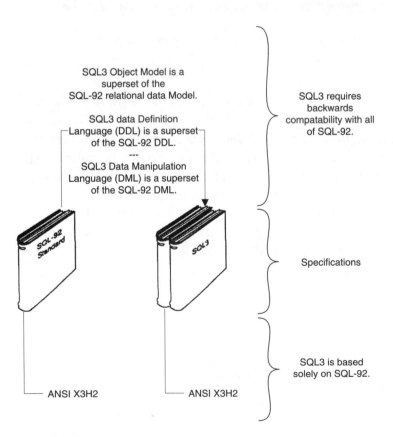

Figure 5.5 *SQL3 heritage.*

In its latest form, SQL3 builds on SQL-86, SQL-89, and SQL-92. This backwards compatibility, critical for SQL3, has impact on how it approaches the use of objects within the historical SQL perspective. SQL3, based on SQL-92, therefore must support backwards compatibility to SQL-92. This is a difficult undertaking for X3H2 since SQL-92 relies on the relational model. Combining objects with all of SQL-92 is technically difficult.

SQL3 differs from the rest of the object industry standards. Its strength and perhaps its weaknesses can be found in its being a closed system, defined only by itself. Contrast Figure 5.5 with Figure 5.2 for ODMG-93. The only foundation for SQL3 is SQL-92 and all the versions of SQL preceding SQL-92. It does not use any of the standards from OMG or the object programming community. A more positive way to look at this is that SQL3 has the full heritage of SQL-92 to rest on—providing backward compatibility with SQL-92.

Great effort went into uncovering a way that SQL's traditional relations and tuples could be related to the newer concepts of objects and the places where objects exist. The X3H2 committee tried to merge the two concepts so that relations of tuples could be viewed as objects and vice versa. This ultimately

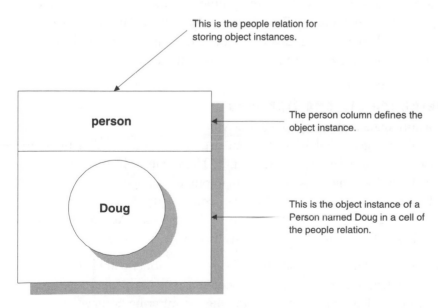

This is the people relation for storing object instances.

The person column defines the object instance.

This is the object instance of a Person named Doug in a cell of the people relation.

Figure 5.6 *SQL3 instance object definition.*

failed. The SQL3 specification was still in flux at the time this was written. Objects in the SQL3 object model, at this time, are stored in special kinds of columns in particular relations. Elsewhere only references to those objects via their unique identity are permitted. The result is separate relation and abstract data type facilities, and the definition for an object that is illustrated in Figure 5.6. In other words, objects are not "first class" because they cannot exist separately from relations, which has an effect on operations such as queries. You cannot access an object directly in SQL3—you must go through the relation. As a result, a query for Figure 5.6 would read: select * from people where person..name = "Doug". In contrast, a similar query in ODMG-93 for Figure 5.4 would be: select * from person where name = "Doug". The extra step of going through the relation is not needed. This may seem minor at first, but if you are traversing large data structures, the extra step can negatively affect your application's performance.

The two salient features of SQL3—full backwards compatibility with SQL-92 and closed system status—result in an object model that is different from most other object models in the industry. This is a *generalized object model* where the types of *all* arguments of a routine are taken into consideration when determining dispatching of what routine to invoke. Although this can be elegant, it is in contrast to the *classical object model* in use by the rest of the object technology industry. The classical object model approach was introduced in Chapter 1. The classical object model dispatches on the first argument, which is the type of the object to which the message is being sent.

Convergence of Specifications

You can anticipate that the specifications will converge in some areas and not in others. Convergence will occur to some degree on object models and to a large degree on query syntax and semantics. There will be little or no convergence on definition languages and data manipulation languages. Jim Melton, the SQL3 editor, presented an ideal view of convergence in a paper he wrote for ANSI X3H2 ("ANSI Discussion Paper X3H2-95-161, Accommodating SQL3 and ODMG," April 1995). His idea is shown in Figure 5.7.

The ODMG-93 object model and the SQL3 object model will likely converge only to the extent necessary to allow the convergence of the query syntax. That in itself is a big undertaking considering the differing heritage of the specifications in everything but SQL-92 query syntax. The ideal goal here

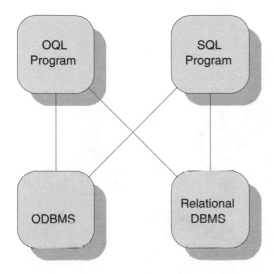

Figure 5.7 *Goal of single query language for the industry.*

also came from Jim Melton and is shown in Figure 5.8 where the SQL3 object model would be a subset of the ODMG object model. To do this would require a big change in SQL3, but there is some point short of this ideal where convergence of a single query language possible.

Convergence between ODMG-93 OQL and SQL3 is very likely given both the similar heritage of the specifications in SQL-92 queries and the effort on the part of both the ODMG and X3H2 to converge the necessary portions of the respective object models. A single query language will most likely apply

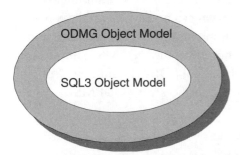

Figure 5.8 *Ideal relationship of the ODMG and SQL3 object models.*

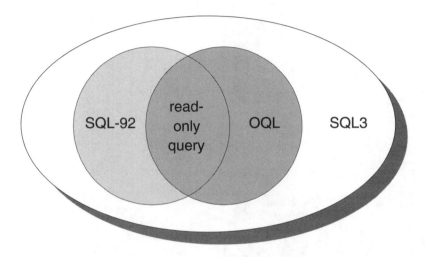

Figure 5.9 *Desired relationship of SQL-92, OQL, and SQL3.*

only to the read-only portion of queries. This is a very significant step for the database industry because it means one query language for the entire industry—whether object or not. This simplifies the work of any third-party vendor who is developing software tools for the database industry. It also means people only need be trained in one query language that will work for any DBMS product. Figure 5.9 shows the desired relationship of a single read-only query language to all of OQL and all of SQL-92 in relationship to all of SQL3.

There will likely be no convergence on aspects of SQL3 such as the SQL Data Definition Language and SQL Data Manipulation Language. This difference will always be there because of the heritage of SQL3. It does not make sense for ODMG-93 to adopt all the relational data definition and data manipulation of SQL-92 when it is trying to be as compatible as possible with OMG standards for data definition and object programming standards for data manipulation. This does not mean the ODBMSs cannot use SQL-92 or SQL3; in fact, many allow the use of SQL-92 right now. Just consider SQL-92 to be another language that interfaces with ODBMSs.

Why Standards Matter to You

The information in this chapter has been provided to help you sort through what is happening in the DBMS standards arena. Compliance to standards

Feature	SQL3	ODMG-93
Object Model (OM)	Generalized	Classical (OMG Common OM)
Data Definition Language (DDL)	SQL3	ODL (OMG IDL)
Query Language	SQL3	OQL (nearly SQL-92 query only)
Data Manipulation Language (DML)	SQL3	C++ Smalltalk

Figure 5.10   *Overview comparison of SQL3 and ODMG-93.*

often creates a set of checklist items for the prospective DBMS products to meet. This chapter provides a background and a likely direction these standards will take when you consider the possible checklist items in Part III. Figure 5.10 provides a reference to the key concepts covered so far.

There are some additional ideas to consider when looking at the checklists in Part III. Your priority may be to ensure that all (or most) of your existing SQL-92 code will work on the DBMS in the future even if it is storing objects. If this is true, look at products that follow a large subset SQL-92 (no one product does it all) with plans to follow SQL3. This approach allows you to take advantage of that backward compatibility mentioned earlier.

Another approach is to achieve transparent integration with object programming languages. Products that follow ODMG-93 would meet this need. Using these products would save considerably in development time and will likely provide better performance, as mentioned in Chapter 4.

In the future, your decision will be less clear-cut. That's because the vendors will continue to evolve their products. SQL3 vendors are likely to work out some type of tighter program language integration than embedded SQL. It is, however, unlikely to be as transparent as ODMG-93. The ODMG-93 vendors are likely to provide SQL-92 access to their products. The degree to which your old SQL code will execute unchanged will vary by the vendors. It is unlikely that you could get by with as few changes as you would with SQL3 vendors.

The ODMG is likely to come up with a language binding to SQL3 because it could be viewed as just another object language, much like the C++ and Smalltalk language integration ODMG-93 already has in place.

A Few Words About ODBC

Many tools and products are targeting the use of Microsoft's Open Database Connectivity (ODBC) because it reduces the number of different ways to connect to different databases. Many people, however, think that ODBC only works with RDBMSs. That is not true. Many ODBMSs also have ODBC interfaces, as illustrated in Figure 5.11.

On the surface ODBC would look like an ideal solution for accessing both RDBMSs and ODBMSs. The advantage of ODBC is that it is a common interface. The main disadvantage is that you are limited in what you can do with it. Imagine a narrow funnel through which data can flow; that is what using ODBC could be like. This is especially the case for ODBMSs. If you are using an object programming language and an ODBMS, it would be unwise to use ODBC because it would not allow you to take advantage of the transparency that many ODBMSs provide for object programming languages.

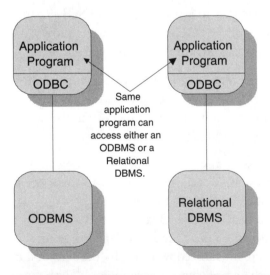

Figure 5.11 *ODBC works for either ODBMSs or RDBMSs.*

One of the best uses for ODBC interfaces to ODBMSs is to use third-party tools that work with ODBC. An ODBC interface allows these tools to use some ODBMSs as well as RDBMSs.

The bottom line is that if you have a very good use for an interface such as ODBC you are not limited to either a RDBMS or an ODBMS. You can make a selection on other criteria. If you need more than what ODBC offers, then you need to look at the respective ODMG-93 and SQL3 specifications. Keep in mind the likelihood that they may converge in the future.

Programming Standards

For people considering an ODBMS, the choice of object programming language is often very important because many ODBMS products are transparently integrated with these languages. Because nearly all language-based products such as compilers meet the language standards at about the same level, programming standards such as C++ and Smalltalk will be mentioned only briefly here.

These object programming standards are extremely important and the ODBMS vendors track them very closely because of the transparent integration ODBMSs have to the programming languages. For example, the ODMG has liaison relationships with two object programming language standards bodies just to ensure that the ODMG standards are synchronized with the programming standards. Those two standards bodies are ANSI X3J16 for C++ and ANSI X3J20 for Smalltalk. Because of the work of the ODMG, you do not need to be too concerned about the nature of the integration of the languages to the ODMG-93 standard. SQL3 at this time, however, does not integrate with object programming languages and will likely use the database sublanguage approach shown in Figure 5.1.

Object Request Brokers

I am often asked what the relationship of ODBMSs is to Object Request Brokers (ORBs). The CORBA specification for ORBs, from the OMG, allows objects to communicate in a distributed environment as shown in Figure 5.12. In this configuration, all communication among the objects in the client

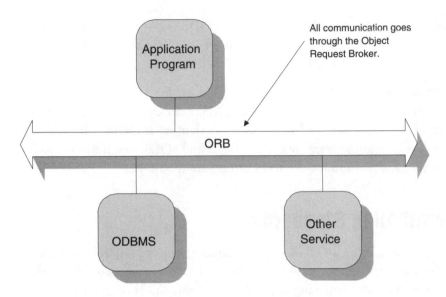

Figure 5.12 *Object Request Broker.*

application program and the various services goes through the ORB. In simple terms, the ORB acts as middleware in the movement of communication between the ODBMS or other services and the client application.

For those familiar with OMG's ORB specification, there are various services: They include persistent services, query services, transaction services, and so on. When you read this list, it appears similar to what a DBMS does.

A common question is whether an ORB (when all services are available) can substitute for an ODBMS. The answer is that once all the services for an ORB are available, it can substitute for an ODBMS only if you are willing to accept slow performance. ODBMSs normally store lots of relatively small objects. They have features to provide your application with high performance on high volumes of these usually small objects. An ORB requires many more system calls to do the same work as an ODBMS. These calls cost you performance. So, on high-volume, small objects, an ODBMS will always be considerably faster than an ORB.

A second question is whether objects in the ODBMS can be registered with the ORB and whether client applications can access those objects. The answer is yes. You might have a reason to judiciously allow some objects in the ODBMS to be used this way. This connection is shown in Figure 5.12. Be careful, however, to limit this use because an ORB has a much larger overhead that will give poor performance compared to what an ODBMS can do with a direct connection.

A third question is whether ORBs and ODBMSs can cooperate beyond just registration of ODBMS object in the ORB. The answer is absolutely! As a comparison, look at Figure 5.13. It shows the same configuration as Figure 5.12 except that a direct connection is made from the client application to the ODBMS. This connection is used when the high-performance access for which ODBMSs are noted is needed. This allows the application to use the caching and other features the ODBMS provides when the performance is required. It also allows some of the objects in the ODBMS to be registered with the ORB if other applications want to access these objects through the regular ORB process.

In addition, the ODBMS is one way to implement the persistent services of the ORB if that is desired. This particular persistent service technique is based on the ODMG-93 standard. The configuration in Figure 5.13 also

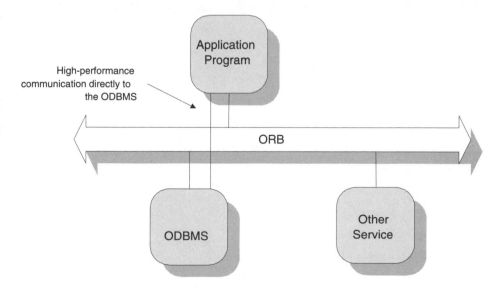

Figure 5.13 *ODBMS use in an ORB environment.*

allows objects in the ODBMS to access other services through the ORB. So an ORB and an ODBMS can be a good combination in many ways.

Summary

Standards are important. They make it possible for you to create products with longer lifetimes; as standards develop, they maintain backward compatibility so your existing software products do not need to be rewritten. Standards also help the industry grow because there is less perceived risk in choosing one of many products that have similar interfaces.

Standards will always continue to evolve, however, and it is important to keep track of where the standards are headed. In the DBMS industry, there are two standards groups of particular importance—the ODMG and ANSI X3H2. Both groups are working toward convergence of object query languages while maintaining backward compatibility to their respective heritages.

For those heavily into object use, three standards to be particularly aware of are ODMG-93, SQL3, and OMG's CORBA standard for object request brokers. In Part II of this book, you will concentrate on the activities involved in selection and deployment of an ODBMS. Understanding about standards provides a perspective to evaluating the features needed for successful application deployment.

PART TWO

Selecting and Deploying Object Databases

This Part provides the process for making ODBMS selection and deployment decisions. Building on the foundation concepts and terms introduced in Part I, a selection and deployment process is introduced in Chapter 6. The steps needed to set the stage for success are the focus of Chapter 6. The heart of the selection process is introduced in Chapter 7. Feature interaction, a vital topic to selection, is the subject of Chapter 8. In this Chapter, in-depth examples illustrate two features and the impact that their interaction has on successful project implementation. Chapter 9 outlines deployment issues that relate specifically to ODBMS deployment. Chapter 10 focuses on an issue of interest to readers with a relational modeling background—how to convert a relational schema to an object schema.

The material in Part II provides a level of understanding that will make effective use of the checklists in Part III possible. Only by gaining a thorough understanding of the material will effective selection and deployment take place.

Setting the Stage for Success

At the end of the 1994 Winter Olympics, several of the figure and speed-skaters got together for a pickup game of hockey. Afterwards, one of the medal-winning speedskaters said jokingly, "It was lots of fun, but because of my speedskating training, I can only turn to the left. That really limits my hockey success." What a humorous, yet significant thing to say! A habit built in by experience and training can indeed be a limitation in a new context.

This chapter focuses on preliminary steps to achieve successful ODBMS selection and deployment. Ironically, some of the training and habits learned in the context of RDBMSs, data modeling, and programming can be limitations in the ODBMS world, just as speedskating training might be a limitation when playing hockey. Having a clear strategy and identifying and training a team early in the process will help to overcome these limitations, as you will see in this chapter and the next.

This chapter introduces a model that has proved to be successful for fielding applications that use ODBMSs. If you follow this model, you will be putting in the front-end research needed to have long-term success. The focus of this chapter is the first two stages of a four-stage model for successful selection and deployment of an ODBMS—strategy and team identification and development. As you will see, these are important stages that need addressing prior to selection and deployment in order to overcome the limitations of prior training and experience. The final two stages of the model—selection and deployment—will be covered in Chapters 7, 8, and 9.

The key points of this chapter are:

- Two of the four stages of the process are introduced—strategy and team identification and development.

- Ways to minimize unexpected rework are presented.

- Much less of your time will be spent in deploying your application if you use this process properly because most of the hard work is up front.

Implementing ODBMS Projects: The Big Picture

Selecting an ODBMS product may seem to be a daunting task. There are, however, several tasks to be completed prior to actual selection that are critical to successful product selection and later deployment. The stages are illustrated in the process model in Figure 6.1. You may recognize that some of what is presented in this model applies to a broader part of object technology than ODBMS project implementation. Much of what is described here can apply to other projects. Implementing an ODBMS project is after all a software development project.

In my experience, lack of attention to the first two stages—strategy and team identification and development—is common and can be disastrous to a suc-

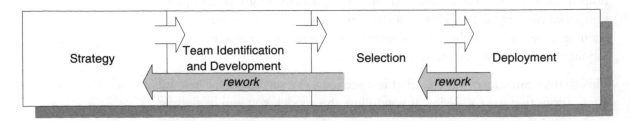

Figure 6.1 *Stages in the ODBMS implementation process.*

cessful outcome. In fact, if you take a look at Figure 6.1, you'll note that there are arrows pointing in both directions. Naturally everyone wants to move forward. If the first two stages are ignored or glossed over, backtracking commonly occurs. This can lead right back to the first stage. For example, a telecommunications firm had to drop its first-choice ODBMS because the effect that normal customer usage would have on the structure of their data had not been studied. In this case, selection of an ODBMS was done first by upper management based on sales presentations; then a team was assembled. The team's first task was to do a quick single-user benchmark. Performance on that benchmark looked fine, but because they still had not studied their data usage and structure, the benchmark gave them erroneous and misleading information. As they started to deploy beta versions of their system, the team noticed it was unacceptably slow in a multi-user environment. They had to start over. After seriously studying the structure and usage of their data, the team chose a different ODBMS that better met those needs.

The point of this story is that taking the time to pay attention to the early stages makes backtracking unnecessary. Those backward-pointing arrows cost you time and money, and they can be avoided. The company in the story thought it had done its work by doing an early benchmark, but because they had not studied their data they didn't know what to benchmark at the time. The benchmark did not test what had to be tested, and the company ended up re-doing much of their development.

The model in Figure 6.1 shows the two most common areas where rework can occur—selection and deployment. The selection process cannot move forward properly if the application needs are not properly defined in the strategy stage. This requires returning to the strategy stage. During deployment, if the known application needs along with the possible features of the ODBMS product were not properly studied, it becomes obvious that the product is not a good fit, based on deployment problems. This requires returning to the selection stage. If it turns out upon returning to the selection stage that the application needs were not properly defined in the strategy stage, you may be back at the beginning.

These first two stages in the ODBMS implementation process—strategy and team identification and development— are where you can best ensure that the last two stages—selection and deployment—are executed properly. Those backward arrows coming from the selection and deployment stages can be terribly expensive in many ways. They can cost you not only money, but lost time and missed market opportunities.

Let's take a close look at the first two of the stages in the ODBMS implementation process and see what you can do to maximize the likelihood that you will be successful in deploying an application that uses an ODBMS, and to minimize your rework.

Strategy

The decision to use an ODBMS is a strategic one that has a broad range of implications for your project and your company. Before even thinking about which ODBMS to use or even if an ODBMS should be used, you must consider what your project is intended to accomplish. How does it fit your overall company strategy? What goals is it intended to meet? The choice of using object technology and which ODBMS product to use should be considered in light of those strategic goals. Will this technology help you better meet those goals? Because these questions are so critical, you'll note in Figure 6.2 that the strategy stage is the first stage in the implementation process. It's enticing to jump right into product selection and benchmarking, but without the answers to those strategic questions, it will be hard to identify any product that will meet them.

Not every application requires an ODBMS. This section will explore four strategic characteristics that point to an appropriate use of an ODBMS, including the impact a company's competitive position can have on this decision. These characteristics are illustrated in Figure 6.3. They include business needs, the kinds of data needed, and how that data is used and stored. In

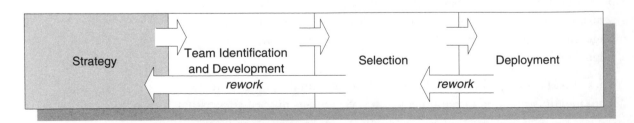

Figure 6.2 *Strategy stage in the ODBMS implementation process.*

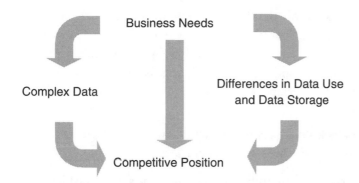

Figure 6.3 *Characteristics that identify appropriate use of an ODBMS.*

addition, these factors must be accounted for in evaluating the effect the development project may have on your company's competitive position and the timing of the development effort.

Business Needs

The first characteristic in determining your strategy is an analysis of your business needs. Does your situation require an ODBMS? The answers to a few simple questions help to identify those situations that are appropriate for ODBMSs. First of all, does your application need a DBMS at all? You should seriously consider some type of DBMS if the data will be shared among multiple people at the same time, yet must maintain the consistency and integrity of the data. Sure, you can program all that yourself, but that is what DBMSs are meant to do. These capabilities are provided by the ACID properties of DBMSs, which were described in Chapter 1. The ACID properties apply to either RDBMSs or ODBMSs.

If your decision is that business needs drive the use of either an RDBMS or ODBMS, you face the additional question of whether or not an ODBMS is appropriate for your application. The complexity of your data will point you toward an appropriate decision.

Complex Data

Having a clear understanding of your data and its complexity is a critical part of the strategy stage. In fact, the level of complexity of the data is the second characteristic to consider. Not recognizing how complex your data is will likely lead you to take a misstep that will cause problems later. Knowing the complexity of your data is literally a strategic understanding that makes it possible to make strategic decisions throughout the process. Although complex data was treated in depth in Chapter 2, here is a list of questions to consider. If you answer "yes" to most of the following questions, you probably have complex data:

- Does your data lack inherent unique identification? An example would be an address entity or a node on a graph.

- Do you have a significant number of many-to-many relationships? An example is a model where a student can take many courses and a course can be taken by many students.

- Do you have to access data using traversals? Examples are a bill-of-materials or a network diagram. The data is accessed by traversing a graph structure that represents the data.

- Do you use many type codes in your processing? An example is an employee type code to indicate full or part-time and programming that checks the different type codes to determine the appropriate processing are examples.

Beyond the complexity of your data are your data storage needs. Do they demand an ODBMS? The only way to be sure is to model your data. Successful deployment of an ODBMS application *does* require you to develop an understanding of the structure of your data at this early strategy stage. You do not need to do an entire model, and you do not need to have someone trained in object modeling at this point. You can use relational modeling if you prefer, but you simply must do enough to understand whether or not you have complex data. For example, you can model the basic entities without getting every attribute or field down. Another way is to model the entities that represent the core or most likely used data in your business without working out all the peripheral data that a full model would require.

This data modeling will provide signs that indicate an ODBMS is needed. You should consider an ODBMS seriously if your model has the characteristics of complex data described in Chapter 2.

Developing the data model for strategic purposes is actually your initial foray into early stages of what is traditionally implementation. As you will see later in Chapter 9, this early effort will make deployment simpler and easier. A word of caution at this stage: Do not assume you have simple data. As we saw in Chapter 2, there is complex data all around us. Data modeling is a way to find it.

Differences in Data Use and Data Storage

Having differences in data use and data storage is a third characteristic to consider in strategy. Using an object programming language but storing the data in an RDBMS is one example. This can affect the performance of your application. The difference between the format of data used in the object programming language and the format in which the data is stored in the RDBMS somehow must be reconciled. The performance cost of translating the data format of tuples to objects and back to tuples is called impedance *mismatch*, which was described in Chapters 3 and 4. Figure 6.4 illustrates impedance mismatch; the client application uses complex data as objects in a graph format yet stores the data as tuples in an RDBMS. Most ODBMSs, on the other hand, do not have this impedance mismatch with object programming languages.

Impedance mismatch does not mean you automatically have to consider an ODBMS. You should, however, consider an ODBMS if this performance cost becomes too high, causing your application to perform poorly. It may seem like the safe solution to use an RDBMS with an object programming language but I know of several companies that realized, late in the development, the impact that impedance mismatch can have. Most of those projects were simply trashed when they missed the window of opportunity to field an application that would have enhanced the competitive position of the company. It was deemed too late or too expensive to go back to the strategy stage and rework the application to use an ODBMS. In the end, it proved to be more risky to use an RDBMS with an object programming language than to use an ODBMS, which does not have the impedance mismatch problem.

Competitive Position

The competitive position of your application is the final critical characteristic in the strategic decision. In thinking about your application, two important issues to consider are its potential performance—how will it stack up com-

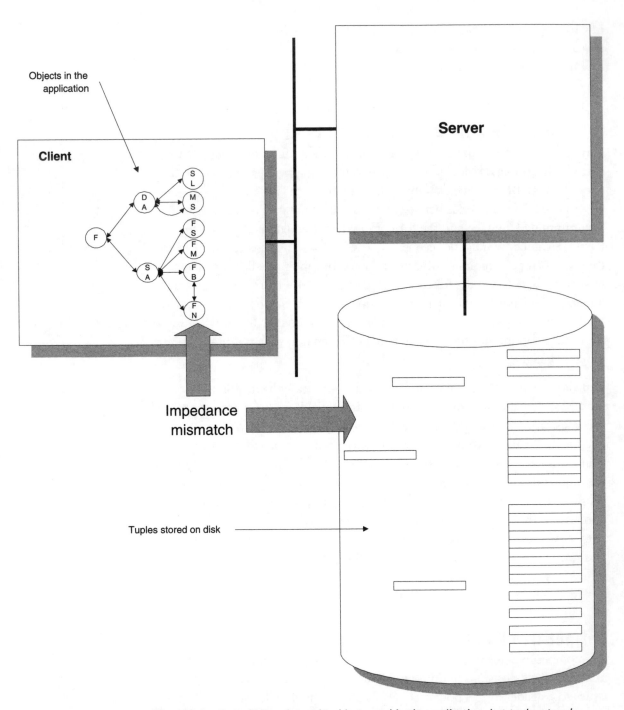

Figure 6.4 *Impedance mismatch: objects used in the application, but tuples stored on the disk.*

pared to other products—and the time needed to field the application so that you can get the application to market quickly enough. The impact of the ODBMS decision on both of these considerations follows.

Performance

The competitive bottom line for using ODBMSs is to achieve performance with complex data. For the most part, it is possible to store complex data in products other than ODBMSs. But, as mentioned in the last section, you will not have the same level of performance. What kind of difference in performance is this really? Looking at my clients' benchmarks on how ODBMSs are planned to be used compared to RDBMSs shows the ODBMSs running from ten to a thousand times faster. It depends, of course, on the nature and use of the data. This performance is based on the mechanisms in ODBMSs to process complex data. First, traversing graph structures in an ODBMS usually is performed by some form of reference technique that is considerably faster than the successive index searches on joins likely required in an RDBMS to do the same traversal. Second, dispatching (see Chapter 1) often executes faster in an ODBMS than application code that would use, for example, a case statement to determine the correct execution based on type code data stored in an RDBMS. Finally, impedance mismatch can lead to performance lags because of the time needed to transform data from application format to database format and back.

This all adds up to considerable performance gains using an ODBMS if you have complex data. If speed of processing enhances your bottom line or competitive position, you should consider this as part of your strategy. I'm familiar with a stock trading firm that uses this speed to make money. This firm uses an historical database stored in an ODBMS to determine what trades to make as they receive a feed of stock information. Reducing the lag time between the new data coming in and the trades being issued based on that data saves them a lot of money.

Time to Field an Application

A critical consideration in strategic decision-making is the amount of time it will take to get a product to market. If you are starting fresh and are new to object technology, it will likely take you two years to evaluate ODBMSs, gain experience, and field your first product. If an ODBMS will be strategic to your commercial products in two years, you should be looking seriously now. Experience does take time.

Based on my clients' experiences, two years is a reasonable time to field a commercial application using an ODBMS. This allows for the inevitable learning curve for object technology, evaluation of programming languages, selection of DBMS product(s), and developing prototypes using the chosen language and DBMS. You need the time for gaining experience with the products, selection of the initial application, design and development of the application, testing, and deployment.

If at this point, your data and competition do not provide pressing business reasons for getting into ODBMSs, you should stop. These products are new on the block and do not yet have the wealth of tools around them that you can find with RDBMSs. On the other hand, if you do see pressing business reasons for getting into ODBMSs, this book will help you get started.

World Wide Framastats: A Case Study

A case study will be woven into this chapter and the next, in order to give a more tangible sense to this material. The company featured, World Wide Framastats, is a fictional one struggling with problems and decisions similar to those of many companies today.

After 20 years in operation, World Wide Framastats (WWF) is a major player in the Framastat business. The Framastat industry is reasonably lucrative and, up until recently, has not been terribly competitive. In a new development, however, technical discoveries have made flexible Framastats possible. In addition, the way business is done is changing. WWF must study its options if it wishes to retain its industry leader status. In this case study, we'll focus on how WWF will be obtaining and processing customer orders. In particular, WWF will consider using an ODBMS in its order gathering and fulfillment processes. As we work through this case study, we will be following the ODBMS implementation process.

In the past, WWF has relied on salespeople to call on its industrial customers, gather information about specifications, and then return to the office to process a bid. There has been talk in the industry about using laptop computers at industrial sites, which would allow immediate customer response with costs and shipment dates for customized flexible framastats. WWF must decide if this is the right choice for them and, if so, how it should be implemented.

First, WWF looked at their business needs. They determined that speed of responsiveness was critical for them. Although they were able generally to fill orders within one month, their customers were finding that this was too long. Their customers were asking for two-week fulfillment. Among other possible strategies, WWF decided to provide their sales representatives with the latest information on laptops that they could carry into the customer site. They hoped to be able to connect to a central system with the customer's requirements, analyze the Framastat data, and determine the price and shipment schedule while the salesperson was still in the office. Removing the time lag and paperwork shuffle would cut at least a week from the fulfillment process.

Next, WWF looked at the complexity of their data. They realized how complex the data was and that they needed good performance on this complex data if the salesperson could respond quickly to the customer. The complexity of the data reflects the additional data needed to support flexible framastats—both in the definition of specific framastats and in the manufacturing and shipment data.

Another consideration for WWF was the way the data was used and stored. WWF had hired a new person to work on the laptop development. He convinced management that the only way to do what they needed on the laptop was to develop programs in C++. (He liked C++ because he knew the language well.) C++, like other object programming languages, was well suited to complex data such as that needed for flexible framastats. This person, known as the Advocate, pointed out that there is a problem using data in object form on the laptops, storing it in relational form in an RDBMS and then expecting to get high-performance responses for salespeople sitting in customers' offices. The Advocate argued that data should be stored in the DBMS in the same form as it is used in the application. He saw it as a simpler way to develop the application as well as providing better performance.

Finally, in looking at their competitive position they knew a major competitor, Framastats Unlimited, was embarking on a program to support flexible framastats. That meant WWF had to take steps to maintain their leadership position in the industry.

After this analysis WWF tentatively decided that an ODBMS might be an option in developing a fast-action order and fulfillment system.

Team Identification and Development

In many situations that I have witnessed, someone decides that ODBMSs should be considered for a project for the first time. At that point, the best technical people are called together and asked to look over what's available. They spend some time looking over brochures and listening to the vendor's marketing and salespeople. Then, somewhat confused, they make a decision and go back to their regular jobs. At a later time, when it's time to develop the application, some other people work on that project. This may work in some situations, but it doesn't work in the implementation of object technology, particularly if the project is one of the first times the technology is going to be used in a company.

After developing a strategy of considering ODBMSs, you must start assembling a team for selection and deployment. Ideally, this team will evolve into the people who will do the selection of the ODBMS product and the deployment of the application. There is a big learning curve in object technology, so it is best to stick with the same people in whom you have invested the time and effort for this learning.

As mentioned in Chapter 1, most computer professionals have some sort of blind spot about a technology that is not their specialty. At this stage of the development of the object technology industry, that means many technical people have some sort of blind spot about object technology. At a minimum, they lack solid knowledge, understanding, and experience. For this reason, it's a good idea to commit to serious training of the people who will be doing the selection and deployment of the technology. That means they should be identified early in the process and dedicated to the team for the duration of

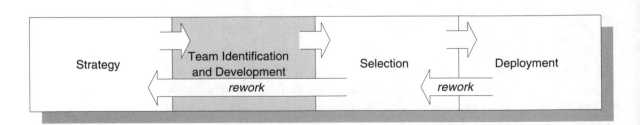

Figure 6.5 *Team stage in the ODBMS implementation process.*

the entire process. The only other alternative is to train successive waves of people working on and then leaving the project—and this will probably guarantee the project will not be done on time because of the learning curve each person will have with object technology.

Figure 6.5 illustrates where the team identification and development stage falls into the entire implementation process. The best scenario is that this same team will participate in both the selection and deployment stages by the time they are done.

Team Member Characteristics

At the heart of a successful application development using ODBMSs is a team of people who are flexible and willing to take a fresh look at how to get the job done. Whom you choose to be on your selection team is important. All team members must be aware of their blind spots and willing to consider all options. By considering all options it is possible to ensure that all application needs are considered when looking at the products available. You can expect that all the vendors are sure their respective products are a good fit; it is your team that will make sure the product chosen really will *be* a good fit. The team also will work through deployment of the application.

What Makes for a Successful Team?

Team theory states that a relatively small number of people—not more than seven—makes a successful team. In my experience with clients working on ODBMS selection, that tends to be true in the real world as well. The general groups of people to draw from for the team members are illustrated in Figure 6.6. One of the key considerations for all team members is their flexibility and willingness to look at things in different ways. As I outline the type of background that is required for each team member, note how important flexibility is within each skill set.

Database Crowd

One team member must come from what I term the "database crowd" and have data modeling experience. This is critical because of the importance of data modeling to the selection process. Data modeling will make understanding data possible, which is critical for successful selection and deployment. If the database person has a background strictly in relational modeling, he or

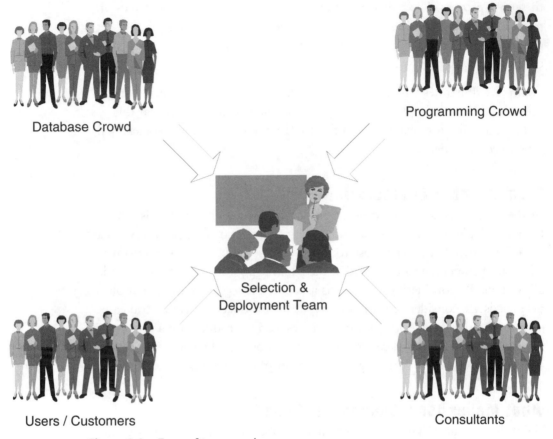

Database Crowd

Programming Crowd

Selection &
Deployment Team

Users / Customers

Consultants

Figure 6.6 *Types of team members.*

she must be aware of this viewpoint and be willing to change the way data is modeled. You may find someone familiar with modeling objects; that would be a major asset—especially if you plan on storing your data in an ODBMS. The object schema needed for your object programming language is the same as the one used for your ODBMS. Someone with object modeling experience will give you a leg up on this aspect of your work.

People with years of successful relational modeling experience can find it very hard to understand the object model because it requires a drastic change in thinking. This is an example of the old saying, "If the only tool you have is a hammer, everything looks like a nail." But if you learn to use other tools such as screwdrivers, saws, drills, and so on, you can see things differently—

there are many things in the world that are not nails! It is a big challenge for anyone to change the way he or she sees things. It can be surmounted, but keep this possible difficulty in mind as you select this key team member.

Having someone on the team with experience in using ODBMSs would be helpful, but be careful that he or she is not too tied to a particular product that was used on a prior project. He or she may think that particular ODBMS product will work for anything, which is not necessarily true (it's that proverbial hammer again). If the person has an open mind, his or her experience may be very useful. Unfortunately, people with ODBMS experience are sometimes hard to find, as it is a new market. So you should expect to develop your own expertise through training and work on your application. Be forewarned, though, that you may very well lose your people with ODBMS experience once your project is done, because of the high demand for them. This will be discussed in Chapter 9.

Programming Crowd

A second team member must have programming experience, commonly in C++ and/or Smalltalk. As I note in Chapter 7 on the selection stage, you may already have a programming language in mind—so consider this in selecting a team member. If you do not have someone with object programming experience, you must find someone willing to change the way he or she programs. Keep in mind that object programming is very different from procedural programming such as C, COBOL, or FORTRAN. In particular, if you are considering C++, watch out for people who think they are writing C++ when they are really writing C programs using a C++ compiler. This is very possible with C++. Because of the nature of programming in C, someone with a strong C background has a hard time avoiding this without some effort. It may be necessary to send a C programmer to a Smalltalk training class to shake up his or her thinking. Unlike C++, Smalltalk forces you to think in terms of objects. C++ will allow you to continue writing procedural C code. It is tremendously hard for any of us to change the way we think. Sometimes changing the environment helps, and in this case the new environment would be Smalltalk.

Users or Customers

One team member must have experience in the problem domain, either as a user or customer. This is critical because this person actually understands the problem. Be careful to choose someone who is not so heavily invested in the current system that he or she cannot see a better way. Look carefully at the role he or she had in the development of the prior system and ask him or her what perspective he or she has on the old system. Responses to this kind of question should give you insight into how flexible he or she might be.

Consultants

An external consultant can help to round out the team by providing a fresh, outside perspective. At this stage, beware of someone who is tied to a particular vendor or product or who has primarily worked with certain types of projects, unless that is the type of project you are doing.

An external consultant with a wide range of experience using a variety of products and projects can save you months of effort in the process. In particular, this help can shorten the lengthy effort it takes to iterate in the center section of the selection model, which you will see in Chapter 7. They can also act as mentors to your team members.

Avoiding Possible Pitfalls

There are a few pitfalls that must be avoided if successful selection and deployment are to take place. In each case, these are the pitfalls that turn the team's effort into a waste of time.

Watch for overactive skepticism. Don't choose people who have been very successful with RDBMSs and are skeptical of ODBMSs. Skepticism can be a healthy trait on a team but constantly debating whether an ODBMS is the right thing will slow you down and lessen team morale. Constant nay-saying that an ODBMS is the wrong way to go adds nothing to the team process. The decision to choose an ODBMS must be made and committed to as part of the strategy stage. By the time the team is getting started, the focus should be on selection and deployment.

Plan to have team members get some training immediately, particularly in those areas that demand a new perspective. If team members have been very successful in procedural languages, for example, you must train them in object programming languages; it's a big jump from a procedural to an object programming language. The pitfall of not getting the training is that your team will struggle to write what might be object program code, when it is more likely they are still writing procedural code. It is critical for those team members who will be working in object programming languages to have object programming skills in place.

Choose people from the user community who are forward-thinking and not locked into the past. This team member must be aware of trends and issues within the user community or he or she will not add value to the process. If he or she believes things should stay as they are or especially if he or she believes the problem domain is too complicated to be explained fully to developers, the person does not belong on the team. The pitfall of having a person who is not forward-thinking on the team is that this person can drag the team down into repeated discussions of "Why are we doing this?" or "This is SO complicated, we can never cover it all!"

What Training Should You Consider?

Because object technology is fairly new and not widely understood, training is an important step in the development of your project team. Before even beginning the selection stage, each team should be knowledgeable on object technology and DBMS concepts. Only then is the team ready to even consider the claims of the various product vendors.

Each team must first get a good understanding of the basics, such as object technology and DBMS concepts. There are many sources of good training available. Check industry magazines such as *Object Magazine* or *Journal of Object-Oriented Programming* for companies advertising training. The special training issues that these magazines sometimes run can be particularly helpful.

Training in object technology takes two forms. The first is object modeling. The second is object programming since this team will also deploy the application.

Training in a methodology for object modeling is critical to the success of the selection effort because only by truly understanding the data through the object schema can the real application needs become apparent. Without this grounding the team may fall victim to the misleading labels that products may carry, rather than understanding the product features and the impact the features have on the completed application. There is a variety of types of object modeling available. In my view, any approach is fine as long as you are reasonably comfortable with it. Folks from both the programming and database crowds should get the modeling training—not just the database people—because the object schema that is used in the application is either stored directly in the ODBMS or is translated in a very specific manner to a non-object format in an RDBMS. All parties have to understand the object modeling issues.

Not knowing how to use a methodology is a serious technical error. The complexity of the problems often being addressed using ODBMSs makes it impossible to just do it through sheer brain power. The methodologies help you identify what the objects really are and how they should behave. Believe me, that is much harder to do than it sounds for many reasons. Also, many people new to ODBMSs believe they know how the object schema should be structured; they are often wrong because they are structuring things in a non-object way. It is not uncommon to look at an object schema and see that it is really a relational schema with intersection entities and type codes. This is analogous to the programmer who has worked in FORTRAN many years and is now using a language such as C++. If you look at the code, it still may be FORTRAN but with a different syntax. The same thing can happen when developing the object schema. A methodology helps break through these patterns. It will also help you identify areas that need more attention. It is usually hard to "gloss over" areas of the application when you are adhering to a methodology.

Training in object programming is also essential for the team, including the database people. This is the inverse of programmers being trained in object modeling and the same reasoning applies. The object programming language and the object model are tightly knit together in this environment. Database people must understand how the data will be used in the object programming language at more than just a superficial level. The object programming language you choose is not that critical; that it is an object programming language is the critical issue. You may or may not have chosen a programming language at this stage. If you have, get training in that one. If you have not yet chosen a language, get training in Smalltalk. Smalltalk training is a great place to learn object technology concepts even if you later decide to use another language such as C++. Smalltalk can be picked up faster than C++.

Be sure to start applying the experience from training immediately and use the training material exclusively, if possible, in order to get through the paradigm shift. Allow time to become accomplished in the new tools, techniques, and ideas. DO NOT let the training sit for a couple of months and think it will come back when needed. I have not seen this work in practice.

When you have narrowed the field in the selection process in stage 3, training in the ODBMS products will be extremely helpful. This is invaluable particularly when you identify a critical aspect of your application and spend some time on it in training for each candidate ODBMS product. You will come to an even deeper understanding of the impact it could have on your application.

Plan a realistic training schedule. Do not plan training in object modeling one week and in object programming the following week. Take the time to really learn and practice your new skills and concepts before going on to new training. Practice the modeling for a while and when you are comfortable with it, move on to the programming training.

Team Identification and Development

Back at World Wide Framastats, progress on the project continued. As is not unusual, WWF decided to look into using ODBMSs to support their effort, although they had little background in this subject. Their engineering group was familiar with programming in C, and their business group was a COBOL shop. Yet, they had an Advocate who was promoting the use of ODBMSs as part of the solution for this business problem.

To get the ball rolling, WWF brought a team of people together. There were some with experience with DBMSs in the past—relational DBMSs—in the COBOL shop. One database person on the team was from that group. A programmer came from the engineering side. Two salespeople saw an opportunity to clean up if WWF could develop a system to support the sales of flexible framastats—they joined the team. The Advocate was there, too. He was fairly new to WWF, but had some experience with object design methodologies and object programming from his last company. The team had five people in all.

The first task of the team was to get up to speed technically. Everyone, including the salespeople, attended training in object design methodologies. What surprised everyone is that the salespeople picked up the object design methodologies faster than the technical people. When asked, the salespeople, said, "Well, it is just the way we think about things—it seems so natural." The technical people struggled because this was not the way they had been developing systems all these years. The database person was having the most difficulty in NOT designing relational data models. But everyone seemed to have some grasp of the concepts of object technology. The technical people also went for C++ training. This nearly killed the project. Of the technical people, those with a C background did not have much difficulty, but the person from the COBOL shop was completely lost. And he let everyone know it— big time. The Advocate worked with him and encouraged him to get some Smalltalk training. This seemed to help his understanding of how to code in object terms. And after some practice, the team was starting to think in terms of object technology.

Summary

This chapter introduced the ODBMS implementation process and explored the first two stages of the process, strategy and team identification and development, in depth. These two stages are essential to successful selection and deployment, which are covered in the next three chapters.

People often ask what is the biggest mistake made in using an ODBMS. The biggest mistake is selecting the wrong ODBMS for your application needs, because this choice inevitably affects how well you can implement and deploy your application. It is a variant of the saying that "the most expensive errors in software development are made up front."

How is the wrong selection made? There are several possible reasons. At the root, the strategy for using an ODBMS may be ill formed. Perhaps those developing the strategy were poorly informed about the technology or did not understand the impact of their decision. A second common reason is that insufficient time is spent in developing the team that will make the selection. An improperly developed team may not have an appropriate understanding of the technology, DBMS facts, programming languages, or the user environment. All of these problems can be overcome with proper attention to all stages in the implementation process.

7

Making a Success of Selection

There are always several ways to approach any purchase. Running out and buying the first thing that looks okay is at one end of the spectrum; deeply researching and gathering a variety of information prior to making a decision is at the other end. There are, of course, approaches between the two extremes. Consider a household purchase such as buying a home theater system. You might buy one on impulse without thinking of the space to be filled or what needs people in the household might have for such a system. At the other end of the spectrum, you might hire someone to come into your home to measure and advise you on the best approach for your needs. And there would be other possibilities in between the two.

You will have longer-term success with your home theater if you look at what are your needs and desires are, as well as the space to be filled. If no research is done, you are likely to have a system that doesn't fit your home or provide the type of performance you want. When that happens, you are likely to replace it as soon as you are able because it won't provide long-term success. Putting some time and effort into the purchase is more likely to provide long-term success. It also provides long-term economy because you won't have to replace it quite so soon.

The same dynamic occurs in the choice of an ODBMS. Prepurchase research to determine your needs and what is available will help you determine the best fit for your needs. That will give you longer-term success.

This chapter describes the selection stage of the model introduced in Chapter 6. It focuses on the type of research you need to do to make an informed selection of an ODBMS.

Key points in this chapter are:

- Matching features to application needs is the best determinant of success.

- Insufficient research into the interaction between your application needs and the ODBMS product features will likely lead to deployment problems.

- Tips to minimize unexpected rework in the process are presented.

In Chapter 6, two critical steps in the ODBMS implementation process—strategy and team identification and development—were covered in depth. If you are turning to this chapter first, flip back to Chapter 6 to get an overview of the first two stages in the process.

When you have identified strategic goals for your project and have determined that using an ODBMS will help you achieve those goals, you have completed the strategy stage. When you have identified and trained a selection and deployment team, you have completed the second stage and are ready to enter the selection stage in the process, as illustrated in Figure 7.1. Following the stages of this process in order will make successful deployment more likely.

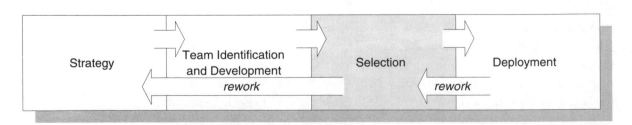

Figure 7.1   *Selection stage in the ODBMS implementation process.*

Selection

The selection stage is illustrated more fully in the model in Figure 7.2. This model been used successfully to select ODBMSs in a variety of industries. The three main steps are followed in a fairly linear fashion, as you will see.

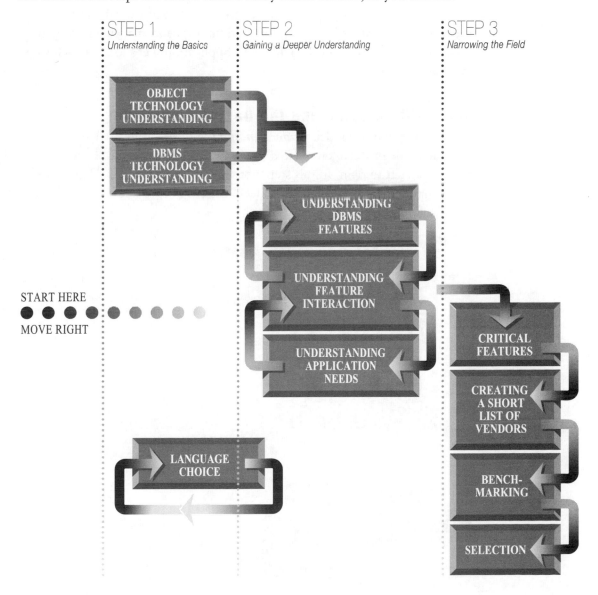

Figure 7.2 *DBMS selection model.*

Understanding the basics of object and DBMS technology as well as choosing a programming language comprises the first step. The second step focuses on gaining a deeper understanding of ODBMS products and your application needs through the iterative process of studying product features, application needs, and the interaction of features and application needs. The final step involves narrowing the field by identifying a list of critical features to use in selecting a short list of vendors and finally, benchmarking/testing in order to identify the best choice for your application. Let's look at each step in greater detail.

Step 1—Understanding the Basics

The first step in this model, *Understanding the Basics*, is located at the far left side of the model and repeated in Figure 7.3; movement in the model flows from left to right. In this step, you must gain sufficient background understanding of object and DBMS technology to move knowledgeably into the selection process itself.

Figure 7.3 *Understanding the basics.*

The choice of a likely programming language, which is often an object programming language, may occur in this step but is not required.

Object Technology Understanding

Everyone on the selection team must have a basic understanding of object technology. Because object technology is quite different from the technology that preceded it, the understanding must be deeper than that which comes from reading a book or taking a course. This depth of understanding usually comes from experiencing it. Generally speaking, this technology must be used to get a sufficiently deep understanding of the impact it will have on the application. A good comparison is the experience that comes from living in a different culture or country, as opposed to reading about it or watching a film. It is not until you have lived in the culture that you begin to understand its subtleties. This is true with object technology as well. Chapter 6 described the training your team needs for developing this object technology understanding. The following paragraphs provide some insight on how people of various computer orientations may experience their first ODBMS project.

Managers will find that object applications/databases are developed in a manner that is significantly different from the way other applications are developed. In developing object applications/databases, most companies spend considerably more time in analysis and design, as well as in testing, than in prior non-object projects. Figure 7.4 shows the changing nature of the implementation phases using object technology on complex data. Trying to force a shorter schedule up front will result in technical problems. The typical outcome of that shorter schedule is that the team may take a more

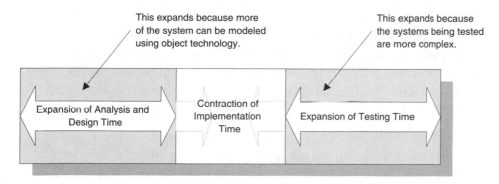

Figure 7.4 *The effect of object technology on the development phases.*

cursory look at products during this selection stage or try to cut corners throughout the entire process. This can mean an incomplete job of object modeling, or object modeling done too late in the process for it to be used for strategic or selection decisions. That will likely result in a poor choice of an ODBMS and rework in the deployment stage.

For data modelers, gaining an understanding of object technology requires doing real object modeling on their actual problem domain. They need to move beyond the examples from the training class. This is because those examples always work so well. Real world problems are not so tidy. They must try object modeling on their own problem domain to confront some of the more difficult—and ultimately rewarding—parts of object modeling. If the data modelers come from a relational modeling background, it will be hard at first for them to think in terms of class hierarchies and the encapsulation of processes as methods attached to classes.

Surprisingly, knowing a great deal about relational modeling can actually be a problem in the selection process. That was my personal experience as a relational modeler. When I first worked with object technology in 1987, it virtually felt as if my head was clamped in a vice and being turned 180 degrees. I had a very hard time seeing the world in anything but relational terms. Moving from relational modeling to object modeling is a significant paradigm shift. You must be aware of that and not assume data modeling is data modeling whether relational or object—it just ain't so.

Similar concepts apply to programmers. They must now program with real data in their application area using the object programming language, not just the examples in a class. As stated earlier, the examples in classes are usually very tidy and very limited in order to complete in the time limits of a class. Programmers must work on more realistic programming issues with the data and processing they will be using. Experienced procedural programmers will find it hard to think in terms of using methods. Some might find it hard to accept that there is little code in their application that shows the DBMS is being accessed.

Because the object schema is so critical to the quality of the work later on in the process, users must bring the real world into the object schema for the object modelers to use. Users should be trained in the concepts of the technology to gain an understanding of how it could be applied to the applications they use. They will need to understand enough to develop scenarios used in the selection process. Again, just reading about object technology does not really give you an appreciation of what it can do.

Selection, Step 1: Understanding the Basics

Back at World Wide Framastats, the team has completed its training and practice as described in Chapter 6. The WWF flexible Framastat team (FlexFram, it was called) had taken several months to get the training in C++ and, later, in Smalltalk. FlexFram then practiced programming first in Smalltalk and then in C++.

They felt ready to make a selection of an ODBMS. The RDBMS person on the team had wanted to make a selection right at the start, but the team managed to wait until they had a better understanding of the technology and concepts. A few people in top management were also pressuring for an early decision, but the Advocate managed to get support for waiting a bit.

They had decided at the outset to use C++, because it was the language the Advocate thought was best for the project. The person from the COBOL shop also had DBMS experience, so they felt ready to look at the ODBMS products on the market. They had been reading the industry journals and had a pretty good idea who the vendors were.

DBMS Technology Understanding

A basic understanding of DBMS technology is important as well. Part I of this book provides an overview. Understanding the purpose of a DBMS, which is to go beyond persistent languages to allow object data to be shared safely in a multi-user environment, is critical to the selection process.

Language Choice

In many situations, a programming language usually has been chosen early in the process. In fact, sometimes it is the first decision made, even though it shouldn't be. More often than not, the object programming language used is the one the team leader favors. Ideally, the choice of language should be dictated by the application needs and those ODBMS features that will be identified in Step 2 that meet those needs. In reality, however, the language usually is chosen first.

In the model, you will see that language choice overlaps Steps 1 and 2. That's because new information is often learned in Step 2 that can change the choice of language. The arrows in Figure 7.2 are circular for that reason. This change can occur when, based on the application needs and the ODBMS with product features that meet those needs, it becomes obvious that a different language is needed. For example, some programming languages lend themselves to dynamic changes in the structure of the data definition. As you examine ODBMS features and your application needs, you may discover that your application may be able to take advantage of this and you may change the object programming language choice.

When everyone on the team is up to speed on the basics of object and DBMS technology, and perhaps a tentative language choice has been made, the team can move into step 2.

Step 2—Gaining a Deeper Understanding
The core of the selection stage can be found in Step 2, *Gaining a Deeper Understanding*, which falls in the center of the selection model. It is shown in

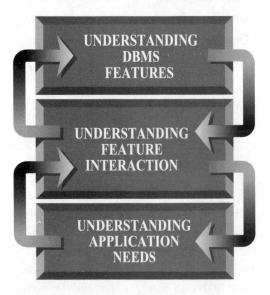

Figure 7.5 *The core of the selection stage.*

Figure 7.5. The greatest amount of time is spent in this step of the model because it is iterative, rather than linear, in nature. It simply takes time to iteratively line up application needs and ODBMS product features. To line up needs and product features, you will use checklists from Part III, object modeling, and prototyping; you will also start to contact the ODBMS product vendors. You will use all this as you study your application needs as well as available ODBMS features in order to determine what ODBMS features will best meet those specific application needs. You will get a deeper understanding of your application needs and possible ways to address them.

This step is particularly iterative because as you consider how a specific feature may impact your application, you may find that your perception of your application needs may change. The deeper you go into understanding possible features, the more impact this new knowledge will have on how you view your application.

Understanding DBMS Features

All ODBMSs are not alike, not by a long shot. Although it seems as if everyone is constantly looking for the "best" ODBMS, the answer is that there is no one ODBMS that is the best. There is no one product that will work for every application, because each application requires a particular combination of features. In my experience, people are often totally unaware of all the possible features they could use in their application development; hence they make very uninformed choices. Making choices based on common knowledge or on the latest industry buzz is not informed decision-making. In Part III of this book, you will find 13 categories of checklists that highlight the broad list of possible features for consideration. These checklists provide the level of detail needed for an informed selection. The key to success is matching those possible features to your application needs.

Features by the same high-level name are not always the same in different ODBMS products. It is important to look beyond the high-level name to the actual functionality of the feature. Every company will put their best foot forward in their marketing activities—that's only natural. It is only by looking at the level of detail provided in the checklists in Part III that you will truly understand the features of any given product.

In this process, you may find that new, unexpected features needed from the DBMS products emerge organically as the application is considered from the point of view of possible features available from the various ODBMS products. The checklists will give you the broadest exposure possible to what is available; use the checklists as a tool to uncover features that might be easily overlooked. As an example, take a look at Checklist 8 in Part III; the feature set is "Versions." This feature could, for example, allow a number of versions of illustrations to be maintained during a design process. Think how might this apply to your application area. Will you need to maintain salary histories? Will you have time-series data? Will you need to maintain revisions of documents? Do you have versions of software? If you have any of these, versioning is a feature than may be important to you. Think about how much development effort could be eliminated by having this feature in the ODBMS product.

As you will see in the next section, it is also critical to understand your application needs, the product features, and how both application needs and features can interact as well as how various features can interact. You must consider what this could mean to your application. This often creates whole new ways of looking at the business problem you are trying to address. I have seen clients revamp the entire application once developers truly understand how some ODBMS features (like versions) can address their application.

Understanding Feature Interaction

Your application needs do not exist in a vacuum separate from the DBMS product features. The features will interact with each other in the application in ways that you may or may not be able to anticipate. The task is to fit the application to the product features and the product features to the application in such a way that the features work well together to provide the functionality needed for the application.

Two features taken together in a unique way in your application could spell disaster—or amazing success. Chapter 8 illustrates how the features of locking granularity, query processing, and method execution can interact to give good or potentially abysmal performance. The use of class-level locking is another example of critical feature interaction. Often, class-level locking is very useful for applications that must dynamically change data definition; yet it can result in locking all the object instances of the class while the change is made. That could result in unacceptable delays depending on the application. On the other hand, the amount of programming code eliminated because of this feature could be immense. Thinking about the possible ramifications is essential at this step.

How do you know if the features can interact and what will happen? This is hard when you are looking at your data and application in a superficial manner. Chapter 8 will illustrate how the concept works with a few critical features that many applications use. It is hard to say how features will interact in all applications. The key is to look at the features in light of your application. In working with clients, the interaction of features becomes obvious as they start to understand the features in light of their application needs. What seems to happen is what I call the "three-way light bulb effect." They are those light bulbs that first come on dimly when you first turn the switch. You turn the switch again, and the light is brighter. The final turn, the light is brightest. What happens in this stage is a dim light appears as you study the features. The light gets brighter as you realize how these features could be used in your application. In the process of looking at various features and various application uses, you start to see how the features can interact given your application. This is when the light bulb is the brightest.

Understanding Application Needs

To start understanding your application needs, there are some basic questions to consider. They include:

- What is the computing environment?

- Will the data be distributed?

- Will the distribution be local or over a larger geographic area?

- How many users will work concurrently?

- How will concurrent users access the data?

- What types of schema changes will be likely?

- How much data is likely to result from your most common queries?

- Will you be using methods as part of your queries?

- Will you be accessing existing data from existing non-object sources such as RDBMSs ?

Your answers to these questions will start you on your use of the checklists in Part III in determining which features are important to your application. As you look through the checklists, you may find features that work differently than you thought. You may also learn about new features that you weren't aware of; these same features might make a significant difference to your application. Some features may even affect the performance of your application because the feature is performed inside the ODBMS rather than outside in your application. Dynamic schema changes (Checklist 4) provide an example of this. Often, the amount of programming code that is eliminated because of this feature can be immense; because the changes all occur inside the ODBMS, it is more efficient than if you programmed it in your application. But it is important only if your application needs this feature.

A second excellent way to start exploring your application needs is to work with the users to develop scenarios of how the new system will be used. These must be developed in detail and should cover the entire application. These scenarios can then also be used as the basis of system testing as described in Chapter 9.

Taking the time to research possible features in the checklists and considering possible application matches will help you come to a much greater depth of understanding about your application and what features will meet those needs. In the next step of the selection process, you will determine which of those features are critical to your application and its success.

Using the Checklists in Part III in the Iterative Process

The checklists in Part III extensively cover the possible features of ODBMSs. These should be used as part of the iterative process of matching ODBMS features to application needs. As you study the checklists representing ODBMS features and your application needs, you start to eliminate some of the checklist items that are not applicable for your application needs. This process is represented by Figure 7.6; the universe of possible feature checklists is winnowed down to a list of useful feature checklists and then to a list of critical and nice-to-have feature checklists.

Object Modeling and Prototyping Assists in the Iterative Process

The best place I have found to start winnowing the features as part of the iterative process is to go back to the object schema. This object schema was started in the strategy stage, where you prepared enough of it to determine if you had complex data. You may not, however, have developed a complete object schema. The team should also have practiced object modeling of something approximating the target application as they went through training in object modeling and the associated object methodology. Now, as part

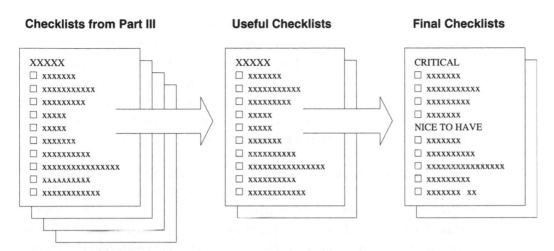

Figure 7.6 *The winnowing of useful features for your application.*

of the selection process, you need to have the requirements and system specifications firmed up. This is where using a methodology pays off; it is much harder to overlook aspects of the targeted application when using most methodologies.

I am also a strong advocate of prototyping aspects of your system to explore these requirements and specifications—also as part of the iterative process. This is where the users are critical. Try things out with them, using prototyping tools and techniques. This is a chance to practice using the programming language you have chosen along with the other tools you plan to use.

The methodology fleshes out the requirements and specifications that give birth to the object schema. The prototypes also test aspects of the model with the users. This in turn affects the requirements and specifications as well as helping to winnow out the ODBMS features you need to consider for your application. Note that you are doing this with no ODBMS at this time. An ODBMS is not necessary at this time to gain the understanding of the features and how they may interact with each other and your application needs. What is necessary is the methodology to develop the object schema and any prototyping to develop the look and feel of the system.

One tip I have found useful when working with methodologies is to purchase a software tool that supports the methodology with more than just a drawing capability. It is especially useful if the software tool can check if the model is well formed and complete within the rules of the methodology. Also, and this is more subtle, I suggest you consider tools that do not make it too easy to customize the notation used for the methodology. It has been my experience that it is so tempting to customize the notation that each member of the team eventually does so and you end up with dialects in your drawings. It is important to stick to the basics of the methodology.

Contacting the Vendors   Once your checklists start to stabilize into a useful subset of checklists, contact some of the ODBMS vendors to complete them. Have them explain in some detail how their system works for some items. The result is a final set of checklists that is separated in to critical and nice-to-have features. Of course, once you know which features are critical, you will need to know what features the products have. Contact the vendors to get each of their individual answers or get a copy of *The DBMS Needs Assessment for Objects*, an annual publication that provides information on which features are provided by the vendors. Information on *The DBMS Needs Assessment for Objects* is contained in the Appendix.

Performance

Following the process of deeply examining features and understanding your application needs before doing any performance work is likely to result in the best performance. I have seen this time and time again with clients. The iteration between application needs and product features provides an understanding that results in an architecture with the best performance possible for your application. The depth of understanding this step provides will greatly increase your odds of a successful application. Later on in the process, however, you must still benchmark to be sure that the performance of that architecture meets your needs. You will see in the next stage that this activity occurs at the end, rather than the beginning, of the process.

Selection, Step 2: Gaining a Deeper Understanding

Back at World Wide Framastats, the FlexFram team was ready to get a deeper understanding, so they contacted a few vendors and before long the FlexFram team was swimming in marketing literature and technical summaries of the products. They felt pretty lost. It became obvious to them that they really did not understand their application needs. Up until now they had been learning about concepts and technology. They had not looked too deeply at what they were going to develop. They got out this book and answered the following questions to begin focusing on features needed:

- What is the computing environment?

  They would be using UNIX servers at the manufacturing locations and laptops for the salespeople.

- Will the data be distributed?

  Yes.

- Will the distribution be local or over a larger geographic area?

  Distribution would be worldwide because WWF manufactures and distributes framastats throughout the world.

- How many users will work concurrently?

  They expected at least 50 concurrent users at each location with at least 10 locations having servers around the world.

- How will concurrent users access the data?

  Most of the access will be reading the engineering data, but manufacturing scheduling and setting shipment dates will require creating and updating data.

- What types of schema changes will be likely?

  The schema changes will be minimal.

- How much data is likely to result from your most common queries?

  Although there are several gigabytes of data at each location, a given query will result in relatively small results.

- Will you be using methods as part of your queries?

  No.

- Will you be accessing existing data from existing non-object sources such as RDBMSs?

  Yes, the DBMSs that were developed in the COBOL shop.

With this foundation of understanding, the FlexFram team was ready to dig into possible features. To do that, they turned to the checklists in Part III of this book. The FlexFram team knew, based on their answers to the questions above, that they needed a distributed DBMS and the queries must execute on the server, given the amount of data queried compared to the size of the query result. They also knew that they wanted database methods to execute on the client side, which ran Windows. These general feature concepts required more study. As they studied the feature checklists, many of the checklist items in Checklist 9, "Distributed Database Systems"; Checklist 5, "Queries and Query Languages"; and Checklist 3, "Procedures and Programming Languages" were added to the Useful Checklists for the FlexFram project. With additional study, some of the checklist items became critical for their project and others were deemed to be nice-to-have.

As is common at this point, there were issues about which they were not yet certain, such as locking granularity and concurrent data access. They had to dig further to make a decision.

In studying the checklists, the team came across private databases and configurations (Checklists 8 and 9). Both were entirely new concepts to the DBMS person on the project, and no one else seemed to know much about them either. They talked with the WWF salespeople on the team about how this could be used, and the team came up with some scenarios. It turned out that the salespeople could envision dialing up one of the servers in the distributed database the night before they called on the customer. They could check out information on the latest configurations of framastats that are available to the private database on their laptop. This would tell them about new ones that were expected to be coming out weekly for some time. The salespeople also wanted the latest information on the customer so they could be knowledgeable on the customer's sales history and current accounts receivable situation. Everyone thought this would be cool. These features might turn out to be critical, but at this point the team put them on their useful checklist.

Step 3—Narrowing the Field

When you have begun to understand DBMS features and how they interact, along with developing a depth of understanding about your application needs, you are ready to move to the final stage of the selection model, where you narrow the field of possible products and prepare to make a choice.

The right side of the model features the final step, *Narrowing the Field*, repeated in Figure 7.7. After iterating sufficiently between your application needs and the DBMS product features to find all the application needs and the DBMS product features you could care about, you are nearly ready for this step. When you have considered the possible interaction among the DBMS product features you are considering, you are ready to determine your critical features.

This step includes determining which of the features are critical to your application, creating a list of vendors whose products include those features,

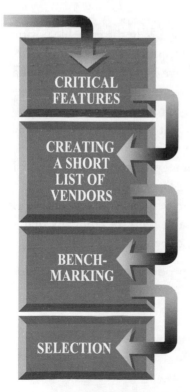

Figure 7.7 *Narrowing the field.*

benchmarking to determine if the proposed product will meet your performance needs, and finally making a selection.

Critical Features

There are some product features that are absolutely essential to your application—your critical features. If a product is missing even one of these features, you should not consider it. This list of critical features will radically reduce the number of products you are looking at. It's important to keep in mind that these critical features will apply only to your current application. Future applications may have a completely different set of critical features. Every application is different. In my experience with clients, I have never seen exactly the same list of critical features.

Creating a Short List of Vendors

Once the critical features—those "do or die" features that any product you consider must have—are identified, you can create a list of vendors whose products have these features.

If more than four vendors remain on the list, you are in the enviable position of using your next tier or nice-to-have features to identify the vendor products you will study in more depth. Once you have included these nice-to-have features, my experience is that no more than two or three products emerge and one of them is usually a clear favorite. Any product on this list has the features to do an adequate job for you. You might want to bring these finalists in for a final questioning based on the deep feature understanding you now have. You may also want to ask them some questions about their business strategies, market segment, and financing. The ODBMS industry is a young one, and it is unlikely that all the current vendors will be in business some years from now. You should be comfortable with the company that makes the product on which you are going to depend.

Another way to gain further insights into the products and their use before making a final selection is to attend a vendor training course.

Benchmarking

After narrowing your choices for selection based on your critical features, the final step is benchmarking, which will help you determine if the top one or two products you are considering will meet your application performance requirements. Without it, you are assuming those performance requirements will be met; this can be dangerous. Benchmarking may very well point out areas of design concern that could be addressed by advanced work from the vendor's consultants.

Many benchmarks are available, but finding one that will actually help you can be quite difficult. The types of benchmarks for ODBMS products include public benchmarks, benchmark data from other companies, or do-it-yourself benchmarks. This next section outlines the types of benchmarks and explains why I believe, in the end, you will probably have to do your own benchmarking.

Public Benchmarks   Public benchmarks are publicly published comparison performance data on ODBMS products. They are, by definition, generic, and therefore cover the range of uses for ODBMSs. Two of the better known public benchmarks are OO1 ("Object Operations Benchmark," *ACM Transactions on Database Systems*, R. G. G. Cattell & J. Skeen, April 1992) and OO7 ("The OO7 Object-Oriented Database Benchmark," M. J. Carey, D. J. DeWitt, & J. F. Naughton, Proceedings of the ACM SIGMOD Conference, Washington, DC May 1993)

There are several important drawbacks to these public benchmarks. The major critical drawback is that they are single-user, which creates an unrealistic comparison for most applications. Another drawback is that these public benchmarks are generic and therefore very unlikely to match your problem domain. These benchmarks use relatively small databases. Most of my clients, however, are looking at multi-gigabyte databases. Even if there is a problem domain match, the comparison data can become rapidly out-of-date as vendors bring new releases to market.

"Benchmarketing" is yet another problem with public benchmarks. This is the situation where the public benchmark is hyped in some vendors' marketing efforts. This has occurred in the RDBMS market, and it has happened in the ODBMS market with both the OO1 and OO7 benchmarks. Based on the marketing literature I've seen, everyone won the OO7 benchmark. Even the University of Wisconsin authors of the OO7 benchmark have shown, for example, how you get different "winners" if you take the number of first places on the tests, a weighted ranking of places, or the geometric mean. Additionally, sometimes vendors are not careful to compare the results from their most recent release with their competitor's most recent release. These public numbers seem to age but never die.

So far it appears that designing a multi-user benchmark is a much more difficult problem than designing a single-user benchmark. This is due, in part, to the fact that the number of dimensions along which the workload can vary is greater in the multi-user case, and in part to the fact that multi-user workloads inherently involve complex interactions of multiple concurrent activities. Also, if there is little agreement about what constitutes the single-user ODBMS workload, there is even less agreement in the multi-user arena. For this reason, coming up with a monolithic workload that generates a single-number system evaluation (*a la* TPC-A or TPC-B) is not likely. The response to date has been to develop a fully parameterized workload that is made up of primitives that can be combined to generate a range of workload with a wide variety of different characteristics. In this sense, a multi-user OO7 Benchmark being developed is really a customizable benchmark generator that we hope will be useful to sophisticated consumers of ODBMSs.

Parameterized Benchmarks As the OO7 authors noted, another option in benchmarking is customizable or parameterized benchmarks. This basically allows you to "set the dials" to get usage patterns that are closer to your application problem domain.

A parameterized benchmark that is available from the Computer Science Research Center at the University of Karlsruhe is the JUSTITIA benchmark (Hartmut Schreiber, Computer Science Research Center at the University of Karlsruhe, Haid-und-Neustrasse 10-14, D-76131 Karlsruhe, Germany). The JUSTITIA benchmark tests concurrent accesses, locally distributed accesses, and the ability of an ODBMS to reorganize its data. Because of its scalability and configurability, the benchmark can be adjusted to a variety of application domains. The JUSTITIA benchmark is the first benchmark that tests both the structural preservation ability and the ability of an ODBMS to reorganize its database during run-time. Locally distributed accesses such as reading of shared data, competing access to shared data, noncompeting consumer-producer situations, and concurrent accesses to physically separated data are supported.

Industry-Specific Benchmarks Parameterized benchmarks are great, but if you do not have the time and want at least some useful preliminary information, there may be another option. Generic benchmarks are unlikely to address the needs of your industry. A middle road that may be useful someday is the effort to do industry-specific benchmarks that have been proposed by Akmal B. Chaudhri at the City University, London. He states that the increasing use of ODBMSs for nonengineering applications requires new metrics to be developed. At City University, an approach is being taken to develop application-specific benchmarks for ODBMSs, by collaborating with users in industry. A multiple case study approach is being used, with a number of alternative research techniques (analysis of system documentation, data collection, interviews, etc.) being used to provide triangulation and external validity. From the case studies, analytical generalizations will be used to develop models upon which the benchmarks can be based (the best source for the latest information is Akmal Chaudri's home page at http://web.cs.city.ac.uk./homes/akmal/info.html).

Benchmark Data from Other Companies   This has to be the most diffi-cult source of data around for two reasons. First, you have to find a noncom-petitor that has application needs similar to yours. Second, most ODBMS license agreements prohibit disclosure of benchmark data without the per-mission of the vendor.

Do-It-Yourself Benchmarks   A do-it-yourself benchmark is the best approach to matching your problem domain. But it can be a huge amount of work. If you go down this path, you must do a multi-user benchmark that, at minimum, tests lock granularity and the likelihood that your data usage will cause lock collisions and reduce performance. As an example of actual costs, consider that it took an ODBMS customer five person-months and required one or two days of technical assistance from each of the vendors for doing just this benchmark on two ODBMS products. As you can see, doing a prop-er benchmark is expensive; this cost is all the more reason to be sure of a strong feature fit prior to committing to the cost of benchmarking.

There are several key feature interactions that should be included in any cus-tomized benchmarking effort. The interaction of the degree of location inde-pendence in a distributed DBMS and security authorization is one example. The interaction of lock granularity, query, and method execution location, which is described in Chapter 8, is another example. A good, do-it-yourself benchmark, should also cover these factors.

Effects of ODBMS Standards   All the benchmarks to date have had to address the problem of the differing product interfaces. A custom benchmark must be created, to some degree, for each ODBMS product. In the future, this will be simpler. The Object Database Management Group (ODMG) has published *The Object Database Standard: ODMG-93* (Morgan Kaufmann Publishers). The vendors that have committed to meeting this interface by late 1995 comprise nearly 90 percent of the ODBMS market.

With ODMG-93, it will be possible to set up one interface for all ODBMS products that covers a large part of the benchmark. This will make comparison benchmarking considerably easier. All the recent benchmarking papers have mentioned plans to use the ODMG-93 specification. Yet, ODMG-93 does not provide standards for all features, so be prepared to create a benchmark that exercises some nonstandard features as well. The nonstandard features may be the reason you are looking at one set of ODBMS products over another.

Some Advice   Once you have investigated ODBMS features and have narrowed your choices, do not buy an ODBMS product on the basis of a single-user benchmark (unless you are doing a single-user database application). Investigate the multi-user parameterized benchmarks before you consider creating a do-it-yourself benchmark. (See the Appendix for reference information.) If you plan to do your own benchmark, make it multi-user and pay attention to the nature and use of your data and the possible effect on performance resulting from lock granularity, along with query and method execution location. (See Chapter 8.)

Benchmarking is a difficult job, but worth doing.

Selection, Step 3: Narrowing the Field

The FlexFram team at World Wide Framastats was getting closer to its product choice. In the discussions and studying of features described in Checklist 9, the FlexFram team also realized they needed to add replication to the checklists and that the DBMS would really need to work on a Wide Area Network. In the area of concurrent access, they realized they could probably use either page or object locking because the conflicts would only occur at the time schedules were being set—they thought page-level locking with MROW would be best, but it was relegated to the nice-to-have checklist. The reason for this lowering of the importance of locking granularity is that configuration data was being checked out to a private database and used offline on the laptop, so there would be no locking conflicts.

Here is a portion of the final critical features checklist the FlexFram team came up with:

❑ Supports multiple database server architecture with multiple clients

❑ Protocol for addressing among the distributed sites on WAN

❑ Strategy for resolving partitioned WANs

❑ If WAN fails, local processing can continue.

Data replication:

❑ Data represented at the physical level by many distinct copies stored at many distinct sites

❑ Users can act as if the data is not replicated at all.

❑ Store and forward—replication occurs on a periodic basis

❑ Solaris server

❑ Windows client

❑ Supports private workspaces or databases

❑ Allows moving entire private databases among the sites in the distributed database

❑ Supports long transactions that can last hours, weeks, months, and so on

❑ Supports persistent long transactions—the long transaction can span system shutdowns or failures.

❑ Contains short transactions—short transactions may occur within the long transaction.

❑ Supports persistent locks that are owned by a user (or something other than the process) spanning sessions and processes

❑ Supports long transaction commit or rollback

❑ Query processing in the servers

❑ Query optimization attempts to break a query into subgraphs for execution in parallel on multiple sites

❑ No need for an application to be aware that the query is being executed on multiple sites.

❑ A single query can obtain objects from multiple sites.

❑ A query successfully returns even if one or more nodes are unavailable—it may also return a message indicating results may be incomplete.

❑ All sites involved in a transaction either commit in unison or rollback.

❑ Distributed concurrency control

❑ Coordination of recovery at distributed sites

❑ Two-phase commit

❑ Distributed deadlock detection

❑ Support for alternative versions or branching

❑ Support for restricting alternative versions or branching so that versioning is linear

❑ Support for accessing the version genealogy

❑ Support for dynamic version binding that references the most recent version

❑ Support for dynamic version binding that references the user selected default version

❑ Support for dynamic version binding so that multiple users may have different contexts such as release 1.3 or release 2.1

❑ Support for a collection of versions that are mutually consistent (configurations)

❑ Support for "freezing" a configuration—making it read only

❑ Support for accessing a specific configuration even when it is not the most recent

❑ Support for configuration hierarchies

❑ Support for branching of configurations

❑ Support for automatic merging of configurations

❑ Support for customized merging of configurations

❑ Support for resurrecting objects deleted in previous configurations for use in another configuration

The FlexFram team used this checklist to evaluate the products on the market. They came up with a list of three ODBMS vendors from about a dozen they could have considered. Each of the vendors was asked to complete the Critical and Nice to Have checklists, in addition to providing portions of their documentation on the items in these checklists. The product that was selected met nearly all of the critical checklist features, and that vendor had work-arounds for the other critical checklist features.

The FlexFram team and management felt pretty confident about the product choice except that they were not sure of the product's performance. They spent several months developing a benchmark to test the distributed query capability in particular because that was so critical for the salesperson's effectiveness in working with the customer. They had to create a benchmark that not only had realistic volumes of data, but could simulate the types of data access they were expecting. (Some people were not sure if page-level locking would provide performance should lock conflicts from concurrent data access occur.) It turned out that the close consideration of architectural needs also provided a product choice that met their performance requirements.

Selection

Selection is, of course, the final step in the selection stage. If you have done your homework, your choice will be obvious to everyone on the team. There should be no doubts. If you do not have this agreement, you probably took a shortcut somewhere along the line. Now is the time to search for what you may have overlooked, not to push a decision.

Be sure, also, to allow enough time for the selection stage. I have spoken with people from many companies who are using ODBMSs. Choosing a vendor and product is never a simple project for most companies. Evaluation usually takes between four and five months of elapsed time because of the learning curves the teams need to go through. On average, two to four products are considered. In many cases, internal benchmarks and testing were used to make a final cut or to verify that the expected performance can be achieved. Public benchmarks do not seem to be commonly considered. The companies that did their own detailed benchmarking took two to five person-months to develop and run the benchmarks.

Summary

In this chapter we have taken a close look at the selection stage of the implementation process. This stage requires the user to understand the basics, gain a deeper understanding, and finally narrow the field. Gaining a deeper understanding is a particularly iterative step. In the next chapter, we will look at feature interaction, an integral part of gaining a deeper understanding of your options in selecting an ODBMS.

Feature Interaction: An Example

Sometimes DBMS concepts play out very simply in our daily lives. This occurred to me while working on this book. My daughter Katie and I decided to visit a new exhibit at the local science museum and take in the latest feature movie at the museum Omnitheater while we were there. I rummaged through my wallet in a fruitless effort to locate my membership card, which I needed to reserve tickets for the movie at the Omnitheater. It was not to be found.

In calling the museum membership line to see what could be done, a cheerful voice at the other end assured me that I did indeed still belong to the museum, a new card would be sent in a week, and I could call the museum ticket line right away with my membership number. Armed with that information I called the ticket line immediately and hit an unexpected snag—they were unable to access my account!

You may be wondering what this has to do with DBMS features. The answer is quite a bit. This is a classic example of two employees who are accessing the same item in the same database at the same time with the net effect that one employee is locked out. Because I called the theater line before the membership worker had completed printing out my new membership card, the theater worker was not able to access my file and make movie reservations. The system was for all intents and purposes on hold, and the ticket line operator could not do anything. We waited awhile and it was still unavailable. I had a vision of the membership person going on a coffee break and forgetting to release my record. Well, the ticket line operator wrote my membership number on a sheet of paper and said she would take care of it later. Now this case was a very minor inconvenience, but what if lots of people were updating membership records? You can imagine the problems it would cause down at the ticket office—the Omnitheater is very popular around here.

This simple, real-life example of the impact of decisions made in project design illustrates the importance of careful consideration of features in the design and selection process. It's unlikely that the designer of the science museum system considered that someone might lose their membership card, call the membership office, and immediately call the ticket office while a new card was being printed. If it had been considered, a capability called MROW, which will be explained later in this chapter, might have been used. Or then again, this might have been deemed too obscure a problem and some other feature might have been thought to be more important.

Think of the impact if the system designer also had included an application that used data from another source to update membership records during the day. That scenario could mean many people might have experiences such as mine when calling the ticket office. What might be a small problem for one person can have large implications if multiplied.

The focus of this chapter is to identify the significance of feature interaction. Two features that should be of interest to anyone considering an ODBMS will be used to illustrate the concepts. This is an example of the type of feature interaction you need to consider in Step 2, *Gaining a Deeper Understanding*, described in Chapter 7. The two features and their possible interactions covered in this chapter are lock granularity and process distribution. The science museum experience, by the way, is an example of the impact of lock granularity.

Lock granularity and process distribution, including the location of method and query execution, are criteria basic to the design of almost any application.

They should be critical in your selection of an ODBMS. Careful examination must go into understanding how these features are handled by the ODBMS and how well that will serve your application. In addition, how these features interact with each other is also critical to the success of an application.

The key ideas of the feature interaction example in this chapter include:

- The aspects of lock granularity that are important to your application.

- Why the location of methods and query execution matter to you.

- The impact on your application of the interaction of lock granularity, methods, and queries.

- Production scenarios to illustrate the complexity of these interactions.

Lock Granularity

The design of the ODBMS locking mechanism and the locking granularity used can affect the performance of your application. Sometimes it is necessary to ensure that only one user at a time can change a data item even though many people are reading the same data item. Locking is a way to do this. Because of locking, all changes to a particular data item will be made in the correct order in a transaction. (See the example in Chapter 1.) Because locking is a very complex topic, the emphasis here will be on how the granularity of locking can impact the performance of applications.

Lock granularity is defined as the amount of data that may be locked with the single object instance or groups of object instances of interest. The types of granularity are illustrated in Figure 8.1. The first three categories of granularity—page, object cluster, and single class—have granularity larger than locking

Locking Granularity				Many Readers One Writer
Page	Object clusters or containers	Single class	Single object	(MROW)

Figure 8.1 *Locking granularity and MROW.*

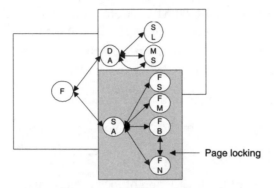

Figure 8.2 *Page locking.*

on a single object. Many Readers One Writer (MROW) falls into a different category; it relaxes some of the locking requirements to allow reading of data even if someone has locked it for writing. More extensive checklists on this subject are included in Checklist 6 in Part III, "Concurrency and Recovery."

In page-level locking, all the data on a particular page is locked, as illustrated in Figure 8.2. In the figure, each rectangle represents a page. A page is a common unit of storage in computer systems and is used by all types of database management systems. If you are unfamiliar with this concept, just think of it being a unit of space on the disk where multiple objects are stored.

Object cluster locking causes all data clustered together (on a page or multiple pages) to be locked at the same time. This is illustrated in Figure 8.3.

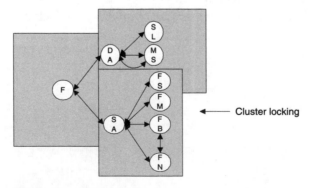

Figure 8.3 *Cluster locking.*

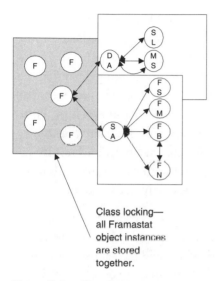

Figure 8.4   *Class locking.*

Class locking, synonymous with RDBMS table locking, means that all instances of a class are locked, usually with the definition of the class itself. This is illustrated in Figure 8.4. This class locking is particularly useful when performing online schema changes.

Object locking, synonymous with RDBMS row-level or tuple-level locks, allows only a single instance to be locked when an object is locked. This is illustrated in Figure 8.5.

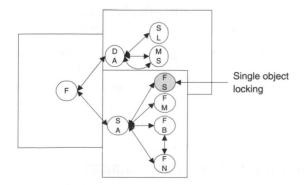

Figure 8.5   *Single object locking.*

Page-, class-, and object-level locks will be recognizable to anyone familiar with DBMS technology. For an example of cluster locking, imagine that you are interested in an entire complex object. The Framastat presented in Chapter 2 provides an example of the differences the various locking granularities will make in an application. If you found and read the object representing an entire Framastat through a query, object cluster locking would lock the entire Framastat. Page-level locking would lock whatever is on the page that the Framastat is stored on—in this case only the Framastat object and not its components. Class-level locking would lock many Framastat objects, but not their components. Object-level locking would lock only the single object, such as an instance of a Fram Sensor.

Which form of locking is best? It depends on how your application will be used. Will one part of a Framastat be used most of the time, all LCDs most of the time, or the entire Framastat most of the time? The answers to these questions will point you in the right direction for the best form of locking for your application.

Which form of locking will give the best performance? The answer depends on the likelihood of lock conflicts and the amount of overhead that locking would use. Lock conflicts occur when two or more users are trying to use the same object/page/cluster at the same time in an incompatible way. An example would be two or more users each attempting to make changes at the same time to either the same Framastat object, a different Framastat stored on the same page or one of the Framastat components. The likelihood of lock conflicts depends on how the data will be used in a multi-user environment. In this chapter, the most common forms of locking will be examined within the context of a multi-user environment: page-level locking, object-level locking, and cluster locking, along with Multiple Readers One Writer (MROW). Each example assumes pessimistic locking—this is when checks for access conflicts occur at the time the lock is requested with some locks queued until the conflicts are resolved. Therefore, no conflicts are present at commit time. This is opposed to optimistic locking—this assumes that simultaneous access to the same objects is quite rare and conflicts are checked only at commit time. Conflicts at commit time may result in an abort or restart.

Page-Level Locking in a Multi-User Environment

Page-level locking, as shown in Figure 8.6, allows all the objects on the database page to be locked at the same time—lock one object and you also lock all the other objects on the page. If the objects are small, then the page may contain many objects. With page-level locking, a single read lock will allow a user to read any of the objects on that page at the same time. That means that the lock-management overhead is relatively light and performance should be better. Figure 8.6 shows two different clients locking different pages so there are no lock conflicts.

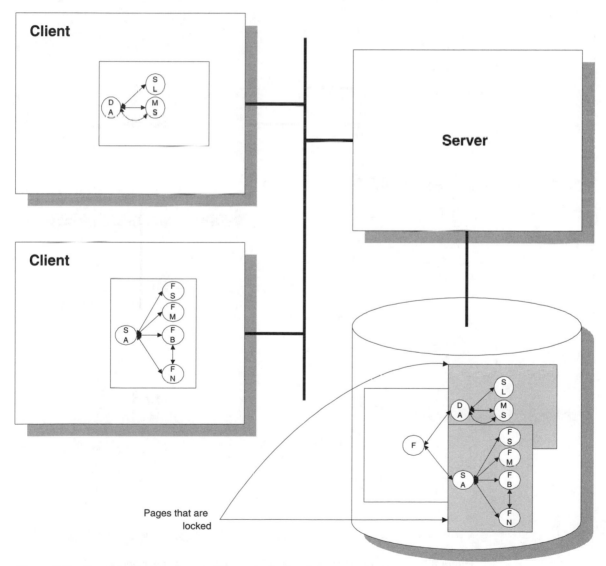

Figure 8.6 *Page-level locking in a multi-user environment.*

On the other hand, if one user is reading an object and other users are trying to update other objects on the same page, performance will be diminished by page-level locking. From a practical point of view, the updating users will

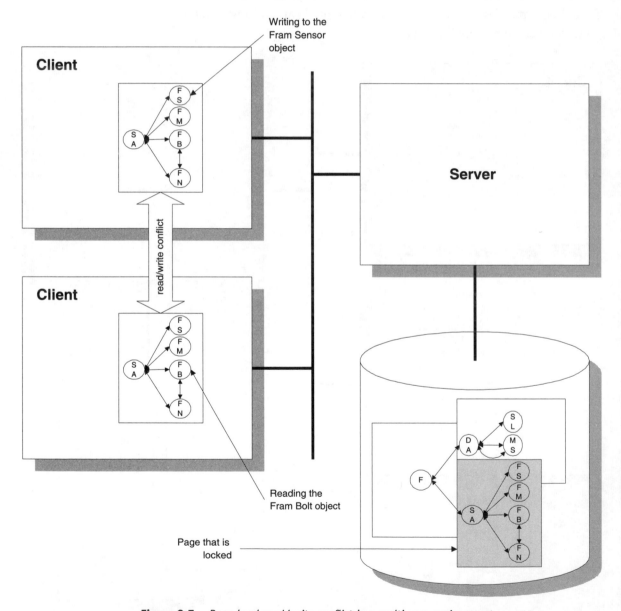

Figure 8.7 *Page-level read/write conflict in a multi-user environment.*

have to wait for the reading user(s) to complete their work and then take turns updating objects as the lock is passed around by the DBMS. This situation, called a *read/write lock conflict*, is illustrated in Figure 8.7. This shows the read/write conflict that can occur when one user is writing to a Fram Sensor object and other users want to read a Fram Bolt object or any other object on the same page. The duration of the read/write lock conflict is determined by how long a client application may hold the lock. This can have a major impact on the overall performance of your application.

Object-Level Locking in a Multi-User Environment

You can lessen the page-level read/write conflict by using object-level locking. Object-level locking sets locks only on the objects that are in use on a page. Because the higher number of locks will require more processing by the DBMS every time a single object is used, locking overhead is higher with object-locking. The higher overhead may reduce overall performance.

On the other hand, object-level locking reduces the likelihood of a read/write lock conflict only to conflicts centered on a single object. This may greatly improve performance relative to page-level locking if your data and the way the data will be used is likely to create page-locking read/write conflicts. Another performance benefit is that client memory is better managed when a few objects on many pages are needed—only the objects required are moved to the client cache. This is illustrated in Figure 8.8.

Multiple Readers One Writer in a Multi-User Environment

Another way to lessen the read/write conflict in page-level locking is Multiple Readers One Writer (MROW). This has an effect similar to, but not the same as, object-level locking. MROW allows multiple users to simultaneously read an object but only one user to write to the object. It is, in a sense, independent of the locking granularity in that it allows for multiple readers and one writer of the objects at whatever level of lock granularity. As shown in Figure 8.9, in MROW a user writing to a Fram Sensor object will not conflict with other users reading a Fram Bolt object or other object on the page.

Nevertheless, MROW differs from object-level locking when multiple users want to write to objects. It is still possible to get lock conflicts, but they are

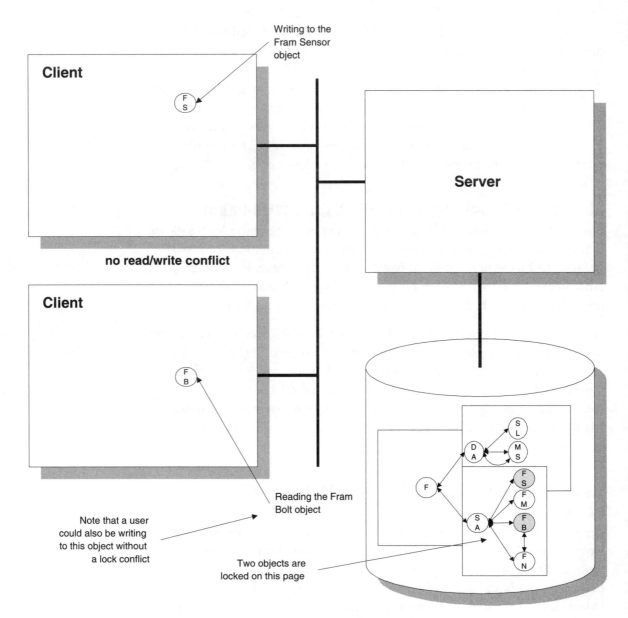

Figure 8.8 *Object-level locking in a multi-user environment.*

the "write/write" variety—two or more users want to write to the same page, for example. Consider the Framastat example again as shown in Figure 8.10. This shows two users trying to update two different parts of the Sensor

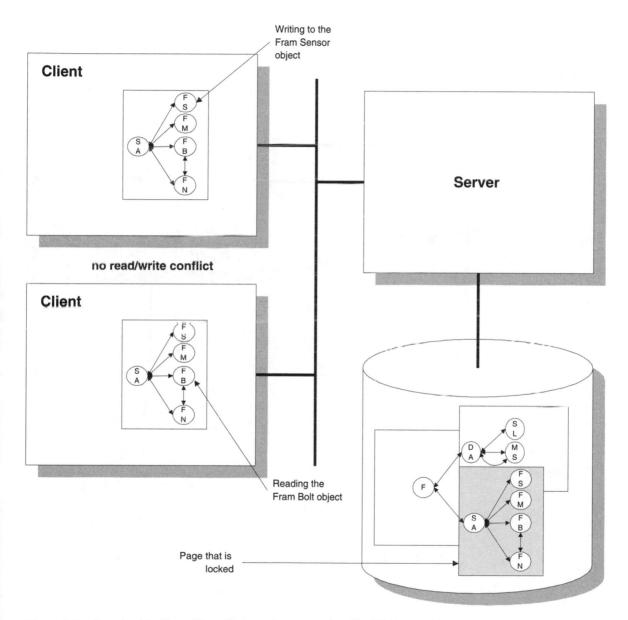

Figure 8.9 *Page-level locking with multiple readers, one writer (MROW) in a multi-user environment.*

Assembly at the same time. One user wants to update data about a Fram Sensor object and another user wants to update data about the Fram Bolt object. The example also shows that the entire Sensor Assembly of the Fra-

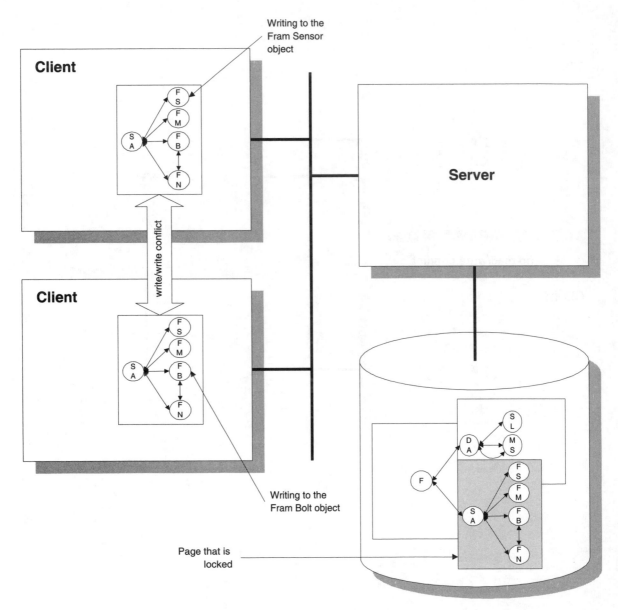

Figure 8.10 *Page-level locking with multiple writers in a multi-user environment.*

mastat is clustered on a single page. The result is a "multiple writers" situation in page-locking; one writer must wait for the other writer to complete before being able to acquire a write lock on the page that holds all the Display Assembly parts. If this is likely to be common, MROW, with page or cluster locking, will provide poorer system performance compared to object-level locking. If a product with object-level locking is used in this example, there would be no lock conflict of any kind because there would be one lock for the Fram Sensor and another lock for the Fram Bolt, as shown in Figure 8.8. The key here is looking for the likelihood of lock conflicts for a given lock granularity and the way the data is expected to be accessed.

MROW and Cluster Locking

MROW is particularly efficient when you can cluster objects in a way to read many of the objects on pages since they are participating in composite objects. Consider an entire Framastat, for example. If you want to access the Framastat object, but the next operation is to access the Display Assembly and then the Sensor Assembly, it would be effective to cluster the parts of a Framastat together. If that clustered object can fit on one or a few pages, you could gain read access with only a single cluster lock instead of one for every page or every object. This is shown in Figure 8.11. Many users could be reading many of the objects on those pages and one user could also be updating any of the parts being read. The result is lower lock overhead, yet an effective object-level granularity for reading objects.

Summarizing Lock Granularity

Locking granularity is one of several key architectural features you must consider when choosing an ODBMS. The determinant for successfully choosing appropriate locking granularity is knowing both your data and how you plan to use it. Page-level locking is generally good if you have large objects or many objects on the same page used primarily by the same user; read/write lock conflicts will be limited in that scenario. Object-level locking is generally good if your objects are small and you expect to have frequent read/write or write/write conflicts on the same page, but not necessarily on the same objects. MROW is a feature that works at all levels of lock granularity. This allows you to have page-level locking while multiple users read objects on the same page even if one user is writing to that page. This same comment also applies to object-level locking and cluster locking. Making a successful choice will require you to think deeply about your data and how it will be used.

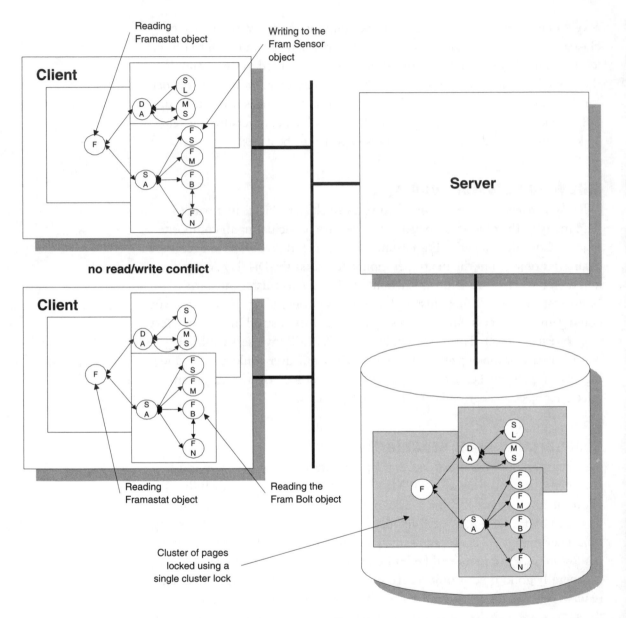

Figure 8.11 *Cluster locking with multiple readers, one writer (MROW) in a multi-user environment.*

Process Distribution

The location of method and query execution in the client/server environment can have a serious impact on performance as well. This section covers where these processes can be distributed in the client/server environment.

Where Methods Execute

Another feature that is important to performance is the location of database method execution. Database methods are those methods that execute on the

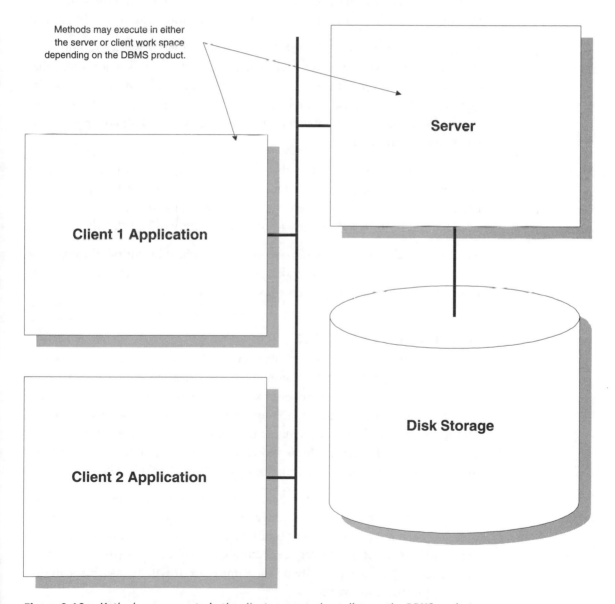

Figure 8.12 *Methods may execute in the client or server depending on the DBMS product.*

data stored in the database. Since database methods are logically encapsulated or attached to the data in the database, they can execute either in the client application workspace or on the server with the ODBMS that stores the data, as shown in Figure 8.12. Whether the server-based methods execute in the ODBMS itself, or via an external call to a routine outside the ODBMS yet still on the server, can further complicate the choices. At this point, however, only the performance impact of database method execution location will be studied.

Executing database methods in the client application workspace requires that the data move from the server to the client application workspace. Once the data has been moved, the execution of database methods on this data can be very fast. Client database method execution is also effective if you are executing the same methods repeatedly on the same data. It will all take place in the client application workspace.

Executing database methods on the server does not require the data to move very far—it is all local. Server database method execution is effective if you are executing methods on different data or over a large volume of data because it minimizes the movement of data and network traffic.

This simplified example of database method execution location illustrates some of the choices you must make. Again, your data and how it will be used among the concurrent users must drive your decision.

Where Queries Execute

Another feature important to performance is database query execution location. The impact of the location of query execution is very similar to the impact of method location. Database queries are those queries that execute on the data stored in the database. They can execute in the client application workspace, on the server with the ODBMS that stores the data, or partially on the client and partially on the server. This is shown in Figure 8.13. Only the performance impact of database query execution location will be considered here.

Executing database queries in the client application workspace requires that the data move from the server to the client application workspace. Once the data has been moved, the execution of database queries on this data can be very fast. Client database query execution is also effective if you are executing the same queries repeatedly on the same data. It will all take place in the client application workspace.

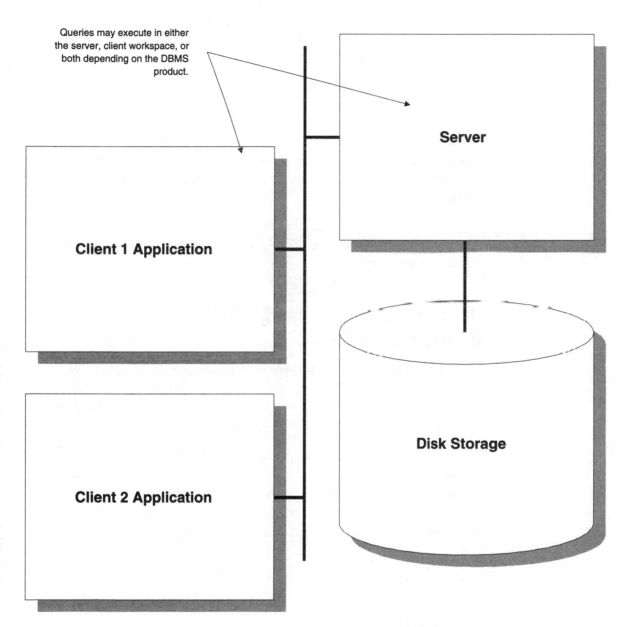

Queries may execute in either the server, client workspace, or both depending on the DBMS product.

Figure 8.13   *Queries may execute in the client or server depending on the DBMS product.*

Executing database queries on the server does not require the data to move very far—it is all local. Server database query execution is effective if you are executing queries on different data or over a large volume of data because it minimizes the movement of data.

Sometimes the query capability is split between the client and the server. Attributes that are indexed provide an example of this. Index searching is done on the server and the rest of the query processing is done on the client. For example, consider indexing state of birth. Selecting all people born in Minnesota causes the server to use the index to get only those people born in Minnesota; all of the objects representing them would be passed to the client for further query processing.

This simplified example of database query execution location illustrates some of the choices you must make. Your data and how it will be used among the concurrent users must drive your decision.

How Locking Granularity and Process Distribution Interact

The ODBMS architecture can affect your application's performance in more ways than merely the sheer processing speed of the ODBMS. The interaction of features, in this case locking granularity and process distribution, have a huge impact on your application's performance as well.

To understand the impact of the interaction of these two features, let's use a simple query as an example. Let's select all people in the database whose ages are 25. In our example, age will not be an attribute of a Person class but a method that calculates age based on today's date and the year of birth that is stored in the object instance as described in Chapter 1 and illustrated in Figure 8.14.

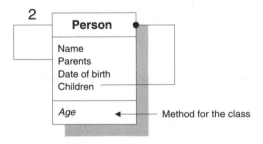

Figure 8.14 *Class definition for example queries.*

To process this example query, an age method must be executed. Let's assume our DBMS locks queried objects with a read lock so that no one can change the year of birth on objects queried. Such read locks are another part of maintaining a consistent view of the data for a DBMS user. See the ACID properties described in Chapter 1 for a description of what is meant by a consistent view of the data. The following production scenarios give a clear picture of the impact of the interaction of these two features.

Production Scenarios for Feature Interaction

The first scenario features a small database with a single user. Locking is not an issue here because it is a single-user system. Locking should be turned off if possible. Most if not all object instances of the Person class shown in Figure 8.14 might fit into the client application workspace because the objects will be small and in this scenario the entire database is also small. In this instance, an ODBMS that executes database methods on the client would likely provide the best performance for this query, especially if more queries of the Person class will be processed subsequently.

In the second scenario, a single user accesses a large database. The comments from the first scenario apply here as well because there is only a single user. The issue becomes the amount of data that must move to the client application workspace to execute the database method as part of the query. All the object instances of the Person class must move to the client workspace because every Person object in the database must be examined to execute the age method. The age must be calculated each time the query is processed. This time, however, the database is too large for all object instances of the Person class to fit into the client application workspace. In this instance, an ODBMS that executes database methods on the server would likely provide the best performance for this query because the movement of the data would likely be too costly.

The focus in scenario three moves to a large, multi-user database featuring object instances of the Person class located compactly on pages. Now the locking issues become important because there is more than one concurrent user who may want to access object instances of the Person class. Let's assume our ODBMS executes database methods on the server. The target data (those people whose calculated ages are 25) is congregated on pages. In this instance, the ODBMS with page-level locking would likely provide the better performance for this query because read locks would be set at the granularity of pages, resulting in a lower locking overhead than object-level locking.

The fourth scenario is a large, multi-user database with object instances of the Person class dispersed widely on pages. This still assumes our ODBMS executes methods on the server. Now, however, the target data (again, those people whose calculated ages are 25) is dispersed on pages. Page-level locking with some ODBMSs could cause many, if not most, pages to be locked since at least one object on the page qualifies for the query. Under page-level locking, it would be nearly impossible for another user to make an update to any object as long as this query transaction was active. In this instance, an ODBMS with object-level locking or MROW would likely give the best performance for this query.

In the final scenario, a large, multi-user database with target data widely dispersed on pages is managed by an ODBMS that executes database methods on the client and uses page-level locking and does not have MROW. All the data for the Person class would need to be sent to the client application workspace to be scanned even though it is too large to stay in the client workspace. Most update activity is shut out until the transaction that contains the query commits because most pages are locked. Subsequent execution of a similar query would mean sending all the data again to the client workspace, effectively causing what is known as *thrashing* behavior. This scenario would give very poor performance.

These five scenarios illustrate, in a simplistic way, the importance of looking at the interaction of features in the design of your application. These are make-or-break features that will have a huge impact on the success of your application.

Summary

This chapter highlighted the importance of studying feature interaction through an in-depth discussion of lock granularity and process distribution. This is the type of study that needs to occur in Step 2, *Gaining a Deeper Understanding*, which was discussed in Chapter 7.

Deployment Issues

There is a common saying in business circles: "Ready, fire, aim." It's so common probably because it describes so well what we often do. In fact, in most projects we are often itching to get to that final stage of implementation. Often, however, we don't do the necessary preliminary work to make the implementation go smoothly.

This scenario applies to software development too. If you think of "Fire" as standing for deployment and "Aim" as analysis and design, you get a glimpse of why we typically see deployment as a long, arduous process. In many projects, we begin deployment before we've done an adequate job of analysis and design. In fact, part of what passes for deployment often *is* analysis and design. If the ODBMS implementation process is followed, you will find yourself in the situation of "Ready, Aim, Fire."

Deployment is the final step in the ODBMS implementation process. If the effort put into the earlier stages in the process seemed excessive to you, deployment is where the payoff takes place. In the strategy stage, you identified the strategic goals to be reached and determined if an ODBMS was an appropriate choice to meet those goals. In the team identification and development stages, you identified appropriate team members and got them trained to do the best job possible. That team worked through the selection stage and made the ODBMS product selection.

Key points in this chapter are:

- If you've followed the model, your deployment work has already begun.

- Your best deployment team has been working together through the whole process.

- More time will be spent in analysis, design, and testing, and less time will be spent in implementation, than in non-object technology projects.

- There are some things you can do to protect your investment.

- There are some tips that can make technical issues easier.

Deployment

The deployment stage, as illustrated in Figure 9.1, is the culmination of the implementation process. Much of ODBMS deployment is similar to any software project deployment. The focus in this chapter will be on what is different about it, what are the issues that you particularly need to be aware of for success.

Deploying Specific Products

There are important differences between ODBMS products, as you've seen in earlier chapters. Once you have made your product selection, you'll want to work with the vendor to make sure you have whatever product-specific information you need. Specific deployment plans for each ODBMS product on the

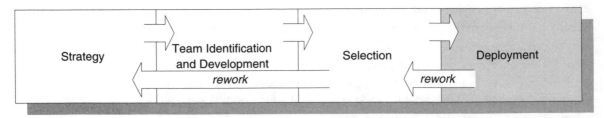

Figure 9.1 *Deployment stage in the ODBMS implementation process.*

market are not included in this book because each product has its own specific information. This is similar to the situation with RDBMSs; anyone who has browsed the DBMS section of a bookstore has noted there are separate books on deployment for each of the major RDBMS products. Instead, this chapter will provide advice that should apply to all ODBMS products.

You Have Already Started

Putting the level of effort required into the first three stages should mean that you have a trained team ready to implement the object schema modeled in a system that's already had some prototyping. This should make deployment a simpler experience than it's ever been before. You have a great deal of the work already completed. This is illustrated in Figure 9.1. If you look at most software development life cycle models, you'll note that the feasibility, requirements, system specifications, and design and program design stages are nearly completed. In moving forward in the deployment stage, you will, of course, be revisiting and fleshing out the analysis, design, and any prototyping work completed in the earlier stages as part of project management. Then you will go on to implement, test, and deliver a completed product, as shown in Figure 9.2.

The shaded side of this model shows activities already conducted in earlier stage—object modeling and prototyping. They are included in the illustration because these activities continue in an iterative manner and are completed in this stage. Implementation proceeds after the object schema is well in place. Prototyping will have exercised the object schema. Implementation and testing iterate until the system is ready for delivery.

Managing the Project

Deployment is essentially composed of project management tasks. The primary tasks of project management, such as project planning, scheduling, and budgeting, are beyond the scope of this book and are readily available from many sources. The focus in this section will be on specifics that will help make managing an ODBMS project more successful—particularly people issues and managing expectations.

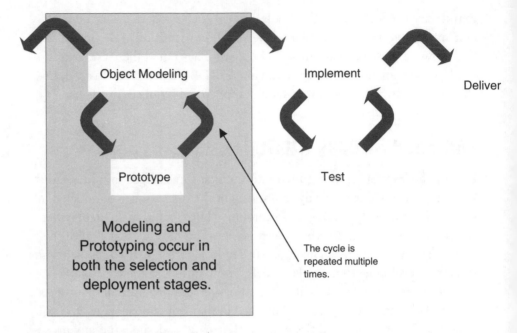

Figure 9.2 *Expansion of the deployment stage in the process.*

People Issues

Your team of people will be important to success in fielding your application. Your best deployment team will be the people you put together as a selection team. The worst scenario is to start fresh with a new team for deploying the application that will use an ODBMS. If you need some particular expertise at this stage, however, you may choose to add a new member.

One important new team member to consider at this time is a consultant from the ODBMS vendor you chose. Get this consultant in early—before implementation is started. This works better than waiting until you reach some hard spot that will require rework. You will find these vendor consultants most useful at two points in the process. When you are nearing completion of your object schema, have this model inspected by the consultant. He or she will likely make suggestions that will permit the ODBMS product to work more efficiently with your object schema. The second point is when you are tuning the system to get the best performance possible from the ODBMS. For example, I know of a company that achieved a 500 percent improvement of the performance of their fielded application by partnering with the vendor's consultants on tuning their system.

Keep in mind that most successful teams stay fairly small—seven people or less. This makes it possible to have smooth communication between team members without adding cumbersome formal communication methods. At this size, team members will chat naturally with each other about their tasks and progress.

Protecting Your Investment

Even in stable industries, some companies change their product lines or go out of business over time. The ODBMS industry is young, so the risk that this might happen is a bit greater. There is, however, a way to lessen the risk that such a change might affect you or your application.

One way to do protect your investment is to program the application as closely as possible to the ODMG-93 specification, which is described in Chapter 5. By doing this, your code will be more portable. Of course, your ODBMS has features beyond the ODMG specification, so you will probably end up with 80 percent portable code. That is a significant percentage should you find you must switch to another ODBMS for some reason.

Avoid the tendency to put a great deal of effort into designing a layer of software on top of the ODBMS to hide the other 20 percent or so of code. Throughout my career I have noted programmers working on "dynamite" application program interfaces. They may be great interfaces, but they are nonstandard. That means they typically are not documented, nor well understood by anyone else. After a little time has passed and the programmer has gone on to something else, they are practically unmaintainable and unusable. It is easier to program directly to the underlying software.

Most often this is done in an effort to make all the code portable. This may be of some help, but in reality one of two things is most likely to happen. First, the odds are that you will stick with your original choice and have no need for the extra layering. In fact, in this case the layering has probably lessened your performance speed. The second possibility is that you will have to change products. If that happens, you may find that the layering didn't really protect you. You would still have to write specific code under the layer for the new product, so you might as well write to the ODBMS product directly.

My advice is to avoid doing your own layering. It is one of the myths in our industry that layering helps. Although layering may help for a year or two, it always seems to cause problems in the end because it is a nonstandard solution not supported by any vendors. In the end, you will have large investment in maintaining this layer.

Another way to protect your investment is in your documentation and code comments. There tends to be a great deal of employee turnover after ODBMS projects are completed. Insisting on what may appear to some as excessive documentation and comments in the code will soften the effect of turnover.

Setting Realistic Expectations About Reusability

One of the strong points of object technology is the reusability of code. While this is a plus, it is something you are more likely to achieve after several projects have been completed. Do not expect to reuse much, if any, code in your first project. The learning curve is too steep, and it creates an unreasonable expectation that cannot be met.

One common mistake is to expect that the class structure can be designed early on and then simply reused. It won't happen—even high in the hierarchy. Let your prototyping show you what you have overlooked. And yes, expect to design the initial class library a couple of times before you are even done with the prototyping. Let it stabilize on its own and do not freeze it too early. You will have convoluted code to show for it if you freeze it too soon.

Setting Realistic Expectations About Timing

Yet another issue is the amount of time allotted to the entire process from strategy to deployment. Some people fail to recognize the amount of time involved in fielding an application using this new technology. From data that I have compiled in talking to my clients, the elapsed time to deliver an application ranges from one year to three years averaging out at two years, depending upon the complexity of the data and the application. The time includes getting the team together, training, object modeling, and selecting the ODBMS product. The amount of time required to field an application may lessen in the future, but at this point in the development of the industry, the learning curve is steep. Ignore that learning curve at your peril.

In fact, the biggest mistake you could make in this process is selecting the wrong ODBMS. You can recover from this but it will cost you time and money. You will essentially be backtracking through the entire process—a wasted effort in rework. If you feel you do not have time to go through the whole process the first time, remember that you may discover you are forced to find time to do it all over!

Changing Development Culture

A relatively small, but established, company in California took a long-term approach in putting together their team. Rather than throw people at a project and ask them to rush through it, this company decided to do it right. Several new people with ODBMS experience were brought in to work with one of their visionary people to prototype a major change to their product. Once the prototype was evaluated, the company committed to making the change to an ODBMS.

The new people became an internal training group and provided training designed specifically for the company needs to every member of the development staff. Each staff member then implemented some small, but relevant project using C++ and an ODBMS. During this time, the new people functioned as mentors supporting the rest of the staff and that was the only task assigned to these new people. When this phase was over, all of this work was thrown away as version zero, as we were all taught to do in our software engineering classes at school but have rarely done. Then the company went about the development work to create the product they currently sell.

What struck me about this approach is the level of commitment by the company to changing their development culture. This company recognized the need to bring in new expertise and yet retain the expertise in the existing people, by giving people strong support to make the change to an ODBMS. Through this process, they lost only one development staff member.

Technical Advice

If the first three stages in the process have been worked appropriately, you are well positioned to address the remaining detailed technical issues that will surface in analysis, design, implementation, and testing. This section provides advice in each of these areas.

Analysis and Design

Analysis and design is at the heart of any software project. From a technical standpoint, the main difference in managing an ODBMS project will be the greater amount of time spent on analysis and design up front as part of the object modeling. If this is done properly, coding almost will seem like an afterthought. I believe this comes about by being forced to model BOTH your data and your process in the object schema. You have the data structured as a result, but you also have the method code structured for the process portion of the model, and the method code is associated with the data. You are likely to have a major portion of your code in these methods. In the applications I have studied, they average between 50 and 100 classes with more than 400 methods for the database. I expect to see this number start growing now as more complex applications emerge.

This structuring of the code with the data is significant. I lived through the structured programming days; I cannot count the number of times code was "re-structured" late at night in the programmer's cubicle—and then "re-structured" again a few days later. The object schema forces you to look at the interaction of the data and the process (method code) much more closely—and you are less likely to have code re-structured during midnight sessions late in the implementation process.

Prototyping

Prototyping is essential to the success of any project. It will make it possible to get a clear understanding of how the system will work and it also makes it possible to get input from the user community. You will likely do several prototypes while you are doing your object modeling as illustrated in Figure 9.2. At this stage, however, you are doing it with the ODBMS in place. This will help you understand how the system works. Some prototypes will simply be small test examples while others may be more significant. There are several reasons to do this. Prototypes provide practice for the team in its new skills learned in training. Some prototypes allow the team to practice with the various ODBMS features deemed to be useful during the selection stage. Prototypes help your developers get over some initial internal resistance to the new technology. In my experience, many developers are more resistant than they care to admit, even to themselves. It may take even two rounds of prototypes before they become comfortable with this technology.

It's also a good idea to plan to complete a major prototype that covers significant portions of the application. This can be used to get feedback from the user or customer community. A prototype provides users or customers with a more tangible view of what's being proposed; don't underestimate how much useful information you can get through this practice. This is another good reason for doing prototypes as early as you can. But do expect to throw this away as version zero. It is a mistake to hope you can enhance such a prototype into a product. Go back to analysis and design and change your object schema based on what you have learned. Then move into implementation.

Implementation

Implementation is the stage where "real" programmers used to do their work. In following the ODBMS implementation process, much of the code will now be in methods and that code will generally be quite simple because of the level of design decomposition that comes with the object model. If properly modeled, each method will perform one action. It is simpler to write this kind of code. The object model also hides the internals of each method from other methods so you have a good shot at eliminating the tendency to write code that "knows" what is going on inside another routine. Again, it is simpler to write this kind of code that is not enmeshed with other routines. When code is simpler to write, you reduce the number of times you end up rewriting the code. The upshot is that this becomes the smallest part of the entire process.

Testing

Testing is yet another topic beyond the scope of this book. From an object technology perspective, do not underestimate the time this will take. As systems become more complex, so does the testing process. I commonly have seen projects where more time is spent on testing than on implementation; yet, in looking at the schedule, testing is invariably expected to be a quick task done at the end.

As your object schema stabilizes, consider incremental testing of objects (both code and data) as they are developed. This is something that the object model supports better than prior models. You have relatively simple data in a single object that is acted on by relatively simple methods. Think of it as component test where each component is in a sense a very small application that can be tested separately.

The flip side of each object being simpler is that the systems that use these objects are more complex. Testing the implementation of the object schema is challenging when you need to consider all the possible interactions the objects can make with each other in a complex system. Your user team members become invaluable here to exercise the system through whatever user interfaces you provide. The most effective approach that I have seen is using the scenarios developed earlier in the selection stage as the initial basis to test the system. One caution—be sure to do multi-user testing under reasonably representative workloads. It should seem obvious to do this, but I have seen this overlooked often.

Lessons Learned

What lessons can we draw from the pioneers who have successfully fielded applications on ODBMSs? Here is what they say:

- Take time to make an informed decision on which DBMS product to use. Be sure the product you select has an architecture that fits your needs. Make sure you are considering all of the features you need.

- Get training on the product and get it early; fielding a production application on an ODBMS is not the place to "wing" it.

- Get the vendor's consultants in early—waiting for a problem before you call on them means you will probably make some bad decisions early in the process. You will have to take some steps backward before you can move forward past your problem.

- Plan to spend more time than usual on analysis and design—many people look back and say they should have involved their vendor's consultants early on, when they are finalizing their object schema.

- Keep your development team small—less than seven people. With a small team, you can all stay on the same track—an important task in a challenging situation.

After Delivery

Everything worked out well. You have successfully deployed an application using one of these products. What should you expect now? What may happen to your team members? Will they stay or move on now that they have this experience? What changes might you expect to the database you have just constructed?

What Has Happened in Other Companies

The best people leave if you do not have another challenge for them—this is a hot industry and as you have probably found, it is hard to find experienced people. Your development team just improved their marketability. They know the technology, have the training, and have participated in a successful ODBMS project. They are just the people you were looking for when you started your project. Other employers are looking for them now. If you want to keep them, look at what it takes to do so. Look for new technical challenges in your company. Also, work with your human resource department to see what kind of a long-term package you can put together.

If you aren't able to keep them, you can expect to be looking for new people and training them. They too may leave after several projects. The positive side to this is that each new person comes in with a different set of experiences, so the new people may bring a perspective that can improve the ODBMS-based system in a way that has not been considered before.

What Changes Might You Expect to Your Database?

It is my experience that good, accessible data is like honey for ants. People will want to use your database in new and unusual ways. While this will create new demands on you and your system, it is a sign you did a good job. This happened to me early in my career. One of the things I did in my first job after undergraduate school was to participate in the development of a statistical database for people collecting unemployment insurance in Minnesota. The system that was being replaced was entirely a handcount system with no statistical detail on individuals appearing in the handcount data. The new database received its data from the system that processed the unemployment applications and checks—with statistical detail on individuals. After a short time, the word got out that we could cut the data by differing age categories, by zip code, by differing occupational categories, and so on. There was hardly a week that went by without some type of special request. All because we built a better system.

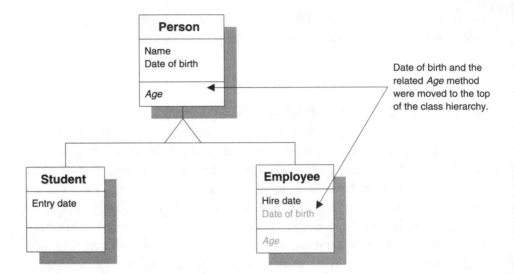

Figure 9.3 *Changes to the object schema.*

As people use this newly available data, they will want more—new attributes and new methods, at a minimum. It is not uncommon to find the need for modifications that could even change the class hierarchy at a high level. Figure 9.3 shows an example of such a change. Assume that the original object schema that was implemented did not carry Date of birth information for the Student class. After the system was in place, someone realized that adding that data to the Student class would be useful. This can occur by moving Date of birth and its associated Age method higher in the hierarchy. Now the Student class can use it and yet the Employee class is unaffected since it now inherits the definition from the Person class.

Summary

Successful selection begins with clear strategy, early team identification and development, and careful selection. Attention to these activities will allow you to minimize rework, which will save you time and money. Focus on the beginning of the entire process and minimize mistakes early. The most costly mistakes sometimes come out of developing a strategy to use ODBMSs that isn't based on a clear understanding of the data and its intended use. A lack of understanding of the ODBMS features that would assist you in meeting the business strategy is the second most costly area. That can come from a lack of knowledge of what features might be considered. Take the time to study the features and how they impact your application needs. If you don't, you may make a poor ODBMS selection and, during deployment, find yourself catapulted back into the selection or even the strategy stage. That is very costly indeed.

10

Using Existing Relational Schema: An Example

As mentioned at the opening of Chapter 2, I was working on a personnel system in the mid-1980s that required all the walls of a conference room to model the data in its relational schema. The system required a model of that size because the huge number of many-to-many relationships required huge numbers of intersection entities. You may recall intersection entities as one of the signs of complex data. Since learning about ODBMS technology, I have often thought how much easier it would have been to convert that relational schema to an object schema and use an ODBMS.

People who are just getting into object technology often ask what they can do with existing relational schemas that they have built and how they might handle the data that they already have stored in an RDBMS. This chapter will show you how to convert the data models and will explain two choices for using the existing relational data. The first choice is to convert the data to an ODBMS and the second choice is to keep it in the RDBMS but access the data as needed.

This chapter will focus on the issues and techniques in reworking relational schema into an object schema.

Key points in this chapter include:

- How to use type codes and relational views to get ideas about the object class hierarchy.

- A step-by-step example of converting a relational schema to an object schema and checking to ensure no information is lost in the process.

- Adding method code that was not in the relational schema to the object schema.

- Ways to convert data or simply access the data in place.

Type Codes

In a relational schema, type codes are commonly used to classify data. For example, type codes might be assigned to types of birds, employees, students, parts, or any other groups of things that could be classified in multiple ways. These type codes are often in numeric or alphanumeric form, but to simplify our examples here, the types will be spelled out in words rather than in the typical numeric or alphanumeric codes.

In Chapter 2, an example of complex data represented in a relational schema focusing on university teachers and students was introduced. The portion of

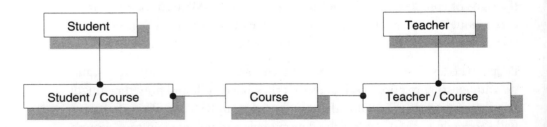

Figure 10.1 *Relational schema for university example.*

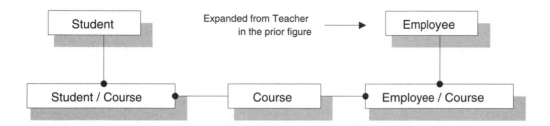

Figure 10.2 *Modified relational schema for university example.*

that data definition that will be used for the example in this chapter is shown in Figure 10.1.

To get a sense of how to adapt a relational schema into an object schema, this university example will be expanded in this chapter to model more closely what a university data structure is really like. As used here, the concept of Teacher has been expanded to include all employees of the university, including support personnel as well as teachers. There will be only one type of support personnel for this example. The types of teachers will be instructors, professors, or graduate students in a workstudy program at the university. In this example, however, one set of type codes is used for all of these types of employees.

Figure 10.2 shows the data definition in a relational schema for the data at the university. It shows Employee where Teacher was in Figure 10.1.

The base table for Employee in Figure 10.2 is shown in Figure 10.3. A *base table* is the way the data is stored physically using an RDBMS. Note the use of Employee Type in this base table to distinguish various types of employees at the university. This is a common way to efficiently store data in an RDBMS.

Employee

Name	Date of Birth	Employee Type	Hire Date	Tenure Date
Don	12 Feb 1960	Support	22 May 1993	
Pat	1 Sep 1965	Instructor	10 Jun 1990	
Donna	11 Nov 1948	Professor	15 Aug 1978	15 Jan 1985
Kim	22 Jul 1972	Workstudy	20 Sep 1994	
Fred	15 Mar 1955	Professor	17 Jul 1985	22 Jan 1992

Figure 10.3 *Employee base table.*

```
if type is Instructor then
      ... specific processing for Instructor ...
else if type is Professor then
      ... specific processing for Professor ...
else if type is Workstudy then
      ... specific processing for Workstudy ...
else if type is Instructor, Professor, Workstudy then
      ... specific processing for any of these ....
else if type is Support then
      ... specific processing for Support ...

... and so on ...
```

Figure 10.4   *Programming code that uses type codes.*

There are two ways to determine if there is type data present—by inspecting the data definition or by inspecting the programming code. In the university example in Figure 10.3, type data clearly is being used in the data definition. Sometimes, when the term "type" is not used, it is hard to identify type codes in the data definition. You can then look at the programming code. When you see code structured as it is in Figure 10.4, this indicates type code processing.

Using Type Codes to Construct Tentative Classes

Type codes provide hints about the nature of the class hierarchy to be constructed. Type codes provide a good place to start creating a class hierarchy as you consider converting the data definition from a relational to an object schema. A class hierarchy in an object schema takes the place of type codes in a relational schema. In an ODBMS, type codes are known and "understood" as the class hierarchy. In a relational schema, type codes are embedded in the data and are not actually "understood" by the DBMS. In this section, the data in the university example will be examined carefully to illustrate how type codes can be used to construct a class hierarchy.

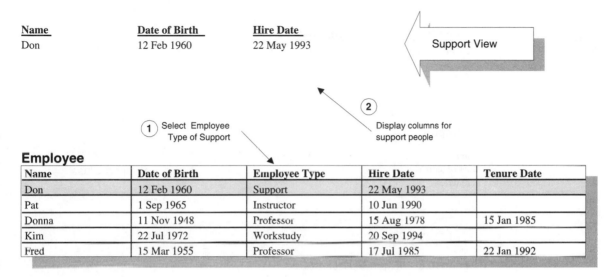

Name	Date of Birth	Hire Date
Don	12 Feb 1960	22 May 1993

Support View

① Select Employee Type of Support

② Display columns for support people

Employee

Name	Date of Birth	Employee Type	Hire Date	Tenure Date
Don	12 Feb 1960	Support	22 May 1993	
Pat	1 Sep 1965	Instructor	10 Jun 1990	
Donna	11 Nov 1948	Professor	15 Aug 1978	15 Jan 1985
Kim	22 Jul 1972	Workstudy	20 Sep 1994	
Fred	15 Mar 1955	Professor	17 Jul 1985	22 Jan 1992

Figure 10.5 *Support View.*

First, let's look at the situation where one type code cannot be further decomposed. In the university example, all employees who are not teachers of any kind are classified as "support." Support provides one type code that is not further decomposed or divided in any way in this example. One way this can be determined is by looking at the code. A second, and probably easier way to determine if there is only one type code, is to look at the views defined. A *view* is a virtual table defined in the base table that, in this example, is the Employee base table in Figure 10.3. Figure 10.5 shows the definition of the Support View. It selects only one type code of "Support."

The data used in this Support View can provide our first tentative class definition, as shown in Figure 10.6. This is simply a direct translation of the columns (in relational terms) or attributes (in object terms) to the class definition. This is the initial step in translating a relational schema to an object schema.

We can follow the same process to create additional tentative classes for the object schema definition. Inspecting the view definitions, it can be seen that the views for Professor and Instructor also select on single type codes. So the columns in the views can be used to create the attributes for the tentative class definitions of Professor and Instructor as well. Figure 10.7 shows the

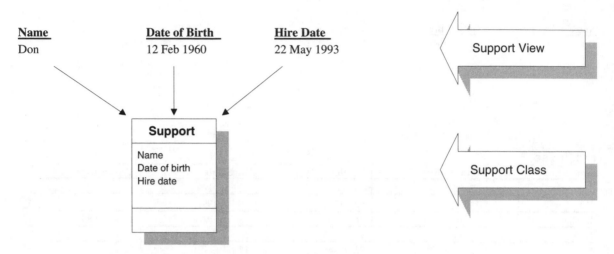

Figure 10.6   *Tentative Support Class.*

Professor View is based on a selecting a single type code. Figure 10.8 provides the tentative Professor Class.

The same process was followed again with the Instructor View. The Instructor View in Figure 10.9 selects on a single type code. The columns in this

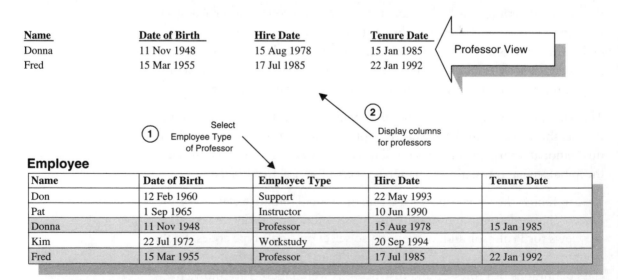

Figure 10.7   *Professor View.*

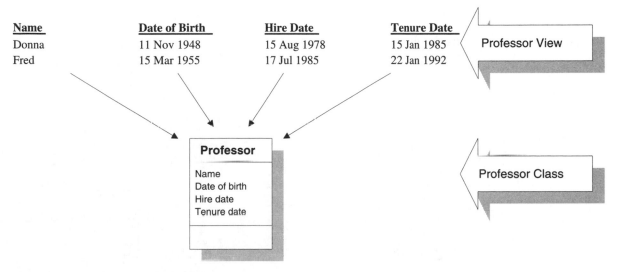

Figure 10.8 *Tentative Professor class.*

view are used to define the attributes for the tentative Instructor Class definition, which is shown in Figure 10.10. Note that although the process for defining the Instructor and Professor classes was the same, the actual definition differs because the Professor View and the Instructor use different data. The Professor View has Tenure Date where the Instructor View does not.

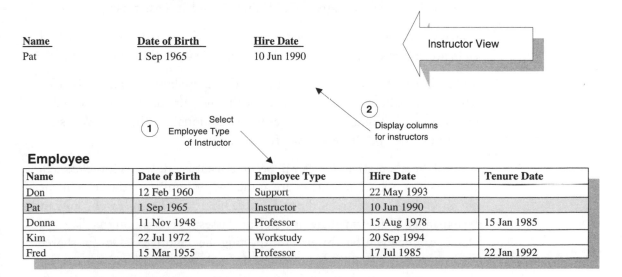

Figure 10.9 *Instructor View.*

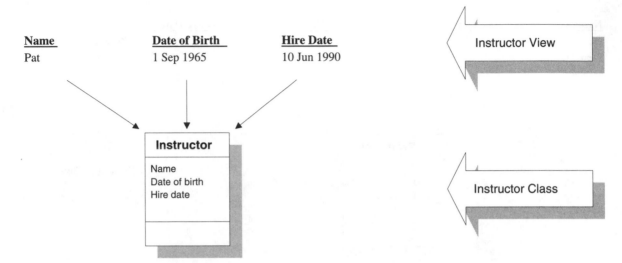

Figure 10.10 *Tentative Instructor Class.*

The final example of an individual type code in the university example is Workstudy, in this case a graduate student who also teaches at the university. As you can see in Figure 10.11, this view is constructed differently from the ones we have seen so far because it requires a join between the Student base table and the Employee base table in order to get all the necessary columns. A new column, Entry Date, comes from the Student base table.

As we saw in the other examples, the attributes for the tentative Workstudy class are drawn directly from the Workstudy View, as shown in Figure 10.12.

So far, four tentative classes have been created, as shown in Figure 10.13. The same attributes—Name, Date of birth, and Hire date—are repeated in each class. Additionally, two classes have additional attributes—Workstudy has Entry date and Professor has Tenure date.

Each of these tentative classes will become what is known as leaf classes in the class hierarchy. Leaf classes are at the end or bottom of the class hierarchy much like leaves are at the end of tree branches. The hierarchy now must be expanded to intermediate or non-leaf classes. Potential intermediate classes can be identified by either inspecting the tentative classes for shared attributes or using multi-type views as defined in the relational schema. In the university example, we will use multi-type views to define new classes.

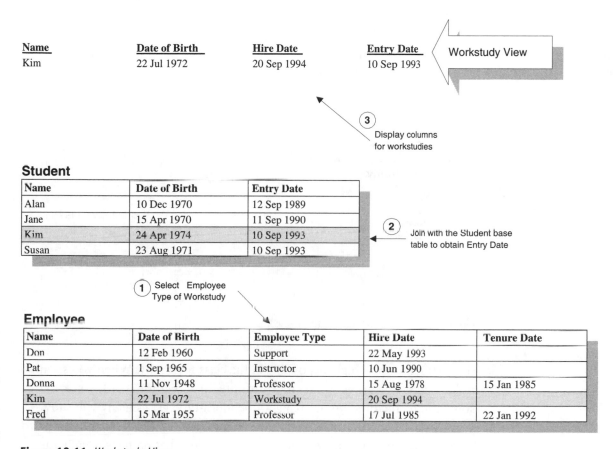

Figure 10.11 *Workstudy View.*

Multi-Type Views

In the prior examples, we looked at the views that selected one type code at a time. It is also possible to have views defined that select on several type codes at a time. These are multi-type views. You might have multi-type views such as the Teacher View shown in Figure 10.14 and the Employee View shown in Figure 10.15. The Teacher View is a multi-type code because there are several types of teachers. The Employee View is a multi-type code because there are several types of employees. These can be used as hints for creating intermediate classes above the leaf classes shown in Figure 10.13. Inspection of these views will provide ways for factoring attributes up higher in the class hierarchy. The term *factoring attributes up* refers to moving the definition of

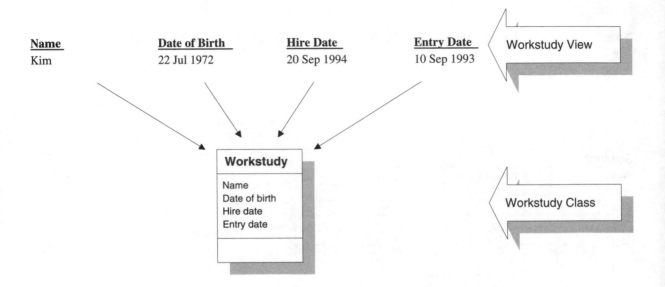

Figure 10.12 *Tentative Workstudy Class.*

the attributes up as high as possible in the class hierarchy. When you see multiple tentative views with the same attributes as in Figure 10.13, you know some can be factored up. Looking at the multi-type views likely will show you which attributes can be factored up and what name you should assign to the new intermediate classes above the leaf node. That name is usually the same name as the multi-type view that you are using.

To create the intermediate classes above the leaf classes, simply add the Teacher and Support Classes above the tentative classes from Figure 10.13 and factor up the common attributes based on the multi-type views. This is shown in Figure 10.16.

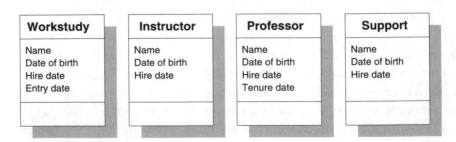

Figure 10.13 *Tentative classes.*

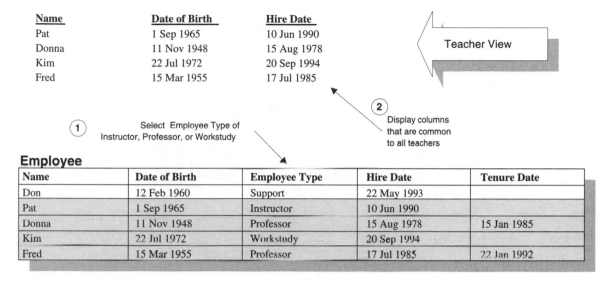

Figure 10.14 *Teacher View.*

In order to have a more complete class hierarchy, we must take into account that a university has not only employees, but students as well. To add this, refer to the Workstudy View in Figure 10.11, which shows the attributes in the Student relational base table. From this, the Entry Date can be factored up

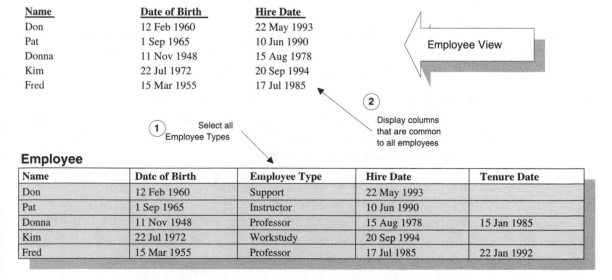

Figure 10.15 *Employee View.*

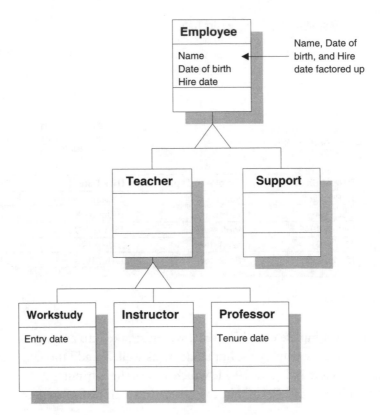

Figure 10.16 *Creating class hierarchy by factoring attributes.*

into a Student Class as shown in Figure 10.17. This introduces multiple inheritance to this object schema. Workstudy is a type of Teacher and a type of Student. The Workstudy class inherits attributes from both Teacher and Student.

Redundant attributes between the Student and Employee Class, which were not addressed in the original relational schema, still exist. They are the attributes of Name and Date of birth. They can be factored out into a Person Class, as illustrated in Figure 10.18.

Almost everything from the original relational schema, except for Course, has been included in the class hierarchy. This is straightforward addition since intersection entities are not necessary in an object schema. (See Chapter 2 for a description of intersection entities and why an object schema does not need them.) Figure 10.19 illustrates the completed object schema for the university example, as outlined in the original relational schema.

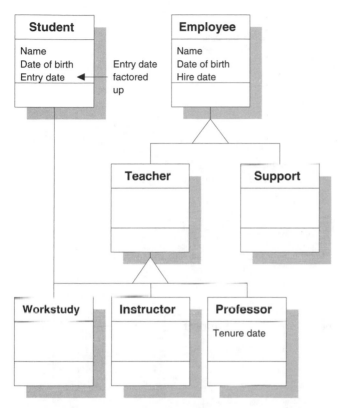

Figure 10.17 *Adding the Student Class to the hierarchy.*

Checking the Class Hierarchy

After completing the object schema, make sure no information has been lost. To do this, check the class hierarchy against the original views defined in the relational schema. First, look at the Support Class in the class hierarchy. It inherits the Name and Date of birth attributes from the Person Class. It also inherits Hire date from the Employee Class. Querying the Support Class in the object schema would, therefore, provide exactly the same results as shown in the relational schema in Figure 10.5 if the same data were stored in the object class definition. This is shown in Figure 10.20.

Moving deeper into class hierarchy, we can see that the Professor Class inherits from the same classes as the Support Class, plus it inherits from the Teacher Class. Figure 10.21 shows the view equivalent to the one shown in

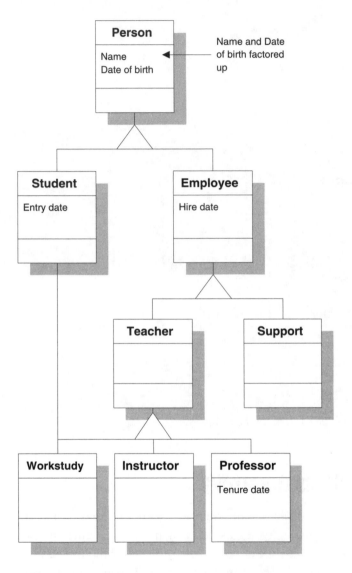

Figure 10.18 *Adding the Person Class to the hierarchy.*

Figure 10.7. You will note that the Teaches attribute has been filtered out for this example. This is because Teaches is a many-to-many attribute that is supported directly by the object schema; it would require the use, in one way or another, of intersection entities in a relational schema. Although it could have been included in the view equivalent without any filtering, it was left in so that you could see it is possible to get back to the original view.

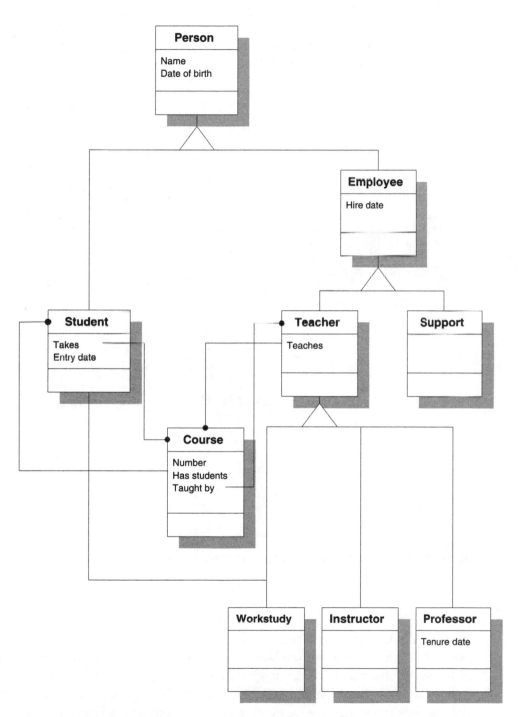

Figure 10.19 *Object schema for original relational schema.*

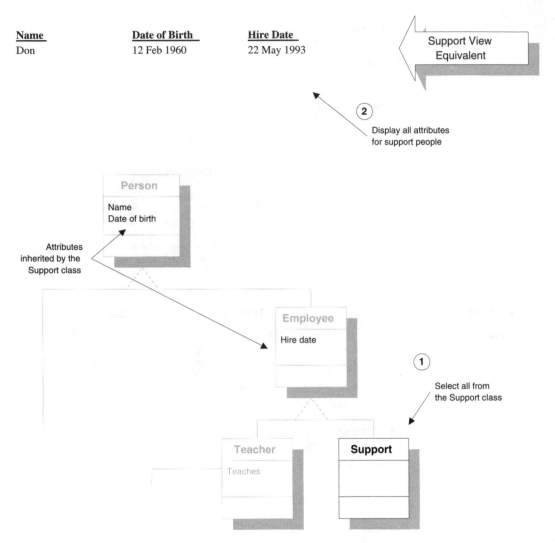

Name	**Date of Birth**	**Hire Date**
Don	12 Feb 1960	22 May 1993

Support View Equivalent

②
Display all attributes
for support people

Person

Name
Date of birth

Attributes
inherited by the
Support class

Employee

Hire date

①

Select all from
the Support class

Teacher

Teaches

Support

Figure 10.20 *Support View equivalent from the class hierarchy.*

Turn to the Workstudy Class to continue checking the class hierarchy against the original relational views. You will recall the relational Workstudy View required the joining of data from both the Employee and the Student base tables. In the object schema, as it has been constructed, this joining is not necessary. The same data as shown in the Workstudy View in Figure 10.11 can be obtained by simply querying the Workstudy Class as shown in Figure 10.22.

Name	Date of Birth	Hire Date	Tenure Date
Donna	11 Nov 1948	15 Aug 1978	15 Jan 1985
Fred	15 Mar 1955	17 Jul 1985	22 Jan 1992

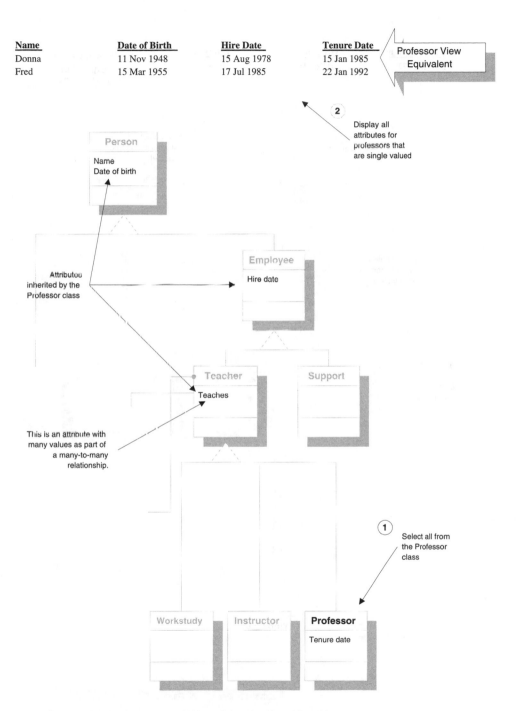

Professor View Equivalent

② Display all attributes for professors that are single valued

Person
Name
Date of birth

Attributes inherited by the Professor class

Employee
Hire date

Teacher
Teaches

Support

This is an attribute with many values as part of a many-to-many relationship.

① Select all from the Professor class

Workstudy

Instructor

Professor
Tenure date

Figure 10.21 *Professor View equivalent from the class hierarchy.*

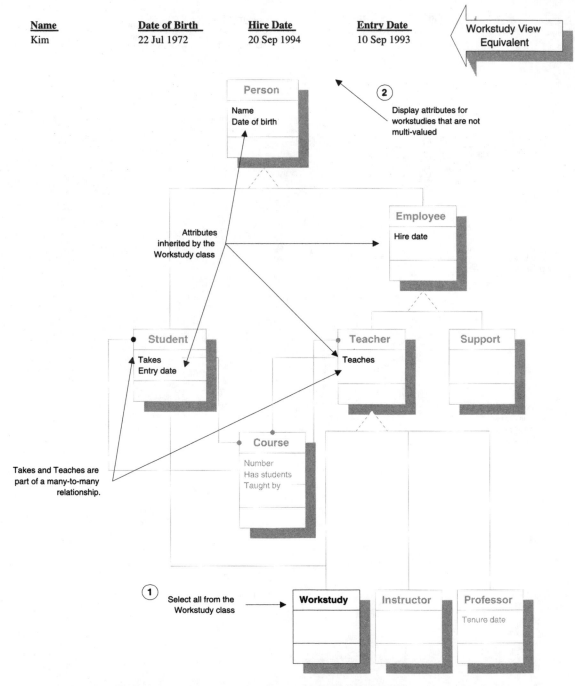

Name	Date of Birth	Hire Date	Entry Date
Kim	22 Jul 1972	20 Sep 1994	10 Sep 1993

Workstudy View Equivalent

Person

Name
Date of birth

② Display attributes for workstudies that are not multi-valued

Employee

Hire date

Attributes inherited by the Workstudy class

Student

Takes
Entry date

Teacher

Teaches

Support

Course

Number
Has students
Taught by

Takes and Teaches are part of a many-to-many relationship.

① Select all from the Workstudy class

Workstudy

Instructor

Professor

Tenure date

Figure 10.22 *Workstudy View equivalent from the class hierarchy.*

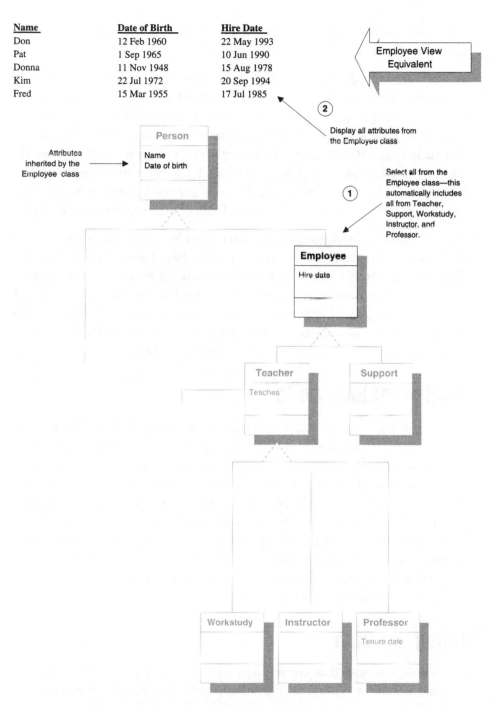

Name	Date of Birth	Hire Date
Don	12 Feb 1960	22 May 1993
Pat	1 Sep 1965	10 Jun 1990
Donna	11 Nov 1948	15 Aug 1978
Kim	22 Jul 1972	20 Sep 1994
Fred	15 Mar 1955	17 Jul 1985

Employee View Equivalent

(2) Display all attributes from the Employee class

Attributes inherited by the Employee class

Person

Name
Date of birth

(1) Select all from the Employee class—this automatically includes all from Teacher, Support, Workstudy, Instructor, and Professor.

Employee

Hire date

Teacher

Teaches

Support

Workstudy

Instructor

Professor

Tenure date

Figure 10.23 *Employee View equivalent from the class hierarchy.*

This is because the Workstudy Class inherits from both the Student and Employee Classes in addition to the Person Class.

Finally, look at the data from the multi-type views used to construct some of the intermediate classes in the hierarchy. The Employee View was selected on the types of Instructor, Professor, and Support. Figure 10.23 shows that querying the Employee Class provides the same results as shown in the relational schema in Figure 10.5. A query at the Employee level automatically queries all the data stored at that level in the class hierarchy or lower so all the types of Employees are included in the query. The only attributes shown, however, are the ones that are defined at the Employee Class or higher in the class hierarchy.

You may want to check some of the other views by simply inspecting the class hierarchy. Note, however, no actual views have been constructed on the class hierarchy at this time. Construction of views in the class hierarchy is not necessary for showing the attributes that are appropriate for each type of data. Remember, class hierarchies explicitly maintain the types of data so it is not necessary to have type codes. As you can see in Figure 10.19, there are no type codes. All that information is in the class hierarchy itself.

Adding Method Code

The final step in constructing the class hierarchy is to add method code. You can find the method code by inspecting the programming code that processes the type data, as was shown earlier in Figure 10.4. In this example, an Age method was found to apply to everyone in the database. It uses the Date of birth and today's date to calculate age. Figure 10.24 shows the Age method attached to the Person class. Also, a method for hiring a new employee is shown along with the method for granting tenure to a professor. There are undoubtedly other methods that can be found. You might also find a different method is necessary for hiring a workstudy so that the method could be further defined for the Workstudy Class.

Using the Data

If you are doing more than converting a relational schema to an object schema, you may also want to use the object schema with data already stored in an RDBMS. Then it's time to consider how to handle that data already stored in the RDBMS. You have two options for this data. In the first case, you can leave

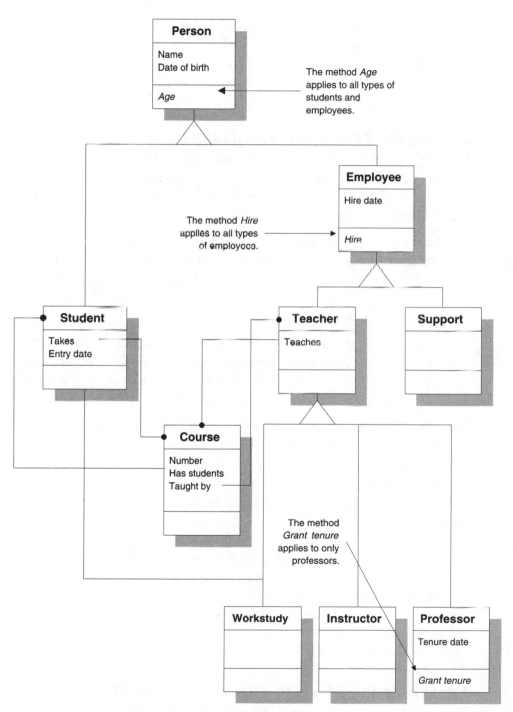

Figure 10.24 *Object schema with method code added.*

the data in the RDBMS and access it when needed, and in the second case, you could convert the data and store it in an ODBMS. In the next two sections we will explore these two options. Either option is possible without losing any details in the relational data. This is the reason we checked to see if we could get back to the equivalent relational views using the object schema.

Leaving the Data in the Relational DBMS

Most commonly, data that's already stored in the database is allowed to remain in the RDBMS and the data is accessed as it is needed. This allows relational data and object data to exist together in the same system without converting the relational data.

The class hierarchy you create for the existing data allows you to access the non-object data in an object manner. In this example, the views used to create the classes at the various levels would be used at run-time to imitate the object structure. For instance, the Employee View would imitate querying the object structure at the Employee Class level.

The upside of this approach is that you can leave all your existing data in place and yet have an object schema of the data that can be used by object applications. This is one of the excellent uses of Object-Relational Mapping products as well as the other ODBMSs that provide access to existing relational data.

The downside of this approach is that you generally will not get higher performance from your data in the object application. You may if you can take advantage of caching the data in the client application, thereby minimizing access to the RDBMS. It is the access to the RDBMS that is not faster—in fact it may be slower because of the additional layer of software to convert relational tuples to object instances. Also, accessing classes using underlying relational views that use joins could still be quite slow, depending how slow the joining operations are in the RDBMS. In the example used in this chapter, the Workstudy Class still requires the use of joins, as illustrated earlier in Figure 10.11. If the application cannot take advantage of caching the results of these joins, there is a potential performance problem. Finally, traversals of references between objects still will use index searches and, in some cases, intersection entities and joins, when the relational data accessed by the objects first comes from the RDBMS.

Converting the Data and Storing in an ODBMS

If you are in a situation where it makes more sense to convert the relational data to the object schema, then the equivalent views discussed earlier in this chapter will again be of use. Each of these equivalent views has a corresponding relational view. The relational view can be used to access the data in the RDBMS. The conversion process, however, will only use the relational views that correspond to the classes at the bottom of the class hierarchy, the leaf classes described earlier. The converted data will be stored in these leaf classes. The classes in the object schema hierarchy above the leaf classes provide alternate ways to view or classify the data that is the equivalent to other views that existed in the relational schema.

To create a conversion program, use the single-valued views (the ones that use only one type code) to get the data from the RDBMS and populate object instances for the appropriate leaf class in the object schema managed by the ODBMS. The upside of doing this is that you get the integration and performance provided by the ODBMS. The downside is that you will either convert the existing applications to access the ODBMS through an ODBC interface or develop new applications. As mentioned in Chapter 5, many ODBMS products provide ODBC interfaces. This allows the object data to appear as relational data, using the view equivalents that were presented earlier.

Summary

One way to translate a relational schema to an object schema was covered in this chapter. The object schema can be constructed from the relational schema and the relational type code information forms the basis of the object class hierarchy. In the object schema, it is possible to drop intersection entities and add method code, which is not possible when using most RDBMSs. Ways to convert relational data to an ODBMS were presented. Finally, this chapter presented a way of having relational data coexist with object data, should you decide to not convert the data.

This chapter completes Part II, which focused on the process to develop a strategy and a team prior to explaining how to select and deploy applications. In addition, there was a detailed discussion of two topics of concern to many considering ODBMSs: the interaction of features with application needs and dealing with existing relational schemas and data stored in RDBMSs. In Part III, exhaustive checklists for determining appropriate feature fit for your application will be presented.

PART THREE

Detailed Selection Checklists

It is an old saying that what you don't know can hurt you. This is true when going through the ODBMS selection process. This Part of the book will most likely expand your knowledge of ODBMS features. It contains detailed checklists of features to help in your analysis of what product will best fit your application. This will help you through the iterative process of understanding ODBMS features and your application needs.

The checklists are aggregated into 13 categories, each of which will expand your understanding of ODBMS features and how they impact your application needs. Examples are provided, often with supporting diagrams. Detailed checklists fully cover the features to help you better *look at the products. References are also provided for deeper understanding beyond what is provided in this book. Read through each list of checklists, along with the comments, and note which features are appropriate to your application.*

CHECKLIST 1 | General Architecture

The basic components of the DBMS architecture are covered in this first checklist.

Client/Server Architecture

The components for client/server architecture are illustrated in Graphic 1.1. This figure provides the basis for the discussion. For an overview of the basic concepts for client/server architecture, see Chapter 1.

○ Supports single database server architecture with multiple clients	*The basis of a multi-user environment is having multiple clients.*
○ Supports multiple database server architecture with multiple clients	*Multiple servers allow for either specialized servers or distributed databases. See Checklist 9, "Distributed Database Systems."*
○ Server is multi-threaded	*Under some circumstances, multi-threading allows for improved performance*
○ Supports single image application and server processes	*You want a "tight" single image that contains both the application (client) and server processes.*

Platforms Supported

Computers and pertinent operating systems are listed.

○ Aviion
Alpha
○ Open VMS
○ OSF/1
○ NT

○ DECStation

HP 9000

   ○ 300/700

   ○ 400/800

   ○ IBM RS 6000 or BULL DPX/2

   ○ MIPS Ultrix

NCR

   ○ System V.4

   ○ 3300

○ SGI

○ NeXT

○ Novell NetWare

Sequent

   ○ NT

   ○ Unix

SPARC

   ○ Solaris 2.0 +

   ○ SunOS

VAX

   ○ Ultrix

   ○ VMS

Intel

   ○ OS/2

   ○ Windows

   ○ NT

   ○ SCO

   ○ MS-DOS

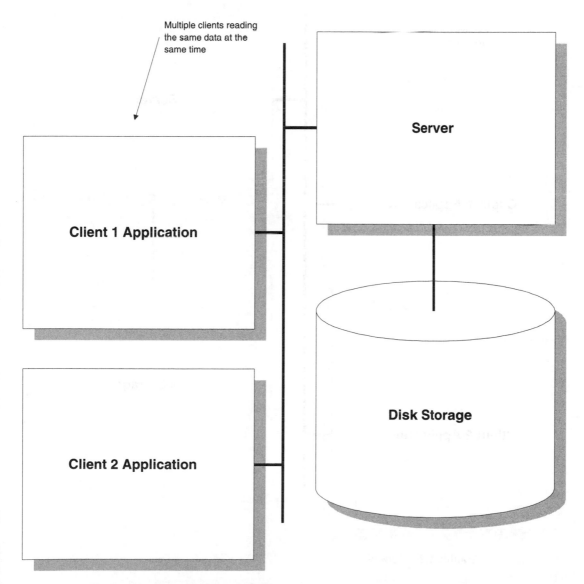

○ NeXT Step
○ Solaris 2.0
○ Mac

Multiple clients reading
the same data at the
same time

Server

Client 1 Application

Disk Storage

Client 2 Application

Graphic 1.1   *Multi-user client/server architecture.*

Networks Supported

The network component to the client/server architecture is illustrated in Graphic 1.2, and network options available are covered in the following checklist.

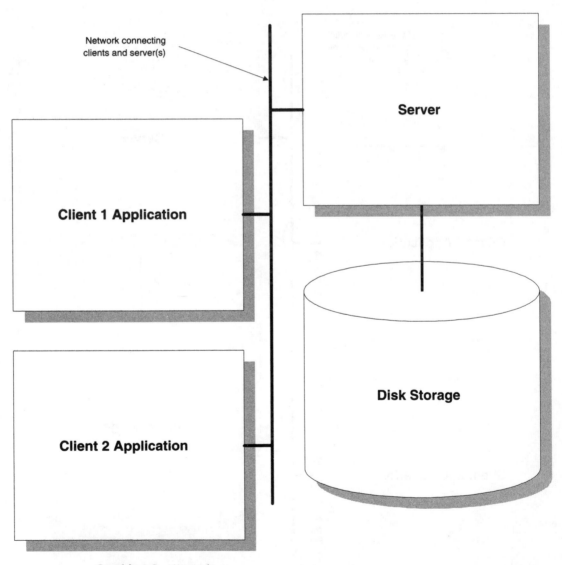

Network connecting
clients and server(s)

Server

Client 1 Application

Client 2 Application

Disk Storage

Graphic 1.2 *Network.*

○ TCP/IP
○ Banyan Vines
○ Microsoft LAN manager
○ Novell Netware
○ DECnet
○ Other

Cache Location

The two types of caching to consider, client-side and server-side, are illustrated in Graphic 1.3 and Graphic 1.4. The unit of caching may vary. See "Lock Granularity" in Checklist 6 and "Unit of Transfer Between Database and Application Memory" in Checklist 1 for other features that interact with caching.

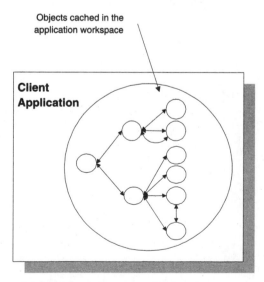

Graphic 1.3   *Client-side caching.*

○ In the server(s)

Almost all products provide some type of server caching—determine if object or page caching is most appropriate when considering your application.

○ In the client/application

This feature may be critical to your application. Review the discussion of the different types of products in Chapter 4.

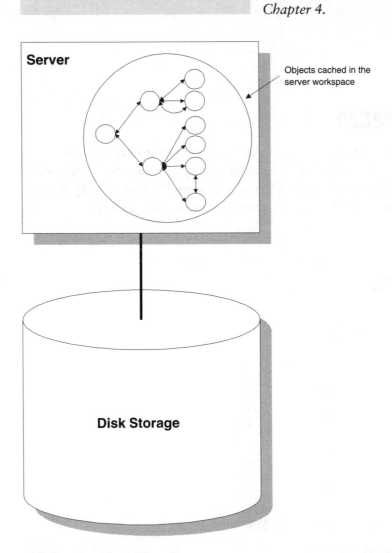

Server

Objects cached in the
server workspace

Disk Storage

Graphic 1.4   *Server-side caching.*

Cache Implementation

How caching is implemented and what your application must do to take advantage of the caching are important. The checklist provides the possible mechanisms that products use for caching.

○ Objects move from secondary storage to the cache automatically as needed without separate explicit commands.	*This is very transparent. Nothing in your application code indicates you are using caching. Referencing the objects in your object programming language causes the caching to occur.*
○ Supports explicit commands to place objects in the cache separate from normal object reference.	*It may be useful to force objects to be cached without explicit reference, as this feature does. The code in the application is affecting the cache.*
○ Objects are removed from the cache or placed in secondary storage automatically without explicit commands.	*This, the inverse of the first checklist item, is equally transparent. You will not see any code in your application to remove objects from the cache because it is under the DBMS control.*
○ Supports explicit commands to remove objects from the cache or place them in secondary storage.	*This allows you to force objects to be removed from the cache rather than waiting for the DBMS to do it. It does require explicit code in your application.*
○ Cache may expand as needed during a transaction.	*This feature allows a cache to increase in size as needed and be managed by the DBMS; sometimes a fixed size is undesirable because it may cause too much thrashing.*
○ Supports multiple client caches for a single application, allowing multi-threaded clients.	*This feature would be useful when you want your client to look like a server to yet another client down the line.*

Unit of Transfer Between Database and Application Memory

This checklist covers the options available for fast data transfer, which is a significant performance concern. The more of the data you want that you

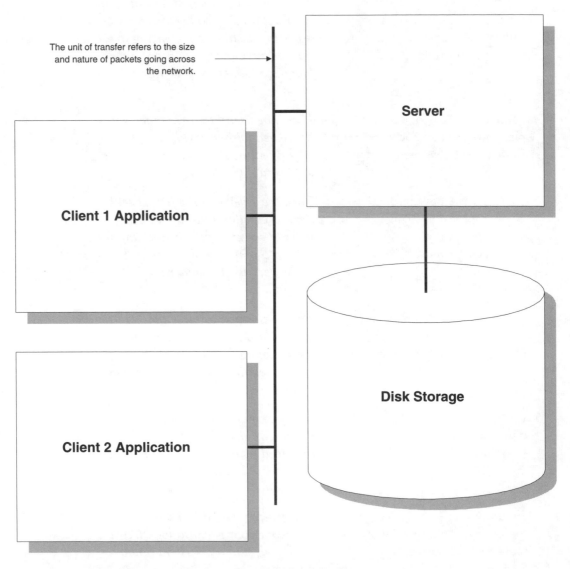

Graphic 1.5 *Unit of transfer across the network.*

can get across the network in as small a unit as possible, the faster the data transfer will be. Graphic 1.5 illustrates the location in the architecture where the unit of transfer is significant.

○ Object or instance	*This, the smallest unit of transfer possible, may be useful when a single object is needed. Unnecessary objects are not sent along, resulting in improved performance. Sending too many objects this way, however, may result in too much overhead.*
○ Logical grouping of objects or instances—for example, query results or composite objects	*This allows dissimilar objects to be grouped together in a unit of transfer—such as collections or containers.*
○ Page	*This is a database page. All the objects on the database page are transferred. This is good when there are many objects needed on the page or if the objects are large. It may be too much overhead if only a few of the many smaller objects on a page are needed.*
○ Many pages (i.e., physical grouping)	*The same comments for a page apply. This is good when you need most objects on multiple pages.*
○ Other	*Ask the vendor what other forms the product may have.*
○ Allows configuration of transfer unit size	*This provides the opportunity to tailor the transfer unit size to best fit the use of your application.*

Memory Utilization

To tune the cache, it is sometimes useful to be able to control the memory utilization. This can be a performance concern if the cache is fighting for enough memory, which will result in thrashing behavior.

⭘ Adjustment of client memory utilization	*This is used by the client cache for all applications.*
⭘ Adjustment of client memory on an application basis	*Each application is able to specify the amount of memory for its cache.*
⭘ Adjustment of each server memory utilization	*This affects the cache on the server side.*

Storage Implementation

Most DBMSs provide options for how data is stored. This checklist covers those options.

⭘ File system	*Database stores data in standard files underneath the DBMS.*
⭘ Automatic expansion should initial allocation size be exceeded	*Databases often expand. Does the product allow the space allocated for the database to expand as needed without human intervention?*
⭘ Manual expansion or reallocation should initial allocation size be exceeded	*This is the inverse of the last checklist item; with this feature a person must be involved if the allocated space for the database must be increased.*
⭘ Raw partition	*This feature bypasses the file system of the operating system to write directly on the disk, which sometimes improves performance but can also increase administrative costs.*
⭘ CD-ROM	*Some products use this for archival data.*
⭘ Database volumes on multiple drives allows parallel I/O by the server process	*The server-side performance is improved by this feature if the nature of your data and how you use it can take advantage of it. This would be useful if you have many transactions involve updating instances of multiple classes. If you store the instances from each class on different drives, this could speed the I/O for your update.*

Storage Management and Garbage Collection

Adding, removing, and updating data stored on the disk can result in portions of the disks with useless space that cannot be used until the garbage in it is collected.

○ Free space recovered automatically	*The product has some way of recovering free space without explicit commands—this may be either online or offline.*
○ Free space recovered dynamically while DBMS is on line	*Some products recover free space while the DBMS is online. Check to see that it does not affect performance at a critical point for your application.*
○ Free space recovered using an explicit command	*Even if free space is recovered automatically, it is sometimes desirable to force a free space recovery to ensure that the disk is as "open" as possible and that the next actions will not cause an automatic recovery of free space that is perceived as slow.*

Continuous Operation

If you have an application that needs to be highly available around the clock, you should review this checklist carefully. This is sometimes called 24 by 7 operations (24 hours a day, 7 days a week). Also see the "Audit Trail," "Disk Media Protection," and "Backup Facilities" checklists at the end of Checklist 6.

○ No need to shut down DBMS server to upgrade to a new DBMS software release	*Some products actually allow this, to varying degrees.*
○ No need to shut down system to add a new site	*This refers to adding a new server to a distributed database environment.*
○ No need to shut down system to remove a site	*This is useful if you need to remove a machine by first migrating its data to other sites in the database and then shutting the server down. See "Location Independence" in Checklist 9.*

○ No need to shut down the system to migrate data from one site to another	*This relates to the previous checklist item.*

Capacity and Scalability

This information is useful if you expect to have a large database and want to make sure the design of the DBMS can handle the data and scale up as needed.

○ Maximum concurrent clients per server

○ Maximum intercommunicating servers

○ Maximum size of database in MB

○ Internal bitsize of OID

○ Maximum number of classes

○ Maximum number of attributes per class

○ Maximum number of methods per class

Licensing and Metering

This checklist covers the types of software licenses used and whether metering is used as an option for licensing.

○ Unit of licensing

    ○ Client-year

    ○ Client-perpetual

    ○ Site

    ○ Host

○ Other

○ Licensing is enforced by software

Method of transferring license

○ License keys

○ Wired in software

○ Honor system

○ Other

○ Software metering supported — *This is a charge-as-you-use approach.*

○ Events metered — *This would charge for certain events as they occur.*

○ Licensing/metering method can be used for other components that use the DBMS — *This would usually occur when a standard software licensing package is used.*

ODMG-93 Compliance

This covers the basic components of the ODMG-93 specification. See Chapter 5 for more information on ODMG-93.

○ ODL—Object Definition Language

○ OQL—Object Query Language

○ C++ binding

○ Smalltalk binding

SQL-92 Compliance

See Chapter 5 for more information on the various forms of SQL. Entry-level SQL-92 is nearly identical with SQL-86. Intermediate-level SQL-92 encompasses about half of the new features of SQL-92, based on perceived market requirements. Full SQL-92 is the whole language.

SQL-92 DDL and DML Compliance

This covers compliance to the SQL Data Definition Language and the SQL Data Manipulation Language.

SQL-92 Data Definition Language

- ○ Entry level
- ○ Intermediate
- ○ Full

SQL-92 Data Manipulation Language

- ○ Entry level
- ○ Intermediate
- ○ Full

SQL-92 Integrity and Query Expression Compliance

This covers SQL declarative reference integrity and SQL query expressions.

SQL-92 Declarative Referential Integrity

- ○ Entry level
- ○ Intermediate
- ○ Full

SQL-92 Query Expressions

○ Entry level

○ Intermediate

○ Full

Other Standards Support

This covers other standards that are often of interest to people working with ODBMSs.

○ OMG Object Request Broker support

○ X/Open XA support

○ ODBC support

○ OLE support

CHECKLIST 2 | Objects, Attributes, and Relationships

Objects

This checklist covers the ways that the object model may be implemented.

○ Object model properties are determined by the object programming language binding

This relates to how closely integrated the ODBMS is with the object programming language.

Object model properties are independent of the programming language

    ○ Support for operations, requests, or messages

    ○ Support for methods that provide the implementation of an operation

    ○ Support for maintenance of the state of objects

Persistence with Programming Languages

This checklist goes into the different ways some of the DBMSs define persistence. For further information, check "Object Language Integration" and "Procedural Languages" in Checklist 3.

○ Supports implicit persistence—the user does not have to explicitly identify, move, or copy objects to make them persistent.

○ Supports explicit persistence—the user can explicitly identify, move, or copy objects to make them persistent.

- ○ Supports both persistent and non-persistent objects of the same class

- ○ Persistence is through inheritance

- ○ Persistence is defined for an object at the storage manager level

- ○ Persistence is by reachability or connectivity from named objects or values that are the persistent roots of a database.

Object Identifiers

See Chapter 1 for a definition of OIDs.

- ○ Each object has a unique, immutable identity that provides a means to denote or refer to the object independent of its state or behavior.

- ○ The system must be able to refer to objects by the unique identity instead of a primary key.

Object Identifier to Pointer Conversion

Swizzling, on the other hand, is the conversion of references between objects from a disk format to an in-memory format. It may have lower overhead if you make many references to the same object.

The DBMS products differ considerably in how OIDs are used with the programming language. One technique is not best for all situations. Hash table lookup, for example, may be faster when references are used infrequently.

O Hash table lookup

Disk representation swizzled to memory representation

O Multiple objects swizzled at the same time

O Objects swizzled upon use

O Use of swizzling is programmer option

O Can store swizzled representation on disk to avoid some conversions

Attributes and Relationships

O Relationships as logical relations between instances of one or more classes

O Attributes

O One-to-one inverse non-composite relationships

O One-to-many inverse non-composite relationships

O Many-to-many inverse non-composite relationships

O Reference from an object in a private workspace to an object in the shared workspace

O Reference from an object in one private workspace to an object in another private workspace

O Attributes on relationships themselves—facets

See "Composite or Complex Objects" later in this checklist for more information.

Literal Attributes

Many products allow the incorporation of classes from either the language vendor or third-party vendors. Also see "Object Language Integration" in Checklist 3.

○ Support for simple entities such as numbers and character strings

○ Support for date data type

○ Support for date arithmetic

○ Support for time data type

○ Support for time arithmetic

○ Support for money data type

Multimedia Attributes

Many products allow the incorporation of classes from either the language vendor or third-party vendors. "Object Language Integration" in Checklist 3 may also be of help.

○ Image classes

○ Nontraditional objects stored and managed in the database

○ Nontraditional objects stored and managed as files outside the DBMS

○ Ability to edit portions of multi-media objects—insert and delete from the middle of an object

○ Ability to version only portions of a single multimedia object

- ○ Audio classes
- ○ Text classes
- ○ Text classes using SGML format
- ○ Full-motion video classes
- ○ Other large binary data

Multimedia Data Manipulation

There are various ways that the multimedia attributes may be manipulated.

○ Nontraditional objects stored and managed in the database	
○ Nontraditional objects stored and managed as files outside the DBMS	*Note that this means they are protected only by the operating system and not by the DBMS.*
○ Ability to edit portions of multimedia objects—insert and delete from the middle of an object	
○ Ability to version only portions of a single multimedia object	*Version Implementation in Checklist 8 may also be of help.*

Collections and Aggregates

Remember that many products allow the incorporation of classes from either the language vendor or third-party vendors. Also see "Object Language Integration" in Checklist 3.

- ○ Sets
- ○ Bags
- ○ Lists
- ○ Fixed arrays

- ○ Dynamic arrays
- ○ Variable length strings
- ○ Stacks
- ○ Queues
- ○ Dictionaries

Composite or Complex Objects

Composite or complex objects are objects that are made up of other objects. An example is an automobile engine. An engine is one object made up of many objects.

The two concepts important for composite or complex objects described in these checklists are well described by their names—containment and dependence. Containment is concerned with one object logically contained in another object; for example, a shelving unit contains a shelf.

Dependence has to do with whether the contained object can exist without the object that contains it. For example, a shelf may exist separately from a particular shelving unit, so it is not dependent on the existence of the shelving unit.

Containment

- ○ Support for specifying that one object contains another object
- ○ Contained object may be in one and only one containing object.
- ○ Contained object may be shared in many other containing objects.

Dependence

- ○ Contained object may exist independently of the containing object.

○ Contained object may be dependent on the containing object.

○ Dependent contained objects are deleted with the contained object (cascade delete).

○ Composite or complex objects may be clustered physically.

Object Clustering

Clustering has to do with the efficiency of transferring data from the disk. The more objects on the fewest possible pages will give you the fastest data transfer. Clustering, however, is usually only a hint to the DBMS. It is not always possible to physically cluster the objects you want to be together because they may be on different servers, or there may be insufficient space in a page to cluster all objects. (See Graphic 2.1.)

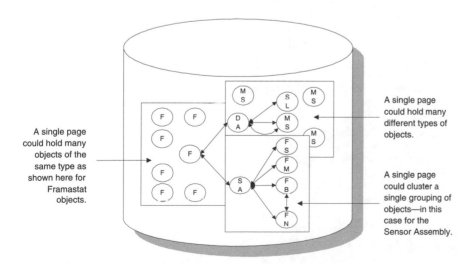

A single page could hold many objects of the same type as shown here for Framastat objects.

A single page could hold many different types of objects.

A single page could cluster a single grouping of objects—in this case for the Sensor Assembly.

Graphic 2.1 *Disk storage.*

230 · CHECKLIST 2

○ Allows system-wide commands
to cluster objects within the same
page

○ Allows application-specific commands to cluster objects within
the same page

○ Allows clustering of composite
objects made up of many types to
be clustered on the same page

Integrity Constraints

Integrity constraints are used to enforce certain rules about the data. For
example, you might want to enforce the rule that all Social Security Numbers
must be unique so that you do not get duplicates. A uniqueness constraint
would be used for this.

○ Only prespecified operations
allowed

○ Constraints on the allowed types
of operands

○ Type constraints on operation
results

○ Type constraints allowed on types
of values

○ Uniqueness constraints

○ Non-null constraint

○ Referential constraints for
creating OID

○ Constraints that ensure referenced object exists

○ Dangling references not allowed

Instance Operations Extensibility

In some cases, these properties are determined by the programming language, not the DBMS. These kernel-level operations may be extended with methods, functions, or some other means so that behavior, not the interface, is modified.

- O No distinction between system-defined and user-defined operations
- O Making new object instances
- O Deleting object instances—also check "Storage Management and Garbage Collection" in Checklist 1.
- O Checking in objects from a private workspace to the shared workspace
- O Checking objects out of the shared workspace into a private workspace
- O Migrating objects from one site in the distributed database to another site
- O Copying instance objects
- O Printing objects

Class Operations Extensibility

These kernel-level operations may be extended using methods, functions, or some other means so that the behavior, not the interface, is modified.

- O No distinction between system-defined and user-defined operations
- O Making new object instances

- ○ Deleting object instances
- ○ Checking in objects from a private workspace to the shared workspace
- ○ Checking objects out of the shared workspace into private workspace
- ○ Migrating objects from one site in the distributed database to another site
- ○ Copying types or classes
- ○ Printing objects

CHECKLIST 3 | Procedures and Programming Languages

This checklist deals with programming languages at both the method and the application level.

Encapsulation

In some cases, these properties are determined by the programming language, not the ODBMS.

External encapsulation

○ Public methods visible outside the database object

○ Public data visible outside the database object

Procedural encapsulation

○ Private methods that can be modified without affecting code outside the database object

○ Private data that can be modified without affecting code outside the database object

Method Implementation

○ Methods operate on a class level.

○ Methods operate on the database level independent of classes.

○ Methods are accessible from query language.

○ Method execution can have impact outside the database.

○ Methods may be called during change notification or triggers.

○ Methods can return parameters.

Method Linking and Typing

○ Method language statically linked

○ Method language dynamically linked

○ Method type errors detected at compile-time

○ Method type errors detected at run-time

Method Execution Location

See Chapter 8 for a discussion of the effects this can have on your application. (See Graphic 3.1.)

○ In the server(s) (server-based)

○ In the client/application (client-based)

Object Language Integration

It may be very important that ODBMS objects appear identical to nonpersistent objects used by the object language in the client application. This can have a major effect on your development time.

○ C++

○ Objective-C

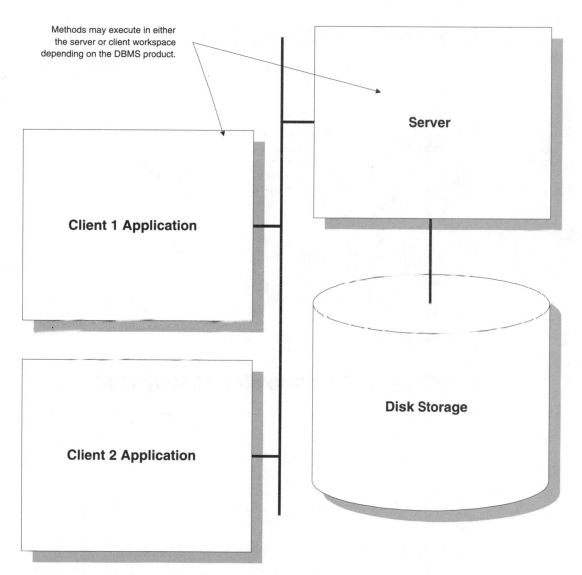

Graphic 3.1 *Methods may execute in the client or server depending on the ODBMS product.*

- ◯ Eiffel
- ◯ Smalltalk
- ◯ CLOS
- ◯ Java

Server-Based Method Language

See Chapter 8 for a discussion of how this feature can affect the performance of your application.

- ○ C++
- ○ Smalltalk
- ○ CLOS
- ○ Java
- ○ C
- ○ Smalltalk language variant
- ○ Lisp
- ○ SQL
- ○ Other language

Client-Based Database Method Language

See Chapter 8 for a discussion of how this feature can affect the performance of your application.

- ○ C++
- ○ Objective-C
- ○ Eiffel
- ○ Smalltalk
- ○ CLOS
- ○ Java
- ○ C
- ○ Smalltalk variant
- ○ Lisp
- ○ SQL
- ○ Other language

Class Libraries

O Description of class libraries that
   work with the product

Object Language Class Reuse by Inheritance

This is the first of several ways that reuse is possible. Only the inheritance
part of the class definition needs to be changed to use class in an ODBMS.

O C++

O Objective-C

O Eiffel

O Smalltalk

O CLOS

O Java

Object Language Class Reuse
by Changing Definition

More than the inheritance portion of the class definition needs to be changed
to use class in the ODBMS.

O C++

O Objective-C

O Eiffel

O Smalltalk

O CLOS

O Java

Object Language Class Reuse Without Changing Definition

Nothing in the class definition needs to be changed to use class in the ODBMS.

○ C++

○ Objective-C

○ Eiffel

○ Smalltalk

○ CLOS

○ Java

Object Language Class Reuse Using Processor

Nothing in the class definition needs to be changed to use class in the ODBMS; the processor makes all changes.

○ C++

○ Objective-C

○ Eiffel

○ Smalltalk

○ CLOS

○ Java

Object Language Class Generation

Application class definitions are generated from the definition in the ODBMS or the Data Definition Language.

○ C++

○ Objective-C

○ Eiffel

- ○ Smalltalk
- ○ CLOS
- ○ Java

Application Language Preprocessors

Sometimes it is necessary to run the application code through a preprocessor before it is compiled so it will work with an ODBMS. This often makes for simpler code writing, but debugging can be difficult because the code that is compiled after preprocessing is not what the programmer wrote and often appears quite different from the original code.

- ○ C++
- ○ Objective-C
- ○ Eiffel
- ○ Smalltalk
- ○ CLOS
- ○ Java
- ○ Ada
- ○ C
- ○ COBOL
- ○ Fortran
- ○ Lisp
- ○ Other language

Procedural Languages

Some of the ODBMS products work with procedural languages in addition to, or instead of, object programming languages.

- ○ Ada call-level library
- ○ C call-level library

○ COBOL call-level library

○ Fortran call-level library

Higher-Level Language

○ A higher-level language is available.

○ Higher-level language allows the expression of concepts not in the host language (C++, etc.).

○ Concepts expressed in the higher-level language can be automatically generated into host language (C++, etc.) declarations.

○ Concepts expressed in the higher-level language can be automatically generated into host language (C++, etc.) method code.

Languages for Simultaneous Access

Configurations of languages that permit instances populated by one language to be read, updated, and populated concurrently by another language (within locking restriction) are featured in this checklist. Other languages may be used via the C interfaces that most languages support. (See Graphic 3.2.)

○ C++

○ Objective-C

○ Eiffel

○ Smalltalk

○ CLOS

○ Java

○ C

○ Lisp

○ Ada

○ Fortran

○ COBOL

○ Other language

Same objects are cached in each of the application workspaces even though the clients use different programming languages.

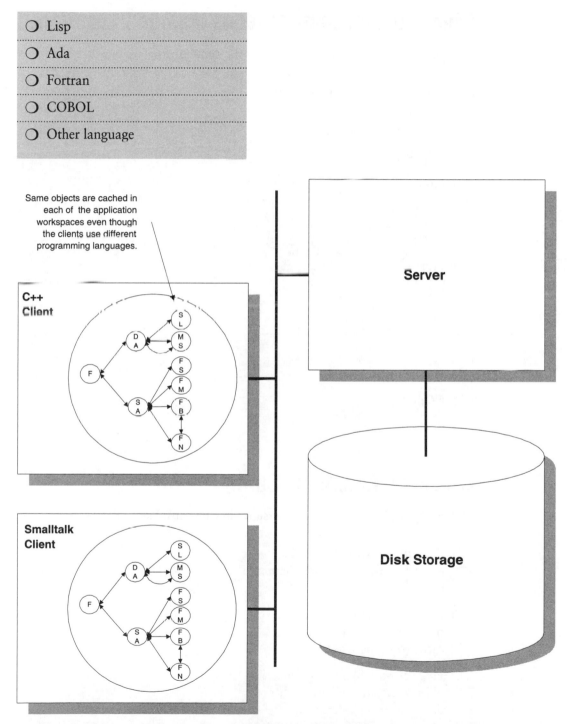

Graphic 3.2 *Simultaneous access using multiple programming languages.*

Languages for Simultaneous Method Execution

Configurations of languages that permit the simultaneous execution of the same database method from multiple languages are covered in this checklist. Other languages may be used via the C interfaces that most languages support.

○ C++

○ Objective-C

○ Eiffel

○ Smalltalk

○ CLOS

○ Java

○ C

○ Lisp

○ Ada

○ Fortran

○ COBOL

○ Other language

Language Reference Safety

"Object Identifier to Pointer Conversion" in Checklist 2 should also be checked.

○ Program variables referencing objects remain valid after commit if locks are retained.

○ Program variables referencing objects remain valid after de-cache (re-fetch object).

○ Program variables referencing objects remain valid after other database or site reference.

Language Type Safety

○ Relationships maintained with type-safety so that compile-time errors occur upon attempting an incorrect type reference.

○ References to all subtypes of same base class allowed dynamically at run-time

Code Management

○ Tracks or manages which applications are using which attributes

○ Tracks or manages which applications are using which methods

○ Manages methods on the server or in the database independent of applications

| **CHECKLIST 4** | Data Schema and Schema Evolution |

This checklist deals with the schema, which is the definition of the data along with what facilities the ODBMS has to allow the schema to evolve or change over time.

Types and Classes

See Chapter 1 for a description of classes.

○ Objects may be grouped into types by commonality of behavior (interface) or into classes by commonality of implementations.

○ Support for classes as first-class objects that may be manipulated in a manner similar to instances.

Binding and Polymorphism

This may be provided by the object programming languages.

○ Support for polymorphism to allow overloading of operations

○ Support for early binding at compile-time

○ Support for late binding at run-time

Inheritance and Delegation

○ Support for deriving new definitions from existing ones by either inheritance or delegation

○ Multiple inheritance in database manager for languages that support multiple inheritance

Logical and Physical View

○ Provides a logical view that allows the mapping of the physical view (byte layout, pointers, floating point number layouts, etc.) without affecting application

○ Allows direct access of the physical view (byte layout, pointers, floating point number formats, etc.)

Schema Update Time

The timing of schema changes may be important to your application. You may have an application that needs to make schema changes dynamically. On the other hand, monitoring on the part of the ODBMS for such dynamic changes may be unnecessary overhead for your application.

Deferred update or lazy evaluation of data instances—schema changes occur immediately, but data changes only upon first read of the data.

○ Automatically without requiring conversion code to be written

○ By writing conversion code as a method or some type of filter

Immediate update of data instances—schema changes occur immediately, and all data changes also as a result of the schema change.

○ Automatically without requiring conversion code to be written

○ By writing conversion code as a method or some type of filter

Batch update of data instances—schema changes and all data changes occur when the database is offline.

○ Automatically without requiring conversion code to be written

○ By writing conversion code as a method or some type of filter

Schema Change Method

○ Schema changes can be issued from within a program.

○ Schema changes can be issued interactively.

○ Schema changes can be made using a graphical user interface.

○ Schema changes can be made using a batch tool to process program header files into schema changes or other data definitions.

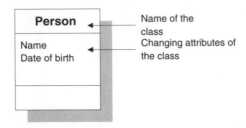

Graphic 4.1 *Changes to attributes.*

Changes to Attributes

Graphic 4.1 shows the part of the class structure affected by changing attributes.

Add a New Attribute to a Class

- ○ With the system offline
- ○ With active users online
- ○ Without recompiling applications that use the class/type or a sub-class/subtype
- ○ Without requiring an unload and reload of class instances

Drop an Existing Attribute from a Class

- ○ With the system offline
- ○ With active users online
- ○ Without recompiling applications that do not depend on the attribute.
- ○ Without requiring an unload and reload of class instances

Change the Name of an Attribute of a Class

- ○ With the system offline
- ○ With active users online
- ○ With recompiling only those applications that use the attribute
- ○ Without requiring an unload and reload of class instances

Change the Domain of an Attribute of a Class

- ○ With the system offline
- ○ With active users online
- ○ With recompiling only those applications that use the attribute
- ○ Without requiring an unload and reload of class instances

Change the Default Value of an Attribute

- ○ With the system offline
- ○ With active users online
- ○ Without recompiling applications that use the class/type or a sub-class/subtype
- ○ Without requiring an unload and reload of class instances

Add a Shared Value Attribute

○ With the system offline

○ With active users online

○ Without recompiling applications that use the class/type or a sub-class/subtype

○ Without requiring an unload and reload of class instances

Change a Shared Value Attribute

○ With the system offline

○ With active users online

○ Without recompiling applications that use the class/type or a sub-class/subtype

○ Without requiring an unload and reload of class instances

Drop a Shared Value of an Attribute

○ With the system offline

○ With active users online

○ Without recompiling applications that use the class/type or a sub-class/subtype

○ Without requiring an unload and reload of class instances

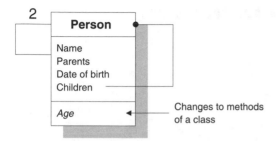

Graphic 4.2 *Changes to methods of a class.*

Changes to Database Methods

Graphic 4.2 shows the part of the class structure affected by changing methods.

Add a New Method to a Class

- ○ With the system offline
- ○ With active users online
- ○ Without recompiling applications that use the class/type or a sub-class/type
- ○ Without requiring an unload and reload of class instances

Drop an Existing Method from a Class

- ○ With the system offline
- ○ With active users online
- ○ With recompiling only those applications that use the method
- ○ Without requiring an unload and reload of class instances

Change the Name of a Method for a Class

- ○ With the system offline
- ○ With active users online
- ○ With recompiling only those applications that use the method
- ○ Without requiring an unload and reload of class instances

Change the Code of a Method for a Class

- ○ With the system offline
- ○ With active users online
- ○ Without recompiling applications that use the class/type or a sub-class/subtype
- ○ Without requiring an unload and reload of class instances

Change the Inheritance of a Method

- ○ With the system offline
- ○ With active users online
- ○ Without recompiling applications that use the class/type or a sub-class/subtype
- ○ Without requiring an unload and reload of class instances

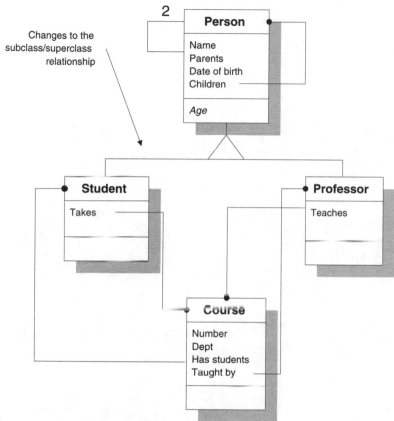

Graphic 4.3 *Changes to the subclass/superclass relationship.*

Changes to the Superclass/Subclass Relationship

Graphic 4.3 shows the location of subclass/superclass changes using the notation.

Add a New Superclass or Supertype to an Existing Class

This is illustrated in Graphic 4.4 where new classes of Employee and Teacher are added above Professor and a new class of Instructor is added as a leaf node.

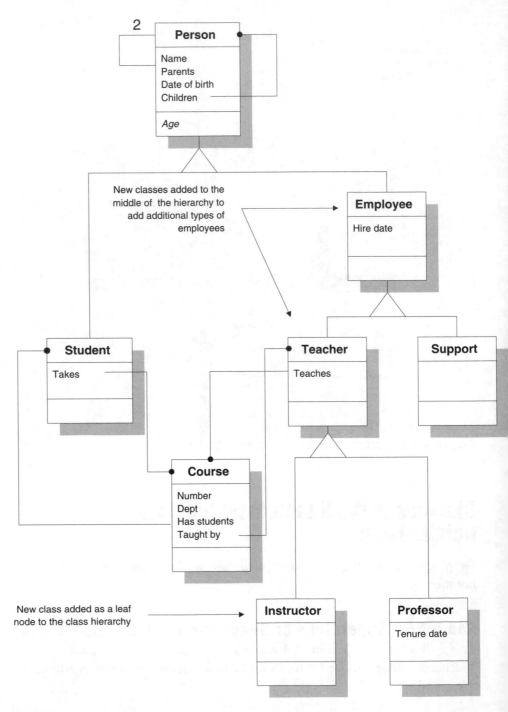

Graphic 4.4 *Adding new classes to an existing class hierarchy.*

- ○ With the system offline

- ○ With active users online

- ○ Without recompiling applications that use the class/type or a sub-class/subtype

- ○ At a leaf node in the class hierarchy

- ○ At any level in the class hierarchy

- ○ Regardless of whether there are instances in the existing class

- ○ Without requiring an unload and reload of class instances

Remove a Superclass or Supertype from Another Class

- ○ With the system offline

- ○ With active users online

- ○ With recompiling only those applications that use either attributes or methods that were inherited only from the class removed

- ○ At a leaf node in the class hierarchy

- ○ At any level in the class hierarchy

- ○ Regardless of whether there are instances in the existing class

- ○ Without requiring an unload and reload of class instances

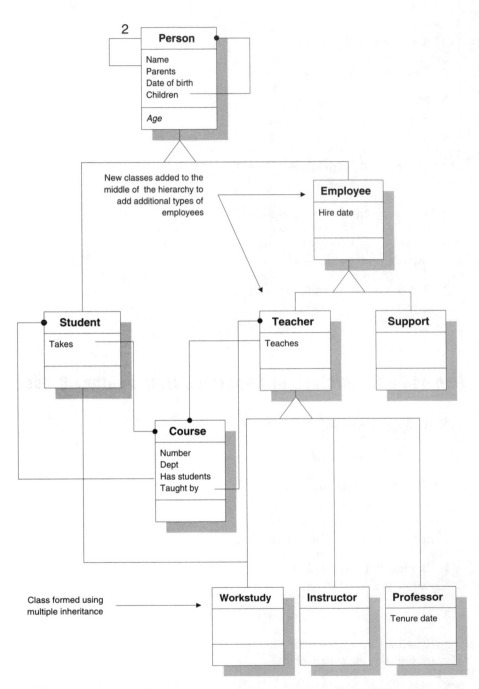

Graphic 4.5 *Multiple inheritance.*

Change the Order of the Superclasses or Supertypes of a Class

Being able to change the order of superclasses is used for multiple inheritance conflict resolution. Figure 4.5 illustrates the Workstudy class formed by multiple inheritance from Employee and Student.

○ With the system offline

○ With active users online

○ Without recompiling applications that use the class/type or a subclass/subtype

○ Regardless of whether there are instances in the existing class

○ Without requiring an unload and reload of class instances

Add a New Class

○ With the system offline

○ With active users online

○ With recompiling only those applications that will use the new class

○ At a leaf node in the class hierarchy

○ At any level in the class hierarchy

○ Without requiring an unload and reload of other class instances

Drop an Existing Class

O With the system offline

O With active users online

O With recompiling only those applications that used the class

O At a leaf node in the class hierarchy

O At any level in the class hierarchy

O Regardless of whether there are instances in the existing class

O Without requiring an unload and reload of class instances

Change the Name of a Class

O With the system offline

O With active users online

O With recompiling only those applications that reference the class by its name

O Regardless of whether there are instances in the existing class

O Without requiring an unload and reload of class instances

Create a New Class as a Generalized Superclass/Supertype of Existing Classes/Types

○ With the system offline

○ With active users online

○ With recompiling only those applications that reference the affected classes

○ Regardless of whether there are instances in the existing class

○ Without requiring an unload and reload of class instances

Partition a Class into New Classes

○ With the system offline

○ With active users online

○ With recompiling only those applications that reference the affected classes

○ Regardless of whether there are instances in the existing class

○ By executing a program to move instances into the new classes

○ Without writing a program to move instances into the new classes should the instances need moving

○ Without requiring an unload and reload of class instances

Coalesce Classes into One New Class

○ With the system offline

○ With active users online

○ With recompiling only those applications that reference the affected classes

○ Regardless of whether there are instances in the existing class

○ By executing a program to move instances into the new classes

○ Without writing a program to move instances into the new classes should the instances need moving

○ Without requiring an unload and reload of class instances

Multiple Schema

○ Multiple, independent schema or subschema can exist in the same logical database.

○ Multiple, independent schema or subschema can exist in private workspace or database.

○ Multiple, independent schema or subschema can be merged into one schema.

Versions of Schema

- ○ Support for playing "what if" with new classes
- ○ Support for versions of class definitions

CHECKLIST 5 Queries and Query Languages

Query Language

Also check "ODMG-93 Compliance" and "SQL-92 Compliance" in Checklist 1.

- ○ Provides a declarative data manipulation language
- ○ Provides associative access
- ○ Query parser recognizes user-defined classes
- ○ Query parser recognizes user-defined methods
- ○ Ability to query both the class definitions (meta-data) as well as the data
- ○ Ability to query over references (path queries such as father.hair.color) as well as simple data items
- ○ Ability to execute programming language methods as part of the query

Query Language Invocation

- ○ Possible to invoke query language from command line interface
- ○ Possible to invoke query language through interactive interface

Query Language Invocation from Programming Language

It is possible to invoke the query language from the programming language. Support for C would also mean any languages that support C function call libraries.

○ C++

○ Objective-C

○ Eiffel

○ Smalltalk

○ CLOS

○ Java

○ C

○ Lisp

○ Ada

○ Fortran

○ COBOL

○ Other language

Programming Language Invocation

It is possible to invoke the programming language from the query language. Generally, languages such as Fortran can also use C function call libraries.

○ C++

○ Objective-C

○ Eiffel

○ Smalltalk

○ CLOS

○ Java

◯ C
◯ Lisp
◯ Ada
◯ Fortran
◯ COBOL
◯ Other language

Query Implementation

◯ Small query results (a few objects) used in the same manner as large query results (billions of objects)
◯ Large query results (billions of objects) handled in a different manner from small query results (a few objects)
◯ The instances in a query result set are always locked
◯ The instances in a query result set are not locked

Data Updates and Queries

◯ Query processing within a single transaction checks both the data in the database and data changed but not committed to the database by the application executing the transaction.	*Generally, this is the most desired approach.*

○ Query processing requires the application to flush data, but not necessarily commit the data, before the updated data can be checked for the query.	*This can sometimes be a problem when developing applications.*
○ Query processing requires any updates to be committed to the database by the application before the data can be checked for the query.	*This can sometimes be a problem for application development because it may not always work well to commit the data before a query.*

Query Processing Location

See Chapter 8 for a discussion of the importance of the query processing location. (See Graphic 5.1.)

○ In the server(s)

○ In the client/application

Query Scope

Also check "Distributed Query Processing" in Checklist 9.

○ Query restriction to a private workspace or database

○ Query restriction to only the shared workspace or database

○ Query restriction to one private workspace or database and the shared workspace or database

○ Query restriction to selected private workspaces or databases

○ Query restriction to selected private workspaces or databases and the shared workspace or database

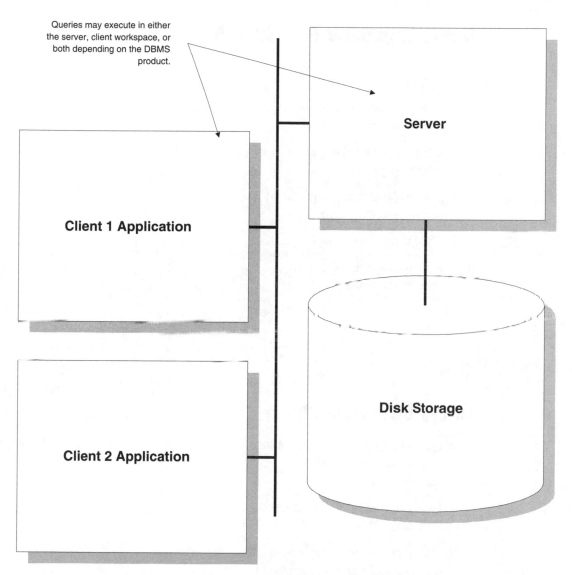

Queries may execute in either the server, client workspace, or both depending on the DBMS product.

Client 1 Application

Server

Client 2 Application

Disk Storage

Graphic 5.1 *Queries may execute in the client or server depending on the ODBMS product.*

- ○ Query restriction to a logical database that is a subset of the physical database
- ○ Query scope to be defined using collections

Query Language Text Search

- ○ Supports pattern matching of text
- ○ Supports boolean logic in combination with pattern matching
- ○ Supports wildcard option for text search
- ○ Supports searching on proximity of words or characters
- ○ Thesaurus support
- ○ Indexing of text contents to support the pattern matching of text

Query Optimization

- ○ Query processor automatically selects best access methods to use for the query.
- ○ Query optimization uses database statistics.
- ○ Query optimizer attempts to take advantage of parallel processing in a distributed network.
- ○ Run-time query optimization.
- ○ Compile-time query optimization.
- ○ Query optimizer can estimate query costs when no methods are involved.

○ Query optimizer can estimate query costs when methods are used in the query.

○ Query optimizer can detect if methods have side effects.

○ Query explain facility to explain the query optimizer's choice

○ Possible to override the query optimizer's access choices

Indexing

○ Ability to define indexes on attributes

○ Ability to define multi-key indexes using two or more attributes

○ Ability to inherit indexes on inherited attributes—sometimes called a *class-hierarchy index*

○ Ability to define indexes for a series of relationships—sometimes called a *path index*

○ Ability to define indexes for a set valued instance variables

○ Ability to dynamically add and remove indexes when a database is in production

○ Ad hoc queries use index

○ Ability to use index for range queries (B-Trees)

Access Methods

○ B-trees

○ Hashing

○ Heaps

○ Other access methods

○ Ability to create new access methods

○ Optimizer understands costs of new access methods

CHECKLIST 6	Concurrency and Recovery

This Checklist covers many of the things that affect how the multi-user environment operates.

Standard Concurrency Control

O Optimistic		*This assumes that simultaneous access to same objects is quite rare and conflicts are checked only at commit-time. Conflicts may result in an abort or restart. This can also be achieved by version branching.*
O Pessimistic		*Checks for access conflicts at the time the lock is requested with some locks queued until the conflicts are resolved. No conflicts are present at commit-time.*
O Concurrency control can be turned off at the system level.		
O Concurrency control can be turned off at the session level.		

Advanced Concurrency Control

O Many readers, one writer (MROW)		*Multiple readers read the pre-state of an object concurrently with one exclusive writer; also called non-blocking read consistency.*
O Read only mode		*Transactions read committed data and never interfere with read-write transactions.*

○ Many readers, many writers	*Conflicts controlled at a sub-object level.*
○ An application can be limited in the time it can hold a granted lock.	

Custom Concurrency Control

○ Custom DBMS concurrency	*It is possible to define custom concurrency control for the entire database manager.*
○ Custom logical database concurrency	*Define custom concurrency control for logical databases managed by the ODBMS.*
○ Custom class concurrency	*It is possible to define custom concurrency control on a class basis.*
○ Custom application concurrency	*It is possible to define custom concurrency control on an application basis.*

Deadlocks

Deadlocks are sometimes called the "deadly embrace." They occur when Process 1 has a lock on object A and wants object B, but Process 2 has a lock on object B and wants object A. One process has to give up by timing out on the wait request and releasing the lock so the other process can proceed.

○ Lock requests requiring polling

○ Lock requests queued

○ Deadlock detection

○ Time-outs supported

○ Time-out time can be adjusted at the system level.

O Time-out time can be adjusted at the application level.

O Time-out time can be adjusted at the class level.

O Support for application specific retry code upon lock conflict detection.

Instance Lock Modes

O S—lock an instance object in Shared mode for read

Shared mode means multiple users can "share" or read the same object at the same time.

O X—lock an instance object in Exclusive mode for update

Exclusive mode means that only the user holding the lock may read or write the objects—no other users have access to the object

Class Lock Modes

Not all products support this type of locking. It is particularly useful for online, dynamic schema changes.

O IS—lock the class definition in Intention Share mode for read and lock instance objects in S mode

O IX—lock a class definition in Intention Exclusive mode for update and instance objects in X mode

O S—lock a class definition for read and implicitly lock instance of the class in S mode

○ X—lock a class definition for update and implicitly lock instances of the class in X mode

○ SIX—lock a class definition for read, implicitly lock instances of the class in S mode, explicitly lock instance to be updated in X mode

Lock Granularity

See Chapter 8 for a discussion of how lock granularity can affect the performance of your application—particularly in a multi-user environment.

○ Data page

○ Index page

○ Group page

○ Segment

○ File

○ Object clusters or containers

○ Isolation of single objects for page or container locking

○ Single class

○ Single instance

○ Attribute of a single instance

Reference Lock Granularity

○ Locking an object locks objects pointed to by the references in the locked object

○ Locking an object does not lock objects pointed to by the references in the locked object.

○ Able to lock an entire composite object

Also check "Composite or Complex Objects" in Checklist 2

Lock Setting, Releasing, and Promotion

○ Locks set automatically by the system such as when an object is dereferenced

○ Locks released automatically by the system

○ Locks set explicitly by the application

○ Locks released explicitly by the application

○ Automatic promotion of locks from read locks to write locks based on activity

○ Automatic demotion of locks from write locks to read locks based on activity

○ Automatic lock escalation to higher granularity such as instance to class if many locked instances

Change Notification or Triggers

This involves notifying an application or person that some event has occurred in the database or triggering the execution of another method.

- ○ Method accessible through change notification or triggers

- ○ Events trigger method execution in the database workspace (active notification).

- ○ Active notification methods can be refined on a class basis.

- ○ Events raise a flag—change found by querying (passive notification)

- ○ Pre- and post-procedure invocation

- ○ Allows for deferred execution of change notification or trigger

- ○ Triggers or change notification can abort transactions.

- ○ Supports prioritization of change notification or triggers

- ○ Events can result in effects inside and outside the database.

Change Notification or Trigger Types Built-in

These are some of the more common events that could be monitored.

- ○ Instance creation notification
- ○ Instance update notification
- ○ Instance deletion or dereferencing notification
- ○ Instance query notification

○ Notification of a checkout of objects from one type of work-space or database to another

○ Notification of a checkin of objects from one type of work-space or database to another

○ Make version notification

Change Notification or Trigger Execution Location

○ In the server(s) (server-based)	*This is useful when methods also execute on the server. It is not necessary to determine all the possible methods that may be invoked ahead of time.*
○ In the client/application (client-based)	*This requires that any methods the notification requires also exist in the application workspace. This can become a problem when a method may invoke another method which in turn invokes yet another method. In such a case, it may hard to determine all the methods to include in your application on the client.*

Server-Based Change Notification or Trigger Language

○ C++

○ Smalltalk

- ○ CLOS
- ○ Java
- ○ C
- ○ Smalltalk language variant
- ○ Lisp
- ○ SQL
- ○ Other language

Client-Based Database Change Notification or Trigger Language

- ○ C++
- ○ Objective-C
- ○ Eiffel
- ○ Smalltalk
- ○ CLOS
- ○ Java
- ○ C
- ○ Smalltalk variant
- ○ Lisp
- ○ SQL
- ○ Other language

Alerters or Named Events

An alerter or named event notifies client applications of events that occur in the database. An application must declare its interest in an alerter or named event by listening for it.

○ Supports alerters or named events

○ Alerters or named events returns parameters or result sets

○ Client application receives notification by polling.

○ Client application receives notification via callbacks causing interrupts.

Checkin/Checkout of Objects

Some products allow objects to be checked in or out of a private workspace or allow some other way of partitioning the database. This makes it possible to keep some instances private when they are checked out.

○ Private instances can be checked in for shared use.

○ Private instances MUST be checked in for shared use access.

○ Private classes can be checked in for shared use.

○ Private classes MUST be checked in for shared use access.

○ Shared instances can be checked out for private use.

○ Shared classes can be checked out for private use.

Audit Trail

○ Supports an audit trail as part of the logging facility

○ Audit trail events may be customized.

Disk Media Protection

Also check "Replication Type" in Checklist 9.

○ Supports rollback recovery

○ Supports rollforward recovery

○ Dual copy disk mirroring provided by the DBMS or by the hardware/operating system

○ Disk media protection can be turned off at the system level.

○ Disk media protection can be turned off at the session level.

Backup Facilities

○ Tool to backup the database

○ Online backup supported

○ Online incremental backup supported

○ Supports distributed database-wide consistent backup

○ Supports online distributed database-wide consistent backup without quieting the DBMS

CHECKLIST 7 Transactions

This checklist provides details for the ACID properties described in Chapter 1. See that chapter for a description of Atomicity, Isolation, Consistency, and Durability.

Atomicity

○ A transaction is a unit of operation—either all the transaction's
   actions are completed or none is.

○ Maintains atomicity in the pres-
   ence of deadlocks

○ Maintains atomicity in the pres-
   ence of database software failures

○ Maintains atomicity in the pres-
   ence of application software failures

○ Maintains atomicity in the pres-
   ence of CPU failures

○ Maintains atomicity in the pres-
   ence of disk failures

*Also check "Disk Media Protec-
tion" in Checklist 6.*

○ Atomicity can be turned off at the
   system level.

○ Atomicity can be turned off at the
   session level.

Consistency

For more on dirty data, see the information on Isolation, also in checklist 7.

○ Degree 0—a transaction does not overwrite data updated by another user or process (dirty data) of other transactions

○ Degree 1—degree 0 plus a transaction does not commit any writes until it completes all its writes (until the end of transaction)

○ Degree 2—degree 1 plus a transaction does not read dirty data from other transactions

○ Degree 3—degree 2 plus other transactions do not dirty data read by a transaction before the transaction commits

Isolation

○ A transaction does not reveal its results to other concurrent transactions until it commits—this eliminates the possibility of lost updates.

○ A transaction allows the option of reading of old copies of data updated by another user or process (dirty data) and allows the updating of that dirty data—this allows the possibility of lost updates.

○ A transaction allows the reading of dirty data, but disallows the updating of that dirty data even after a commit by another user or process—erroneous updates can still occur if the update is to some other data item and is based on the dirty data.

Durability

○ Recovery to the most recent successful commit after a database software failure

○ Recovery to the most recent successful commit after an application software failure

○ Recovery to the most recent successful commit after a CPU failure

○ Recovery to the most recent successful backup after a disk failure

○ Recovery to the most recent successful commit after a data disk failure

Also check Disk Media Protection in Checklist 6.

Transaction Characteristics

○ Commit or rollback

○ Checkpoint commit—the ability to retain the same locks after the transaction commits

○ Pinning and unpinning of objects in the cache during a transaction

○ Savepoints—the ability to establish intermediate points to rollback to instead of having to rollback to the beginning of the transaction

○ Revert—abort, but retain locks

○ DBMS maintains and uses the cache after a commit within the DBMS concurrency mechanisms—cache not always flushed automatically

Long Transactions

Also see "Checkin/Checkout of Objects" in Checklist 6.

○ Support long transactions that can last hours, weeks, months, and so on.

This is the basic definition of a long transaction.

○ Span sessions and processes

○ Support persistent long transactions—the long transaction can span system shutdowns or failures.

○ Contain short transactions—short transactions may occur within the long transaction.

○ Support persistent locks that are owned by a user (or something other than the process) spanning sessions and processes

○ Support long transaction commit or rollback

Shared Transactions

○ Multiple users or processes may participate in the same transaction without locking while logged on to the same machine.

○ Multiple users or processes may participate in the same transaction without locking while logged on to different machines.

○ Users or processes may join or depart shared transactions at any time.

Nested Short Transactions

○ Commits and aborts at one nested level automatically commit or abort the inner nested transaction.

○ Commits and aborts at one nested level do not automatically commit or abort the inner nested transaction.

○ Inner transactions must commit or abort before outer transactions.

○ Locks held by an inner transaction are released upon that transaction's commit or abort.

○ Concurrency control and locking are enforced among nested transactions.

This Checklist covers versions of objects. This capability is helpful to keep versions of things over time. Examples could be configurations of a part of employee salary histories.

If your application can use versions, look at what the vendors provide. The vendor version capability can save you a tremendous amount of development effort. Be forewarned, however, that there are no standards for such version capability and the vendors implement versions in quite different ways. Make sure that your requirements for versioning match the vendor's version capability.

Version Implementation

This covers the basics of version implementation and the terminology used. Graphic 8.1 shows the versions of a Fram Sensor part.

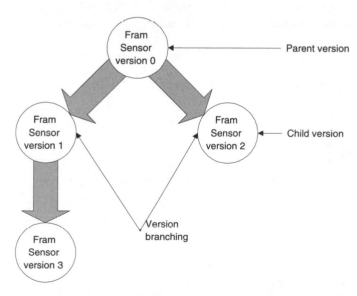

Graphic 8.1 *Version hierarchy and version branching.*

○ Support for alternative versions or branching	
○ Support for restricting alternative versions or branching so that versioning is linear	
○ Support for accessing the version genealogy	*This is the parent and child relationship shown in Graphic 8.1.*
○ Support for status enforcement— only certain version status transitions are allowed.	*An example of a status would be such user-defined statuses as "alpha," "beta," or "released" status. It may not be valid, for example, to move directly from "alpha" to "released."*
○ Support for status upgrade and downgrade	*Upgrade promotes a version from a "alpha" to a "beta" status. Downgrade demotes from "beta" to "alpha."*
○ Storage of only the deltas of versions within an instance rather than making complete instance copies	*Deltas here refer to just the portions of versions that changed—not the entire version.*
○ Support for optionally compressing the deltas into one instance	

Version Binding

Other objects may point to the versioned object. These other objects can point to a specific version or they may be able to point to some type of generic object that always provides, for example, the most recent version of an object. See Graphic 8.2.

Version binding may be used for custom configurations. For automatic configurations, see the next checklist.

O Support for static version binding

O Support for dynamic version binding that references the most recent version

O Support for dynamic version binding that references the user-selected default version

O Support for dynamic version binding so that multiple users may have different contexts such as release 1.3 or release 2.1

Version Configurations

Support for configurations beyond versions requires some type of built-in policy for managing configurations. A configuration is versioning of versions, if

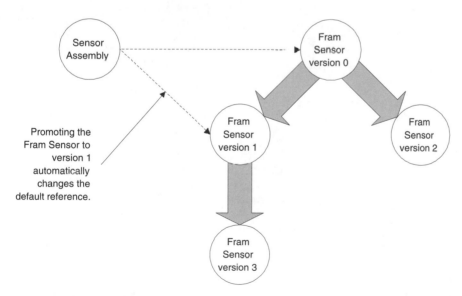

Graphic 8.2 *Version binding.*

you will. This allows for versioning a group of versioned objects. Graphic 8.3 shows various configurations of the Framastat described in Chapter 2.

○ Support for a collection of versions that are mutually consistent (configurations)

○ Support for "freezing" a configuration—making it read only

○ Support for accessing a specific configuration even when it is not the most recent

○ Support for configuration hierarchies

○ Support for branching of configurations

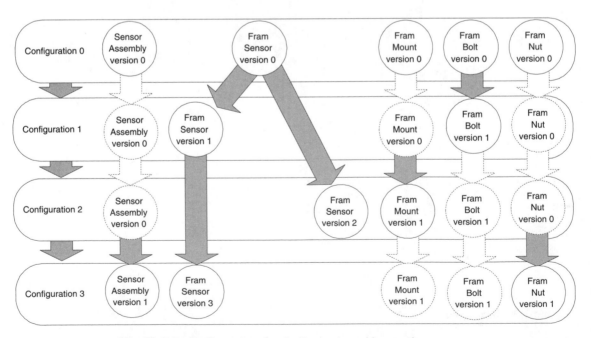

Graphic 8.3 *Configurations for the Sensor Assembly over time.*

○ Support for automatic merging of configurations

○ Support for customized merging of configurations

○ Support for resurrecting object deleted in previous configurations for use in another configuration

Version Configuration Streams

○ Support for named configuration streams—a path through a configuration hierarchy

○ Support for a default named configuration stream

○ Support for overlapping streams—for example, between development and release configurations

○ Support for discontiguous streams—for example between development and release configurations

Version Granularity

Class-level versioning

○ Support for specifying versioning at the time the class is defined

○ Support for turning versioning on after the class has been populated with instances

○ Support for turning versioning off once it was turned on for a class

Instance-level versioning that allows some instances of a class to be versioned while others are not

○ Support for specifying instance-level versioning at the time the instance is created

○ Support for turning instance-level versioning on for an existing non-versioned instance

○ Support for turning instance-level versioning off once it was turned on for an instance

Version Merging

It is often desirable to merge the alternate versions by taking only part of the data from each of the parent versions. (See Graphic 8.4.) This checklist covers some of the support in the ODBMS that may be available for doing this.

○ Support for automatically merging versions

○ Support for custom methods for merging versions—these should have a recognizable name to be automatically invoked by the DBMS.

○ Support for application-based merging of versions, but with the resulting merge available in the version genealogy

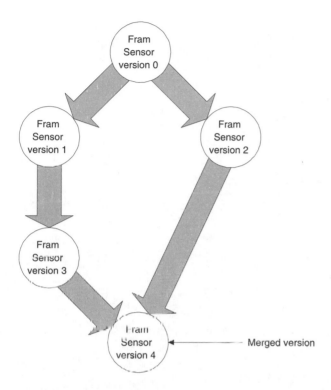

Graphic 8.4 *Version merging.*

Version Extensibility

These kernel-level operations may be extended using methods, functions, or some other mechanism so that the behavior is modified, yet the interface is unchanged.

- ○ Database kernel method for making new versions may be refined to provide customized behavior.

- ○ Database kernel method for making new versions may be refined on a class basis.

- ○ Database kernel method for promoting versions may be refined to provide customized behavior.

○ Database kernel method for promoting versions may be refined on a class basis.

○ Database kernel method for demoting versions may be refined to provide customized behavior.

○ Database kernel method for demoting versions may be refined on a class basis.

Version Queries

Since versions create many of what might be thought of as the same object, it is important to understand how you might query versioned objects and what the results might look like.

○ Versioned objects may be indexed.

○ Queries on versions return all versions that meet the query criteria—even if they are all versions of the same object.

○ Queries on versions return only one version that meets the query criteria—even if there are multiple versions of the same object that might meet the query criteria.

CHECKLIST 9 Distributed Database Systems

This checklist covers distributed database systems. The term "distributed" is used loosely by many vendors. Use the detail in this checklist to see what is really meant by "distributed" for the products you are considering and then consider what is important for your application needs.

Location Independence

One feature of a distributed DBMS is that the application does not need to know where data is located in the distributed environment. Graphic 9.1 illustrates how data can be moved from storage on one server to another server without impacting the way the data looks to the client application.

○ No need for an application to know where data is physically stored

○ Objects can be migrated to another physical location without impacting application code.

○ Database at one location can be migrated to another without impacting application code.

○ Objects stored at one site can reference objects stored at another site in the distributed database.

○ Movement of objects among sites does not invalidate references between objects.

○ Movement of objects among sites requires resetting references possibly after copying the objects.

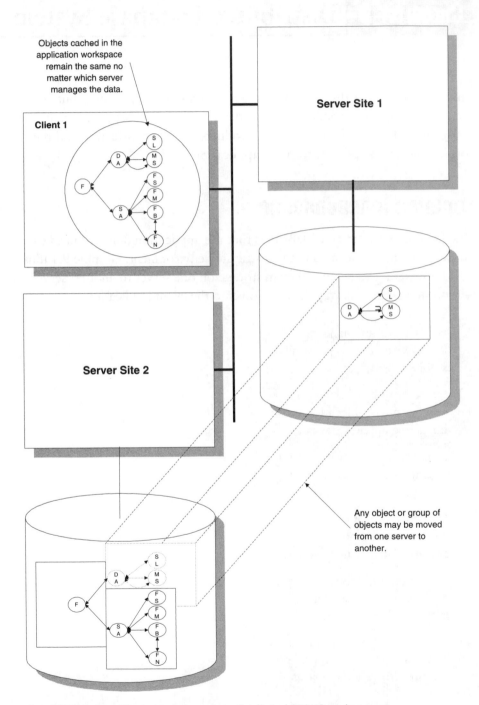

Objects cached in the application workspace remain the same no matter which server manages the data.

Client 1

Server Site 1

Server Site 2

Any object or group of objects may be moved from one server to another.

Graphic 9.1 *Location independence in a distributed ODBMS environment.*

Local Autonomy at Each Site

This checklist focuses on features that keep each site as separate as possible so that other activities can continue locally should a site go down.

○ Local database

○ Local users

○ Local locking

○ Local logging

○ Local recovery

○ Local communications manager

○ Local transaction manager

No Reliance on a Central Site

A central site can mean a single point of failure for the services provided at that site should it go down.

○ All sites are treated as equals.

○ No master site

○ No master global dictionary

Fragmentation Independence

○ Data can be stored at the location where it is most frequently used.

○ Data can be re-fragmented and re-distributed at any time in response to changing performance requirements.

○ Applications can act as if the data were in fact not fragmented.

○ Instances of a single class can be fragmented among multiple sites.

○ Attributes of a single instance can be fragmented among multiple sites.

Replication Independence

Schema replication

○ Schema represented at the physical level by many distinct copies stored at many distinct sites

○ Users can act as if the schema is not replicated at all.

Data replication

○ Data represented at the physical level by many distinct copies stored at many distinct sites

○ Users can act as if the data is not replicated at all.

Replication Type

This refers to data replication only.

○ Real-time—replication occurs as part of the same transaction

○ Store and forward—replication occurs on a periodic basis

○ Time-based—replication occurs at a set time of day

Replication Granularity

This refers to data replication only.

- ○ Entire database, all servers are replicated.

- ○ Selected servers, but all data at the server is replicated.

- ○ All instances of selected classes can be replicated.

- ○ Specific instances of selected classes can be replicated.

Detachable Databases

- ○ A subset of the database can be detached from the shared database yet retain all necessary schema information even if the schema is part of the shared database.

- ○ Multiple independent subsets of the database can be detached.

- ○ Detached databases can be attached to a new or existing database and all necessary schema information will transfer.

- ○ Detached databases can be used by themselves.

- ○ Detached databases can be re-attached to the original shared database.

Private Workspaces or Databases

○ Supports private workspaces or databases

○ Supports multiple levels of private workspaces or databases—group workspaces or databases in addition to the shared workspace or database

○ Allows concurrent users in a particular private workspace or database with full concurrency and locking

○ Allows concurrent users in a particular private workspace or database without concurrency and locking

○ Allows moving entire private databases among the sites in the distributed database

Private Objects in Shared Workspace or Database

○ Supports private subclasses/subtypes of classes/types in the shared workspace or database

○ Supports private instances in the shared workspace or database

Distributed Query Processing

○ Query optimization attempts to break a query into subgraphs for execution in parallel on multiple sites.

○ No need for an application to be aware that the query is being executed on multiple sites

○ A single query can obtain objects from multiple sites.

○ A query successfully returns even if one or more nodes are unavailable—it may also return a message indicating results may be incomplete.

○ Ability to define access methods transparently across multiple sites in a distributed database—it is not necessary to specify the site identifications.

○ Access methods at multiple sites must be defined separately for each site.

Distributed Transaction Management

○ All sites involved in a transaction either commit in unison or rollback.

○ Distributed concurrency control

○ Coordination of recovery at distributed sites

○ Two-phase commit

Also check the next checklist on Two-phase commit optimization.

○ Distributed deadlock detection

Two-Phase Commit Optimization

○ Read-only commit optimization that detects read-only subtransactions that need not participate in the callback portions of prepare, commit, or abort phases

○ Lazy commit optimization where messages and disk writes are piggy-backed

○ Linear commit optimization to arrange subtransactions so that prepare and commit propagate down and back up a chain of participants

Server or Peer Hardware Heterogeneity

○ Aviion

Alpha

   ○ Open VMS

   ○ OSF/1

   ○ NT

   ○ DECStation

HP 9000

   ○ 300/700

- ○ 400/800
- ○ IBM RS 6000 or BULL DPX/2
- ○ MIPS Ultrix

NCR

- ○ System V.4
- ○ 3300
- ○ SGI
- ○ NeXT
- ○ Novell NetWare

Sequent

- ○ NT
- ○ Unix

SPARC

- ○ Solaris 2.0 +
- ○ SunOS

VAX

- ○ Ultrix
- ○ VMS

Intel

- ○ OS/2
- ○ Windows
- ○ NT
- ○ SCO
- ○ MS-DOS
- ○ NeXT Step
- ○ Solaris 2.0

○ Mac

Network Heterogeneity

"Networks Supported" in this category may also be of help.

○ TCP/IP

○ Banyan Vines

○ Microsoft LAN manager

○ Novell Netware

○ DECnet

○ Other

Wide Area Network Support

○ Protocol for addressing among the distributed sites on WAN

○ Strategy for resolving partitioned wide area networks

○ If Wide Area Network fails, local processing can continue.

This checklist refers to existing data managed by another DBMS that is external to the ODBMS.

DBMS Access

Use this checklist for each external DBMS.

○ Read data in the external DBMS from within the ODBMS	
○ Write data in external DBMS from within the ODBMS	
○ External DBMS instances appear as object instances in the ODBMS to the application.	*To the application, ODBMS objects and objects representing external DBMS entities would appear the same.*
○ Changes made to object instances representing external DBMS instances are also automatically made in the ODBMS.	
○ External DBMS access is from the application or client.	*The application will be responsible for interrelating ODBMS objects to objects representing external DBMS entities. This is shown as path 1 in Graphic 10.1.*
○ External DBMS access is from the ODBMS server.	*References from ODBMS objects to objects representing external DBMS entities could be stored in the ODBMS. This is shown as path 2 in Graphic 10.1*
○ Allows schema changes to external DBMS from within vendor product	

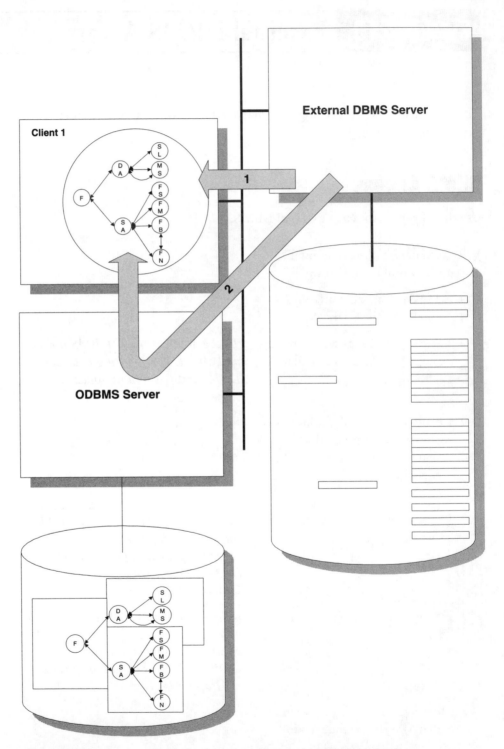

Graphic 10.1 *Two possible paths for external data to be treated as objects.*

DBMSs Simultaneously Open

These are configurations of DBMSs that can be open simultaneously.

○ DB2

○ Ingres

○ Informix

○ Oracle

○ Sybase

○ IDMS

○ IMS

○ VSAM

○ Flat File

○ Other

Multi-DBMS Queries

These are configurations of DBMSs that can participate in a multi-database query.

○ DB2

○ Ingres

○ Informix

○ Oracle

○ Sybase

○ IDMS

○ IMS

○ VSAM

○ Flat File

○ Other

Multi-DBMS Joins

These are configurations of DBMSs that can simultaneously participate in a relational join.

○ DB2

○ Ingres

○ Informix

○ Oracle

○ Sybase

○ IDMS

○ IMS

○ VSAM

○ Flat File

○ Other

Multi-DBMS Updates

Configurations of DBMSs that can participate in a multi-database update are covered in this checklist.

○ DB2

○ Ingres

○ Informix

○ Oracle

○ Sybase

○ IDMS

○ IMS

○ VSAM

○ Flat File

○ Other

Multi-DBMS Updates with Two-Phase Commit

Configurations of DBMSs that can participate in a multi-database update using two-phase commit across product boundaries are covered in this checklist.

- ○ DB2
- ○ Ingres
- ○ Informix
- ○ Oracle
- ○ Sybase
- ○ IDMS
- ○ IMS
- ○ VSAM
- ○ Flat File
- ○ Other

Multi-DBMS Schema Integration

Configurations of DBMSs that can participate in a global schema definition are covered in this checklist.

- ○ DB2
- ○ Ingres
- ○ Informix
- ○ Oracle
- ○ Sybase
- ○ IDMS
- ○ IMS
- ○ VSAM
- ○ Flat File
- ○ Other

Multi-DBMS Schema Integration Conflict Resolution

Configurations of DBMSs that can participate in a global schema with underlying database schema conflict resolution are covered in the following checklist.

Schema conflict resolution refers to those situations when two fields in two different DBMS have the same data but in some different format. For example, say hotels are rated on a 1 to 3 scale in one database and rated on a 1 to 5 scale in another. Schema conflict resolution must come up with a way to create one global meaning for the two different scales on the same subject in two different DBMSs.

- ○ DB2
- ○ Ingres
- ○ Informix
- ○ Oracle
- ○ Sybase
- ○ IDMS
- ○ IMS
- ○ VSAM
- ○ Flat File
- ○ Other

CHECKLIST 11 | Security Authorization

This checklist has to do with the facilities available for authorizing access to the data stored in the ODBMS.

Security Granularity

This is the size of the unit upon which security can be assigned. Generally, the finer the granularity, the higher the overhead. On the other hand, you may not want to have to manage security solely at a database or file level because it may not give you the flexibility you might need.

- ○ Database
- ○ File or partition
- ○ Page
- ○ Segment
- ○ Schema
- ○ Class
- ○ Instance
- ○ Attribute
- ○ Value of attribute
- ○ Method execution
- ○ Long data or large binary objects

U.S. Department Of Defense Certified Security Compliance

discretionary protection
○ C1
○ C2
mandatory protection
○ B1
○ B2
○ B3
verified design
○ A

Security Implementation

This covers how security authorization is implemented for the ODBMS.

○ Uses security of underlying operating system
○ Uses internal software security in addition to or instead of underlying operating system
○ Custom security can be coded into the class hierarchy or in access methods.
○ Protects DBMS objects in program address space

Encoding of Schema and Method Definitions

○ Supports encoding of schema definitions so that the definitions are encoded

○ Supports encoding of method definitions so that the definitions are encoded

Private or Personal Database/Workspace Authorization

○ Supports private workspaces or databases only accessible by the owner of the private workspace or database

○ Owner of private workspace or database may authorize other user access to the private workspace or database.

○ Authorized users other than the owner of a private workspace or database may authorize other user access to the private workspace or database.

User or Role Authorization

○ Authorization attached to a user

○ Authorization is attached to a role

○ Users may have more than one role.

○ A role may inherit authorizations from one or more parent roles.

Implicit Authorization

○ Class authorization implies subclass or subtype authorization.

○ Class authorization implies instance authorization.

○ Class authorization implies method authorization.

○ Instance authorization implies attribute authorization.

○ Write authorization implies read authorization.

Positive and Negative Authorization

○ Positive authorization	*Lack of an authorization on an object means that a role/user cannot access the object.*
○ Negative authorization	*A role/user may be denied access to an object because the role/user has a negative authorization on the object.*

Strong and Weak Authorization

○ Strong authorization	*Guarantees that it and all of the authorizations it implies cannot be overridden.*
○ Weak authorization	*May be overridden by other authorizations.*

Day and Time Authorization

○ Authorization by time of day

○ Authorization by day of week

○ Authorization by a combination of time of day and day of week

CHECKLIST 12	Tools

Schema Browsing/Editing Tools

- ○ Forms-based schema browsing tool (no editing)
- ○ Forms-based schema browsing and editing tools
- ○ Diagram-based schema browsing tool (no editing)
- ○ Diagram-based schema browsing and editing tool
- ○ Multiple schema browsing/editing tools may be executed simultaneously.

Data Browsing/Editing Tools

- ○ Forms-based data browsing tool (no editing)
- ○ Forms-based data browsing and editing tools
- ○ Diagram-based data browsing tool (no editing)
- ○ Diagram-based data browsing and editing tool
- ○ Multiple data browsing/editing tools may be executed simultaneously.

Query Tools

○ Integration with DBMS so that there is no need to retype attribute or member function names

○ Interactive forms-based queries

○ Interactive diagram-based queries

○ Query by example

○ Supports path queries

○ Supports query refinement based on the results of an earlier query

○ Allows query definitions to be saved for future use

○ Multiple query tools may be executed simultaneously.

Version Browsing/Editing Tools

○ Forms-based version browsing tool (no editing)

○ Forms-based version browsing and editing tools

○ Diagram-based version browsing tool (no editing)

○ Diagram-based version browsing and editing tool

○ Multiple version browsing and editing tools may be executed simultaneously.

Screen Development Tools

○ Database manager integration so that there is no need to retype attribute or member function names

This means that attribute or member function names are available in some representation other than manual entry — probably icons or buttons that can be dragged onto the screen being developed.

○ Automatic generation of default screens based on class definition

○ Screen definitions can be edited interactively

○ A single screen can use data from more than one class

○ Provides OSF/Motif look-and-feel

○ Multiple screen development tools may be executed simultaneously

Report Writer

○ Integration with database manager so that there is no need to retype attribute or member function names

○ Automatic generation of default reports based on class definition

○ Report definitions can be edited interactively.

○ A single report can use data from more than one class.

○ Generates graphics such as pie charts and bar graphs

○ Multiple report writer tools may be executed simultaneously.

Multimedia Tools

○ Manipulation of data in image classes

○ Manipulation of data in audio classes

○ Manipulation of data in text classes

○ Manipulation of full-motion video classes

○ Manipulation of other large binary data

○ Hyper-linking among multimedia data

○ Multiple multimedia tools may be executed simultaneously.

DBA Tools

○ Initializing sites

○ Monitoring status of database sites

○ Monitoring status of transactions

○ Clearing of locks

○ Monitoring disk space usage

○ Viewing of the physical layout of object on disk

○ Viewing of the physical clustering of objects on disk

○ Multiple DBA tools may execute simultaneously.

Statistics

○ Data types and storage location

○ Access frequency

○ Access type

Tuning

○ Allows setting page size or minimum unit of disk transfer

○ Allows setting segment size

○ Allows setting cache size

CASE Tool Integration

○ Database schema generated by CASE tool

○ Database schema can be imported to CASE tool

○ Database method code generated by CASE tool

○ Database method code can be imported to CASE tool

○ Entire application can be generated by CASE tool.

4GL

- ○ Employs the database management system directly

- ○ Nonprofessional programmer can obtain results with it.

- ○ Nonprocedural code is used where possible.

- ○ Interactive—designed for online operation

- ○ Designed for easy/interactive debugging

Rules

- ○ Supports backward chaining in DBMS

- ○ Supports forward chaining in DBMS

- ○ Supports truth maintenance in DBMS

- ○ Rules are not associated with a specific function or method in DBMS.

- ○ Rules are not associated with a specific collection in DBMS.

- ○ Ability to query about rules currently being enforced in DBMS

Expert System Integration

○ Implementations where the data-base manager invokes expert system from methods

○ Implementations where the data-base manager invokes expert system from within constraint mechanism

○ Implementations where the expert system uses the database manager

Internationalization

Internationalization of Interactive Tools

This checklist covers the degree of internationalization of tools, error messages, object names, and strings.

○ Interactive tool displays are in French

○ Interactive tool displays are in German

○ Interactive tool displays are in Kanji

○ Interactive tool displays are in Korean

○ Interactive tool displays are in Spanish

Internationalization of Batch Tools

○ Batch tool displays and commands are in French

○ Batch tool displays and commands are in German

○ Batch tool displays and commands are in Kanji

○ Batch tool displays and commands are in Korean

○ Batch tool displays and commands are in Spanish

Internationalization of Error Messages

○ Error messages are in French

○ Error messages are in German

○ Error messages are in Kanji

○ Error messages are in Korean

○ Error messages are in Spanish

Internationalization of Object Names and Strings

○ Object names can be localized

○ Strings can be localized

A p p e n d i x

Information on ODMG Standards

Postal Address:	14041 Burnhaven Drive, Suite 105
	Burnsville, MN 55337 USA
Voice:	+1-612-953-7250
Fax:	+1-612-397-7146
Email:	info@odmg.org
Web:	http://www.odmg.org

Information on OMG Standards

Postal Address:	Object Management Group
	Framingham Corporate Center
	492 Old Connecticut Path
	Framingham, MA 01701 USA
Voice:	+1-508-820-4300
Fax:	+1-508-820-4303
Email:	omg@omg.org
Web:	http://www.omg.org

Information on X3H2 Standards

X3 Secretariat, CBEMA
1250 Eye Street, NW, Suite 200
Washington, DC 20005-3922 USA

Books to Get Started

These are listed in the order they should be read.

Object-Oriented Technology: A Manager's Guide, David A. Taylor, Addison-Wesley, 1992, ISBN 0-201-56358-4.

Object Databases: The Essentials, Mary E.S. Loomis, Addison-Wesley, 1995, ISBN 0-201-56341-X.

Object Data Management, R.G.G. Cattell, Addison-Wesley, 1994, ISBN 0-201-54748-1.

The Object Database Standard: ODMG-93, Release 1.2, R.G.G. Cattell, Ed., Morgan Kaufmann Publishers, 1995, ISBN 1-55860-396-4.

Book Listings with Reviewer Comments

http://web.cs.city.ac.uk/homes/akmal/books.html (also linked from http://www.odmg.org)

WWW Sites with Links to ODBMS Vendor Web Sites

http://www.odmg.org

http://users.aol.com/dbmsfacts/index.html

Industry Trade Studies Comparing ODBMSs

http://web.cs.city.ac.uk/homes/akmal/books.html (also linked from http://www.odmg.org)

Contact Information for *The DBMS Needs Assessment for Objects*

The *DBMS Needs Assessment for Objects* provides completed worksheets on all the checklist items in Part III of this book for the various types of ODBMS products: Object-Relational Mapping, Object Manager DBMSs, Object DBMSs, and Object-Relational DBMSs. It is updated annually. To obtain more information, contact:

Barry & Associates, Inc.
14041 Burnhaven Drive, Suite 103
Burnsville, MN 55337 USA

Voice: +1-612-892-6113
Fax: +1-612-397-7203
Email: DBMSfacts@aol.com
Web: http://users.aol.com/dbmsfacts/index.html
(This web site has sample pages, a listing of tables, and ordering information.)

G l o s s a r y

Abstraction

The distillation of a large amount of information down to its essentials.

ACID Properties

The properties of a DBMS that allow the sharing of data to be safe. The acronym is derived from the four properties: atomicity, consistency, isolation, and durability.

Atomicity

This is the "all or nothing" flavor of an entire sequence of operations as it is applied to the database. The sequence of operations is considered "atomic," either all or none of the updates are visible to the outside world.

Attribute

A characteristic defined for a class.

Base Table

A relational table that is physically stored in the database.

Binding

The association of a name with a class.

Caching

The retention of data usually in the client application to minimize network traffic flow and/or disk access.

Case Statement

A series of statements in programming code whose execution is determined by some type code. This commonly appears as "if then else if" code.

Class

The definition of the structure, methods, and the items of data.

Class Hierarchy

The inheritance relation among classes.

Collection

An aggregate object that groups an arbitrary number of other objects.

Column

A characteristic defined for a table.

Compile-Time Binding

Binding that is done at compile-time. Also called early or static binding.

Composite Object

An object that contains one or more other objects by referencing the contained objects.

Configuration

A configuration is versioning of versions. This allows for versioning a group of versioned objects.

Consistency

The preservation of the integrity of the information in the database despite the actions of multiple users working at the same time.

Container

An object that contains other objects including operations to iterate on those objects.

Data Model

Data types, integrity rules, and operators used for abstraction.

Database

Data stored in a computer system.

Database Management System

Software that manages access to a database.

DBMS
Acronym for a database management system.

Dispatching
Execution of methods based on polymorphism.

Domain
A set of values, all for the same type.

Durability
The ability of the system to recover committed transaction updates if either the system or the storage media fails.

Dynamic Binding
See run-time binding.

Early Binding
See compile-time binding.

Encapsulation
The separation of the external aspects of an object from the object's internal implementation.

Field
Another term for a column in a relation.

Garbage Collection
A mechanism that deallocates memory or frees up disk space for objects that are not accessible or referenced.

Impedance Mismatch
When data is used in one form in the application and stored in another form in the database. This requires a translation process coming from the database to the application and another translation process going from the application to the database.

Inheritance

The mechanism that allows a class definition to include the attributes and methods of its superclass(es).

Instance

In the relational model, this refers to a tuple of a relation. In the object model, this refers to an object that is an instance of the class definition.

Intersection Entity

In relational modeling, it is the introduction of a new relation (or entity) between two other relations that have a many-to-many relationship. The intersection entity eliminates the many-to-many relationship.

Isolation

The series of safeguards that a database management system uses to prevent conflicts between concurrent transactions.

Late Binding

See run-time binding.

Many-to-Many Relationship

In data modeling, this occurs when one entity has some type of relationship with many instances of the other entity and vice versa. For example, a Student can take many Courses (a many relationship with the Course entity) and a Course can have many Students (a many relationship with Student entity).

Method

Executable code that is encapsulated as part of the class definition.

Model

A representation that uses abstractions for the concepts of the real-world situation.

Multiple Inheritance

Inheriting from more than one superclass.

Normalization

The simplification of data to minimize update anomalies. Usually in relational systems.

Object

An instance of a class definition containing data that can be operated on by the methods of the class.

Object Database Management System

A database management system that uses the object model.

Object DBMS

A DBMS that uses objects in the client application and stores objects in server disk.

Object Manager DBMS

A DBMS that provides an application program interface for the client application and stores objects in the server disk.

Object Model

An abstract data model where the predominant data type is an object.

Object Modeling

The process of using the object model to define a specific object schema.

Object Schema

A definition of data that uses the object model.

Object-Relational DBMS

A DBMS that provides nearly any type of interface for the client application and stores either objects or tuples in the server disk.

Object-Relational Mapping

Middleware that allows the client application to use objects by translating relational tuples to objects when data is read from a relational DBMS and translating objects to relational tuples when data is stored in a relational DBMS.

ODBMS
Acronym for an object database management system.

Optimistic Locking
Assumes that simultaneous access to same objects is quite rare and conflicts are checked only at commit-time. Conflicts may result in an abort or restart.

Overloading
Defining more than one method with the same name.

Overriding
Where a method for a subclass adds to or replaces a method of its superclass.

Page
A unit of storage on disk or a unit of memory.

Pessimistic Locking
Checks for access conflicts at the time the lock is requested with some locks queued until the conflicts are resolved. No conflicts are present at commit time.

Polymorphism
A mechanism that selects a method based on the type of the target object.

RDBMS
Acronym for a relational database management system.

Relation
A collection of tuples.

Relational DBMS
A DBMS that uses the relational model.

Relational Model
An abstract data model where the predominant data type is a relation.

Relational Schema

A definition of data that uses the relational model.

Run-Time Binding

Binding that occurs at run-time. Also called late or dynamic binding.

Scenario

A description of application uses—used both for design and testing.

Schema

The definition of the data to be stored in a database.

Static Binding

See compile-time binding.

Subclass

A class that is lower in the class hierarchy than another class.

Superclass

A class that is higher in the class hierarchy than another class.

Swizzling

Changing on-disk object references to in-memory references.

Table

Another term for a relation.

Transaction

Updates to the database where either all or none of the updates are visible to the outside world.

Tuple

An instance of a relation.

Type Code

A value in an instance that is used to categorize data.

Update Anomalies

Inconsistencies that occur when data that is stored in two places is changed in one but not in the other.

View

A virtual, derived relation that is defined in terms of other relations.

I n d e x